positions asia critique

the maoism of prc history:
against dominant trends in anglophone academia

volume 29   number 4   november 2021

Contents

Foreword: The Maoism of PRC History

Aminda Smith

Good PRC history is left history. But hear me out. I do not mean that all good PRC historians are leftist in their thinking, their politics, or their methods; they are not. Nor do I mean that all good PRC history advocates for left positions; it does not. But rather, good PRC history is left history because it takes seriously and elucidates the leftist logics that framed discourses and experiences in socialist China. It grants that Maoist (Maovian?) projects had logics and evaluates them on their own terms, rather than dismissing them as obviously illogical. As Kristin Stapleton and Michael Schoenhals have pointed out, Mao Zedong Thought is perhaps the most important of the theories that inform the study of PRC history (H-PRC 2016). Knowing what Mao and Maoists actually thought, as well as what they tried to do, is all the more important when today's dominant political and economic systems rely, for their very existence, on the falsification of

positions 29:4 DOI 10.1215/10679847-9286636

the ideologies, Marxian and otherwise, that attempt to contest them and hold them accountable. Bad PRC history abets conservative and regressive politics by attempting to erase any positive aspects of the socialist project, by pretending it was irrational, and by demonizing, *reductio ad Maoum*, anyone who disagrees.

Good PRC history resists teleological interpretations of the past by recovering the "infinite possibilities" that Maoism once offered, and that many people pursued, often using Mao's ideas to take them places that even Mao did not want them to go (Badiou 2014; Karl 2010; Wu 2014). When good PRC historians dive into archives and oral histories, they attempt to recapture this history of possibility by moving within the mindscapes of Chinese Communism. They learn to think like Maoists, even as they question Maoist thought. Good PRC history, like Maoism, should make us question what and how we *know*.

Reading sources from the PRC past can challenge our assumptions about how the world is and how it could be. When we are mindful of our own presentist thought categories and work to ensure that we read the sources on their own terms, they can destabilize the naturalized narratives of capitalism, neoliberalism, and imperialism as well as the entities that benefit from some or all of those, including US-style liberal democracies and, importantly, today's proudly illiberal PRC state. As this issue discusses, however, despite important interventions over the past decades, reactionary, red-baiting visions of the socialist past still play an outsized role in PRC history, both in its academic and popular forms. The only way to balance the scales is to unearth and resuscitate the disruptive elements that the dominant emplotments of history necessarily conceal, cast aside, or name as imaginary.

The First Rule of PRC History:
Social Science and Anti-Marxist Positivism

There is an ongoing battle over what PRC history is and should be, complete with camps and several casualties so far. One of the most widely cited visions for the field was articulated in 2016 by political scientist Elizabeth Perry. Her article included a swipe at "Sinological garbology" (buying or otherwise salvaging documents that have been thrown out by archives, institutions, and individuals), a method that counts among its practitioners such field-shaping senior scholars as Michael Schoenhals and Zhang Letian. But Perry suggests that garbology has led younger researchers astray, luring us into a "janitorial role." We seem content, she muses, to "grub for diversity in the dustbins of grassroots society" to tell interesting but ultimately unimportant stories of difference. Meanwhile, according to Perry, "social scientists" continue to do the far more significant work of exploring "the 'commanding heights' of the Chinese state and its policies" (2016: 116). Despite the janitorial metaphor, it is important to note that this critique could also apply to historians who do not do garbology but use similar kinds of grassroots sources from local PRC archives. Perry's concern is that historians, in general, seem to be focusing on minutiae rather than "overarching historical arguments." She notes that this might be "understandable and excusable" among *historians* working in China, "in light of political constraints," but that "the reluctance of many Western historians to tackle the question of the long-term significance of early PRC experiences, notwithstanding their diversity, seems less justifiable" (2016: 114). This distinction, between Chinese historians and non-Chinese "Western" historians is important, as both Perry's critique and ours in this issue are concerned primarily with the latter group.

Perry and others, including Neil Diamant, argue that this problem, in the non-Chinese anglophone field, results from the fact that historians (by which they generally mean scholars trained in history departments) overstate the novelty of our work and disregard (read: fail to cite) all of the social scientists who have already asked key questions of the PRC past (Diamant 2018: 189). I was a bit surprised that some of the most high-profile criticisms of PRC history came from Perry and Diamant, two of the political scientists who work most historically and with whom PRC historians have always engaged. As a graduate student, I initially assumed that Perry and Diamant, as well as Michael Dutton, Patricia Thornton, Joel Andreas, and others were all historians, precisely because they were attuned to change over time, contingency, and most of all to crafting deep, immersive past-scapes.

But those kinds of historically minded scholars are anomalies in social scientific fields that are largely concerned with contemporary questions and which often (mis)use facile descriptions of the past toward that end. Must historians really engage seriously with the work of nonhistorically minded social scientists (read: the bulk of social scientific scholarship) simply because it periodically hijacks a Maoist practice to build models that flatten the past? I would actually caution against engaging with such work because what is there referenced as "history" is most often a teleological preface to a series of assertions about the present. Spending too much time in those thought worlds will introduce into our own work precisely the presentist logics that derail good PRC history and render it fundamentally ahistorical. This will produce bad PRC history, perfectly suited to bolster those End-of-History arguments that laud the inherent superiority of liberal capitalism and the purported implausibility of change.

Perry's scholarship does not fit into this latter category, and the sensitively historical nature of her own work actually undercuts the substance of her critique. But her programmatic statement nonetheless highlights many of the reasons some historians, including those in this issue, have long been dissatisfied with trends in English-language scholarship on the PRC. Perry's concerns offer a useful starting point because they are consistent with the increasing certainty on the part of many social scientists, over the past century and a half, that their ways of knowing are superior to those of scholars in humanities disciplines. The recent disbanding of certain university departments, especially those focused on literary, philosophical, or cultural studies, signals the growing sense that questions and approaches associated with "scientific methods" produce more important knowledge than that arrived at via philosophical inquiries, discursive analyses, and thick descriptions of microsites.

The discipline of history provides a good lens for examining these kinds of claims. It sits uncomfortably between the social sciences and the humanities and reminds us that while there are important distinctions between disciplines, the process of assigning fields to larger institutional categories is also somewhat arbitrary. (History is one of several disciplines that are incorporated into colleges of social science at some universities and into colleges of arts or humanities at others). The false opposition between these ways of knowing also elides the fact that the current forms of all academic disciplines were produced in the same modern era, often quite explicitly to serve the political interests of bourgeois capitalist and imperialist powers. Despite those close connections, however, the fact that humanistic studies of language and culture were linked to the much older studies of classics, while social science was more closely attached to the natural sciences, reified the flawed perception that the latter relied on more "objective" methods of producing knowledge (Dutton 2002).

The allure of the ostensibly superior social sciences intensified during the middle of the twentieth century with the rise of what Vicente Rafael (1994: 91) has called "The North American Way of Knowing." Academics and university administrators pushed for the development of area studies, which would take from the humanities that deemed valuable, especially linguistic competency and cultural understanding, and marry it to social scientific methods, to create a new institutionalized mode of knowledge production. As Rafael (1994: 92) argues, the resulting units and the research they conduct are "fundamentally dependent," to this day, on "the conjunction of corporate funding, state support, and the flexible managerial systems of university governance characteristic of liberal pluralism." Thus, unsurprisingly, social science, as an institution, produces a great deal of knowledge that serves those interests.

Many proponents of this new way of knowing believed that scientific methods in area studies would help to counter the influence of Marxism in the academy. Karl Popper (1957), perhaps the best-known proponent of "positivism" as superior to Marxism, argued that Marx had developed his theories through scientific methods but that over time Western social and natural sciences had proven to be more truly based on observable facts. Of course, as his own analysis of Marxism suggested, Popper and other self-identified positivists were not the only thinkers whose theories could be so labeled. Many twentieth-century epistemologies similarly contended that the only valid knowledge is that attained through the observation and rational interpretation of perceptible, natural phenomena.

For their part, many Marxist thinkers insisted that dialectical materialism was no less fact-based or testable and adaptable than other modern sciences and that so-called positivists were the ones who ignored facts in favor of political dogma. George Novack claimed that Popper was principally motivated by his own, very subjective views on the implausibility of revolution and thus used "arbitrary and essentially reactionary standards" to determine what was scientific. Novack (2002: 165) further suggested, playfully but insightfully, that Popper's brand of "positivism" was in fact "badly named and should be more precisely termed 'negativism,'" for its counterrevolutionary roots and impulses. But nevertheless, the connection between positivism and liberal, anti-Marxist thought lingered, as did the unsubstantiated assertion that positivism produced more reliable knowledge than Marxism (or other epistemologies).

Thusly styled positivists took over North American academia during the Cold War. Their rise was buoyed by a ferocious retrenchment of liberalism, emblematized by Margaret Thatcher's notorious claim that there was "no alternative" to so-called free market economics. A vibrant academic insurrection did erupt during the Vietnam War. Of special importance to the China field was the Committee of Concerned Asian Scholars (CCAS), who rejected the use of Asian studies to abet US liberal and imperialist interests. But by the early 1980s, most of those radicals had returned to the anticommunist fold (Barlow 1993; Lanza 2017). For historians, this was probably predictable. The discipline, as Hayden White (1987: 60) reminds us, was constituted "in the service of political values and regimes that were in general antirevolutionary and conservative," and, with a few notable exceptions, it has more often than not continued in that vein.

It was in this context that, during the Reagan-Thatcher years, many former CCAS members and other anglophone China scholars began to extol the importance of "positivism" and "empiricism" in research. They were, in part, participating in the larger academic reaction to "postmodernism," or what sinologist Geremie Barmé (1999: xvii) has called "the two-line struggle between theory and empiricism." In the China field, the appeal to "facts" was also part of a burgeoning argument against the PRC state, which many had once championed as a positive model, in contrast to the Vietnam War–era United States and its allies. From the mid-1970s onward, China scholars had increased opportunities to visit the PRC, and many there observed phenomena they perceived as flatly contradicting Communist Party rhetoric. It became a mission, for many of them, to evangelize these newfound truths.

It is unsurprising that China scholars became focused on countering Marxist narratives. After all, the loudest narrator of China's past and present is probably the Chinese Communist Party. But because so many members of the anglophone China studies field had once held high hopes for the revolution, when they became disillusioned with that project, they experienced it as a personal betrayal. In the fifty years since, their painful memories of being duped by CCP rhetoric, fused as those memories were to the growing epistemological dominance of the North American Way of Knowing, have shaped the questions, methodologies, and sensibilities of PRC studies, as much as any other disciplinary or theoretical framework. As I argue later in this issue, in a post-disillusionment era, under the tutelage of the betrayed, generations of students learned that the first rule of PRC studies is: never take the Chinese Communists at their word.

* * *

The contributors to this issue were trained in that post-disillusionment era. And although we were too young to have experienced the disenchantment firsthand, many of our more senior teachers shared memories of their awakening. They extolled the importance of looking for stories that did not appear in, and/or manifestly contradicted, official or mainstream narratives about PRC history. This is how we came into what Perry calls our "janitorial role." Our senior colleagues, Perry included, taught us to seek out marginalized voices and nonstandard histories.

When we went into the field, we followed that mandate, hunting for nonstate sources, such as oral histories or diaries. We dug up official documents that the state had hidden or discarded, such as the "garbage sources" that were abundant in flea markets and used bookstores and that often contained classified files, including firsthand reports from grassroots cadres that contested higher-level claims. As we embarked on our field research during the later 1990s and the early 2000s, PRC archives were also more open than they had ever been before or have been since. We were flush with locally produced primers for schoolchildren and for cadres, with work reports from village communes and directives sent by local governments, with personal letters, sketchbooks, and shopping lists. To try to make sense of the disparate and confusing splinters we encountered, we returned to the *People's Daily* and the works of Party theorists, but we also devoured the formulaic textbooks produced by central authorities for their mid-level and lower-level bureaucrats, many of which were also newly available.

As we worked through our documents, we began to realize that many of our methods seemed to further obscure meaning because, of course, Marxism and then Maoism were forged in the same crucible as the modern humanities and social science disciplines. All of those intellectual traditions are interrelated critiques. Chinese Communist praxis attempted to mount a direct challenge to the epistemological frameworks that drove Western liberal and academic thought. Maoism explicitly operated according to an alternative set of logics, logics that were purposefully designed to falsify the "truths" of capitalism, imperialism, and liberalism, among others. It can thus be productive to read liberal positivism, Marxism, and other contemporaneous theories of knowledge in conversation with one another. But they cannot unlock one another's truths in any straightforward way.

Chicken Feathers and Garlic Skins: The Virtues of Dumpster Diving

In a reply to Perry's initial salvo, Michael Schoenhals (2016) pointed out that to see janitorial labor as less important than social scientific work unfortunately and unfairly disparages both PRC historians and the people who keep our workplaces clean and safe. Years earlier, in what now seems a prescient rebuke to the anti-garbology line, PRC policy makers of the time also remarked on the political significance of attitudes about trash. Educational materials, aimed at recalcitrant cadres, explained that proper CCP governance was constantly beset by lower-level agents who thought local stories and individual troubles were nothing more than "chicken feathers and garlic skins" (鸡毛蒜皮 *jimao suanpi*), or the useless detritus that is swept into the trash bin after making a meal. Rectification stressed that such thinking constituted a serious methodological error, which violated the mass line. "The people have many matters which don't seem to be major," cadres were to learn, "but national issues are just accumulations of the small affairs of ordinary people" (L. Liu 1952). When PRC historians begin with grassroots documents, from either flea markets or archives, they are following the first epistemological principle of the mass line: All truth comes from the masses. That principle is crucial to the proper contextualization of Mao-era sources.

Because of its social scientific bent, anglophone scholarship tends to emphasize a relatively functionalist understanding of the mass line, stressing the way policies were supposed to evolve through a back-and-forth exchange ("from the masses to the masses") between the people and the Party. This claim about PRC governance has been dismissed by some scholars as overly idealistic "window dressing," but recent studies in political science have taken the mass line more seriously as a secret to CCP success (Y. Liu 2006; Tang 2016). Social scientists rightly point out that the mass line was very useful to the Party because it enabled both tight control and surveillance as well as a measure of popular participation to ensure continued mass support.

However, the pressure to advance generalizable conclusions has led political scientists to focus on comparisons between, say, mass mobilization in China and Cold War theories of "mass society" (Tang 2016), or between, for example, the PRC's "democratic dictatorship" and "liberal democracy." We learn a great deal from this literature about how the CCP developed its central leadership technique, how that technique ranks against others, and how it has and continues to serve the state well. But this rather dry, social scientific analysis of a relatively specific yet also familiar-seeming set of policies in China leaves one to wonder how *that* mass line connects to the mass line at the heart of Maoism, the mass line that inspired people around the world, leaving its indelible impression on farmers, radical feminists, French philosophers, and Black Panthers, just to name a few. The mass line was far more than a leadership method; the mass line was, at its core, the Maoist theory of knowledge production. It was a guide to radical thinking. And recapturing that epistemological element is essential to understanding Maoism's global appeal, but it is also essential to making sense of Mao-era historical sources.

The basic premise of mass line epistemology is that all truth comes from the masses and any inquiry must therefore begin with close, empirical observations, conducted on the ground and from a "mass perspective" (or through the eyes of the ordinary people). The data thus gleaned is to be considered in the context of the Marxian theories that Mao believed offered the most reliable analyses of history and society. Because the mass line was a way of knowing, it informed nearly every aspect of everything the CCP did, at least in its early years. Whether leaders viewed it more or less cynically did not matter in the sense that the political culture of the Party meant superiors at all levels still had to order, inspire, and even entreat their subordinates to work in accordance with the mass line. As I argue later in this issue, nearly all government records that purport to describe CCP governance and the attitudes, conditions, or behaviors of the masses were created in that context. The reference materials officials used to produce city, provincial, and central-level documents were compiled in consultation with that local data.

The directives, decisions, models, and measures one must use to correctly analyze Chinese Communist governance, its institutions, or its methods, even at the central Party level, make less sense apart from the mass line praxis that informed them. Excavating the forgotten and discarded shards of local experience, which once mattered a great deal (at least discursively) to the PRC state, is crucial to the correct interpretation of that state's written traces and, to a certain extent, the traces of the people it sought to govern. Microhistories are thus central to the mapping of Chinese communism and must be central to any analysis of what went on at its "commanding heights."

To understand the PRC past, we need the chicken feathers and garlic skins of Maoism. Some of those tidbits remain in archives, others can be scavenged from postsocialist rubbish heaps. I agree wholeheartedly with Perry that presenting local anecdotes for their own sake is not the most valuable contribution historians can make. But Ginzburg (1980), Darnton (1984), and Davis (1983) have long since dismissed any sense that *microstorie* do not have macro implications. We *dundian* 蹲点, or "squat in a spot," to gain the deep knowledge of "single points," that early PRC political theorists taught would "illuminate the entire plane." Good PRC history makes a great number of claims about the nature of the "entire plane" of the past because it follows the dialectical logic of the mass line. Particularity is only enlightening when it is united with the universal, and the universal is only universal because of its relationship to many particulars.

In part because of the influence of Maoist thought around the world, including in academia, the past several decades of historical scholarship about China and elsewhere, has increasingly shown that microhistories of single points best illuminate *all* larger planes (Badiou 2014; Karl 2010; Elbaum 2018). In this sense, it is not simply a predilection for sinological minutiae that leads Jeremy Brown and Matthew Johnson (2015) to argue that there was no single "Maoist China" that can be characterized in broad strokes. In fact, social and cultural historians of many pasts around the world have come to similar conclusions. But such a position need not evade "big questions" unless only broad strokes and generalizations count as big answers. The North American social scientific way of knowing might posit just that, but Maoism was a critique of precisely those kinds of claims.

Historical Rupture and Alternative Epistemologies

By taking Maoism seriously, good PRC history raises critiques that shake the smug epistemological certainty of a moment and reveal the unproven assumptions and subjective values hidden in a dominant worldview. Taking mass line epistemology seriously, as we approach our Mao-era sources, offers us the opportunity to reflect on how we *know* and to wonder whether we could know better. For example, one of the things I once found in the trash was a letter written by an actual janitor from a small northern city. "Dearest Chairman Mao," wrote Ms. Wu, who identified herself as a worker on a municipal sanitation team. "I would like to suggest," she began, "that many more people, including cadres and leaders, engage in sanitation work. This kind of work helps develop a mass perspective and offers a chance to participate in the important work of protecting the health of the people." Whenever I read Ms. Wu's letter, or the many more like it, in discussions of Mao-Era political culture, colleagues inevitably wonder how much Ms. Wu could really have understood about political concepts like "mass perspective." My interlocutors tend to question that these kinds of letters are political texts in which people are attempting to engage seriously with Maoist ideas. Does it not seem more likely, scholars ask, that Ms. Wu and her comrades were attempting to navigate an increasingly politicized "daily life," deploying the state's language because they had to do so or because it might be useful in getting what they wanted?

Obviously, historians can never know what Maoism did or did not mean to Ms. Wu. But it is significant that just as social scientific research reduces the mass line to a useful instrument of Party control, so too does post-disillusionment rationale reduce Ms. Wu's use of a mass line conceptual framework to a coping strategy. That otherwise accomplished and thoughtful scholars can confidently advance such undertheorized and undead understandings of "daily life" is indicative of the strong impulse in post-disillusionment PRC history to render Maoist political ideas as disconnected from or in conflict with people's everyday realities. This impulse leads scholars to gloss the Maoist lexicon as inauthentic, even when, as in the case of Ms. Wu, there is no evidence in the source itself to suggest the letter was anything other than participation in Maoist politics.

Post-disillusionment methodology here reveals what Novack called the "congenital vice of positivist epistemology." Positivists, according to Novack, have an apparently powerful method for excising those ideas they do not like—they evaluate them in light of the liberal values that informed the development of the Western scientific method and declare all conclusions that do not support those values to be "unscientific" (or superficial in relation to the scientific). In so doing, however, positivists must violate the rules of their own empiricism; they must exclude certain evidence, or define it as anomalous, and/or they must give certain evidence an interpretation that is not supported by that evidence itself (Novack 2002: 166). Later in this issue, I demonstrate in detail the analytical mistakes produced by this practice. But we can also see the problem quite clearly in the scholarly evaluations of Ms. Wu's letter.

The only thing the source actually contains is a Maoist political and epistemological claim, but post-disillusionment methodology does not insist on the examination of that claim. And, indeed, no evidence is required to exclude the evidence provided in Ms. Wu's letter. This creates an analytical disparity: If, on the one hand, I make a textually supported argument and claim that Ms. Wu was genuinely attempting to think like a Maoist, many readers would remain unconvinced. If, on the other hand, I were to claim that Ms. Wu was deploying the language of the state tactically, many readers would accept that argument, even if I offered no evidence. This sort of analytical imbalance is not quite what David Bloor had in mind when he advocated "symmetry" in analyses of knowledge production (Bloor 1976). But we might invoke a kind of "symmetry principle" to insist that post-disillusionment "common-sense" interpretations offer direct evidence, preferably from the historical source in question, to refute something like the sincerity of Ms. Wu's expression. If they cannot do so, then we might probe their claims a bit more deeply. What kind of analytical work does their profound skepticism of Maoist political concepts *do* for those scholars who insist on it? One answer is that when the words of Maoist speakers are reduced to quaint local expressions of otherwise "universal" human concerns, such as navigating "daily life," this process reinscribes the supposed universality of the very claims about daily life that Maoism sought to denaturalize. Renaturalized, these "universals" make Maoist interventions seem illogical. What logic could there be, after all, in disputing the existence of the "natural" world?

Good PRC History Is Left History

Rafael and Dutton have both noted that the social scientific North American Way of Knowing asserts and maintains its superiority by excluding evidence and offering questionable interpretations to advance not fully substantiated claims about what is "natural," "universal," and "scientific." Distilling alien logic systems into data or sidelining them as epiphenomenal to the "facts," bolsters Thatcher-style no-alternative claims by rendering the alternatives as always already illogical and even imaginary. Discredited as beliefs not based on evidence or as lapses in logic, entire systems of meaning are reduced simply to fragments of data, deployed to give us a false sense of our own epistemological superiority.

Good PRC history attempts to reveal that lie. It seeks to recapture what has been lost, not solely because the contents of the dustbin of history are significant on their own (though we think they are). But, more importantly, because the things in that dustbin are bits of evidence that were excised or ignored by various iterations of the CCP state and the scholars who have sought to know it. To allow all of that purposely discarded evidence to stay in the trash is to abet the exclusion-based superiority claims of both liberal positivism and the illiberal PRC state, which cites an ahistorical version of the mass line as its justificatory epistemology. Indeed, by engaging in such exclusion to reduce the epistemology of the mass line to a mode of governance (which can then be touted by today's CCP or reviled by its critics) social scientific and post-disillusionment approaches have not only oversimplified PRC history but also reified the state and its elites as the arbiters of historical meaning.

Social scientific macrohistories have left us with a view of the early PRC as a time when the CCP used its mass line tactics to establish tight, even totalitarian control and deep surveillance over society. That is certainly what many leaders wanted to do, and they might want us to believe they succeeded. But as local, micro, and "from the margins" cases have shown, there was so much that the PRC state could not control and so many things central leaders never came to know. The post-disillusionment falsification drive has similarly left us with a picture of Maoist political logics as inauthentic and dogmatic, suggesting promises that Mao and other elites either could not or would not fulfill. That vision is certainly key to the perpetuation of liberal capitalist ideology, but it is also contested by the profound and continuing resonance of Mao's ideas. Maybe the "commanding heights" are so high that all observers can see from there are what look to be the teleologies of failure and the capriciousness of individual leaders. But from way down in the weeds we see aspects of the socialist past that were much more radical and subversive.

If we begin, as the mass line instructs, with a sanitation worker in a small city who wrote a letter to Chairman Mao, we may get a glimpse at how ordinary people dared to reimagine their worlds, to contest things as they were, and to demand things be different. And when trash can after trash can and archive upon archive are full of such letters, all that once-forgotten evidence gets more and more difficult to ignore. Good PRC history lets us question the post-disillusionment claims that support the current ideological status quo: *Were* Maoist conceptual categories inauthentic or illogical? *Is* the socialist experiment best read as elite power plays and political lies? When we look more closely at those claims, it turns out that they have been stated loudly and repeatedly, but they are not as evidence based as they purport to be.

Good PRC history can render post-disillusionment emplotments less convincing, by gathering all the chicken feathers and garlic skins that had to be discarded to make those narratives appear true. That does not mean, however, that the counternarratives of their ideological opponents become more convincing, as defenders of the contemporary CCP might sometimes argue. Good PRC history also suggests that Maoism's radical potential never belonged to Mao or the PRC state, and it could not be contained by them or delegitimized by their mistakes. Indeed, as Rebecca Karl (2010: x) has argued, what Mao really offered was a challenge, and "recalling Mao's challenge is to recall a time when many things seemed possible; it is to remember possibility against the pressure to concede to the world as it now appears." We can only recall that time by reanimating its logics, beginning at the grassroots and following as many paths through the Mao era as we can. Good PRC history is thus left history because it can recapture what so many people found most meaningful about Maoism—its inquiry into how we know. *That* vision of the PRC past can still lead us to make genuine and powerful interventions into global conversations about how the world is and how it might be.

References

Badiou, Alain. 2014. "A Dialogue between a Chinese Philosopher and a French Philosopher." December 13. www.leapleapleap.com/2015/03/creative-nonfiction-a-lecture-performance-by-alain-badiou/.

Barlow, Tani. 1993. "Colonialism's Career in Postwar China Studies." *positions* 1, no. 1: 224–67.

Barmé, Geremie. 1999. *In the Red: On Contemporary Chinese Culture*. New York: Columbia University Press.

Bloor, David. 1976. *Knowledge and Social Imagery*. Chicago: University of Chicago Press.

Brown, Jeremy, and Matthew Johnson, eds. 2015. *Maoism at the Grassroots: Everyday Life in China's Era of High Socialism*. Cambridge, MA: Harvard University Press.

Darnton, Robert. 1984. *The Great Cat Massacre and Other Episodes in French Cultural History*. New York: Basic Books.

Davis, Natalie Zemon. 1983. *The Return of Martin Guerre*. Cambridge, MA: Harvard University Press.

Diamant, Neil. 2018. "What the (Expletive) Is a Constitution?!" *Journal of Chinese History* 2, no. 1: 169–90.

Dutton, Michael. 2002. "Lead Us Not into Translation: Notes toward a Theoretical Foundation for Asian Studies." *Nepantla: Views from South* 3, no. 3: 495–537.

Elbaum, Max. 2018. *Revolution in the Air: Sixties Radicals Turn to Lenin, Mao, and Che*. New York: Verso.

Ginzburg, Carlo. 1980. *The Cheese and the Worms*. London: Routledge.

H-PRC. 2016. "Most Important/Influential Theoretical Work for PRC History?" May 12. networks.h-net.org/node/3544/discussions/124969/most-importantinfluential-theoretical-work-prc-history.

Karl, Rebecca. 2010. *Mao Zedong and China in the Twentieth-Century World: A Concise History*. Durham, NC: Duke University Press.

Lanza, Fabio. 2017. *The End of Concern: Maoist China, Activism, and Asian Studies*. Durham, NC: Duke University Press.

Liu, Lantao 刘澜涛. 1952. "Zhonggong zhongyang huabei ju di san shuji Liu Lantao zai chuli Zhang Shunyou shijian huiyi shang de jianghua" 中共中央华北局第三书记刘澜涛在处理张顺有事件会议上的讲话 ("Party Central North China Bureau Third Secretary Liu Lantao's Speech at the Conference on Handling the Zhang Shunyou Affair"). *Renmin ribao*, May 30.

Liu, Yu. 2006. "From the Mass Line to Mao Cult: The Production of Legitimate Dictatorship in Revolutionary China." PhD diss., Columbia University.

Novack, George. 2002. *Marxist Writings on History and Philosophy*. London: Resistance Books.

Perry, Elizabeth. 2016. "The Promise of PRC History." *Journal of Modern Chinese History* 10, no. 1: 113–17.

Popper, Karl. 1957. *The Poverty of Historicism*. London: Routledge.

Rafael, Vicente L. 1994. "The Cultures of Area Studies in the United States." *Social Text* 12, no. 41: 91–112.

Schoenhals, Michael. 2016. "A New 'Document of the Month' (September 2016)." H-PRC, September 1. networks.h-net.org/node/3544/discussions/142037/new-document-month-september-2016.

Tang, Wenfang. 2016. *Populist Authoritarianism: Chinese Political Culture and Regime Sustainability*. Oxford: Oxford University Press.

White, Hayden V. 1987. *The Content of the Form: Narrative Discourse and Historical Representation*. Baltimore: Johns Hopkins University Press.

Wu, Yiching. 2014. *The Cultural Revolution at the Margins: Chinese Socialism in Crisis*. Cambridge, MA: Harvard University Press.

Introduction: The Politics of (Maoist) History

Fabio Lanza

Personally, I have always thought that writing history is a political act—and I have always acted on that principle. Almost all China historians in US academia—and for sure all the historians contributing to this special issue—have been trained within or in proximity to Asian studies departments; we were provided with rigorous language preparation and have all had more than a passing acquaintance with what is unfortunately still called "sinology," meaning the study of "China" as an enclosed, foreign, and distant object. Given that context, Chinese history might look more prone than other national histories to indulge in the curious, the anomalous, or at best the irrelevant: topics such as the horse trade during the Mongol empire and porcelain production in the Ming period are indeed fascinating, but they probably sound, correctly or not, very remote from any contemporary political relevance. Of course, there are also stratified intellectual, racial,

positions 29:4 DOI 10.1215/10679847-9286649
Copyright 2021 by Duke University Press

and political reasons—often subsumed under the category of "Oriental-ism"—why China studies and Chinese history might appear to some to be much less directly political than other fields, a scholarly refuge where research as pure intellectual pastime is still possible. Yet even when we purposely write to move away from politics, to detach ourselves from the "viruses of the present," we engage in a political act (Bloch 1954: 36–37).

I would hold that writing Chinese history is *even more* directly and overtly political than writing any other nation's history. First, the textual reverence, the almost monastic devotion to language learning, and the always implied "esoteric" character of Chinese studies mask the political decisions involved in the choice of historical methodology, the production of situated knowl-edge, and the author's position vis-à-vis the subjects of that history. All these choices acquire even more political relevance precisely because they are concealed in the structural folds of a field whose history is marked by the continuous and stubborn "othering" of its object. While the historical context and the relative positions of China have changed over the decades, one constant of Chinese studies in the anglophone world has been the posit-ing of "China" as a separate location, a place so different that it required its own separate form of knowledge, distinct from other disciplinary fields: that applied equally to the complexities of classical language, the supposed insu-larity of Confucian culture, and the crazed nature of Communist develop-ment. Writing Chinese history is therefore always an act against, acquiescent to, or in support of the layered politics of this academic and scholarly field.

In fact, anglophone historians of China always write in relation to Sinol-ogy, not as the careful evaluation of sources and language, but as the his-torical construction of "China" as an object of inquiry. But they also write in relation to a more recent history, not disconnected from or uninfluenced by sinological precedents, but one with more obvious and direct political implications. In the United States, that history, especially when it comes to modern and contemporary China, has been framed by the concerns and the policies of the Cold War, when Asian studies departments were cre-ated and funded as part of a larger "know your enemy" effort. Profoundly affected by the McCarthy purges in the 1950s, which not by chance began with a virulent attack against the scholar Owen Lattimore, China studies in US academia remained in an uneasy (but ultimately profitable) relationship with US policy in Asia, a relationship alternatively of subservience, willing collaboration, or complicit silence. In the 1960s and 1970s, those scholars who wrote about contemporary China had to accept the "Manichean bi-polar world" that those policies framed and required; proclamations of neutrality and objectivity often served to hide the internalization of anticommunism and McCarthyism (Fairbank and Peck 1970: 56). For others, less contemporary, more "sinological" inquiries—meaning pursuits solidly anchored in the past and in an idea of "China" as a self-contained object of study—offered a temporary respite, an escape from a field born out of government funding and global political confrontation, even if it meant the acceptance of one's impotence.[1] Not surprisingly, three of the articles in this issue, by Jake Werner, Covell Meyskens, and Matthew Johnson, all deal with the long-standing ideological premises that still influence the study of PRC history.

The first major critique to the Cold War–era field of China studies, its practices, the knowledge it produced, and the way it was deployed came in the late 1960s. This coincided with the global crisis spurred by decolonization and US imperialism, of which the Indochina war was the most blatant example. I am highlighting this moment in the history of the field because it shows clearly a paradigmatic shift for which Maoism is central. Young graduate students and professors, united under the collective name of Concerned Asian Scholars, staged an all-out attack against their academic discipline and their teachers, highlighting how their scholarship had constructed Asia in ways that were functional to US imperialistic policies, their alleged neutrality obscuring a very clear political choice of camp (Lanza 2017).

It is not by chance that the attack from the Concerned Asian Scholars came at the time when Chinese (and Asian) people could not anymore be rationally constituted as "passive objects" to be studied, but had come to the fore as unmistakably political subjects, leading the transformations that are closely identified with the "global sixties." Those political subjectivities and the revolutionary upheavals in which they had been produced, however, could not be either recognized or made sense of if viewed within the dominant paradigms of Asian studies, which still privileged modernization theory and anticommunism. To even try to assess the experiments of Maoist China, to "take Maoism seriously," required first and foremost a complete revision of those scholarly paradigms; but, more importantly, if one "took Maoism seriously," that is, if one accepted that the political experiences of high Maoism (from the Great Leap to the Cultural Revolution) were worthy of examination *as politics*, that could not but profoundly affect one's own ideological, political, and intellectual position.

As Aminda Smith points out in the foreword, Maoism was first and foremost a revolutionary epistemology—that is, a theory (and a praxis) of the production of knowledge—under the conditions of continuing revolutionary struggle while at the same time guaranteeing the continuation of that struggle. In addressing how correct knowledge could be produced, Maoism directly questioned the relationship between those who work with their hands and those who work with their minds—be they the cadre, the intellectual, or the teacher—and claimed the right of the former to speak and be listened to. As such, Maoism, especially the Maoism of the Cultural Revolution, presented what was perhaps the most radical challenge to the positions of intellectuals and scholars, the stability of their pedagogy, and the very structures of disciplined knowledge. It was not simply Red Guards attacking the stultified pedagogical system in Chinese schools; it was farmers moving into the realm of agricultural scientists (Schmalzer 2016), workers taking over factory management, peasants producing art, all also and at the same time engaging in philosophical debates. And, in the long 1960s, this was not just a rhetorical and theoretical challenge, nor was it limited to China. Maoism provided a vocabulary (or sometimes *the* vocabulary) for the colonized to subvert the language of the colonizer; for French workers to articulate demands that went beyond a salary increase and shorter hours; for black radicals across the United States to position themselves as part of a global struggle for anticolonial liberation (Kelley and Esch 1999). It also gave young people, and specifically students across the world, the language and the praxes to critique and potentially disrupt not only the contents of the educational system but also the very essence of its pedagogy, the stable positions at its foundation (who teaches, who is taught), its social function, and the universal validity of the knowledge it produced. The fact that students from Paris to Turin to San Francisco insisted on calling themselves Maoists (or "*chinois*") was the result of something more than a simple infantile affectation. In France, the encounter with the Cultural Revolution shaped the thought of major philosophers, from Deleuze to Foucault, from Badiou to Rancière: the granular issues of Maoism were thus encoded into "French Theory," and it was in this disguised form that they later entered US academia (Cusset 2008).

In the context of the global sixties, then, it was impossible for radical American scholars, for whom contemporary China was both a topic of research and a political inspiration, not to be forced to rethink their own assumptions about their scholarship, their field, the structure of US academia, and what it meant to be a scholar. By the time the Vietnam War generation of Asianists came to consciousness, it had become evident that producing scholarship, and especially scholarship about Maoist China, was unavoidably a political act. To learn and teach Maoism required an explicit critique of the institutions of learning, the mechanism of production and transmission of knowledge, and one's own position within them. This often placed the individual scholar in an untenable bind between politics and the practices of academic life. For US scholars in the sixties, those contradictions were exacerbated by the fact that China, while politically close, remained physically inaccessible to Americans.

Obviously, the Maoist subversion of pedagogy was never complete, and it often ended up producing violent and unsustainable results. Even Maoist epistemology itself came to be betrayed, at times by the very Maoist leadership who professed it. Similarly, the search for a new approach to Maoism within US academia remained elusive and was then brutally interrupted by the late 1970s with the collapse of revolutionary hopes worldwide and the actual end of Maoism (Lanza 2017). The legacy and significance of that brief "Maoist" moment, when China scholars found themselves at a center of a global political reflection, was not fully explored and evaluated in its aftermath, in large part because the end of Maoism coincided with a sudden closure of all the political and intellectual possibilities of that period, in China and around the world, what Aminda Smith has aptly called "the post-disillusionment era."

I wanted to single out that moment in the sixties, not so much because I think we are in a comparable political situation, but because I believe it offers a perspective into the ideological background, the promises, and the perils of the "new PRC history." First and foremost, like that earlier generation of scholars, by "taking Maoism seriously," (good) PRC history must take on the challenge that Maoism presents to fixed categories (the Party-state, the people, China itself), to the disciplined production of knowledge, and to the very figure of the intellectual and their relationship to the subject/object of their inquiry. In that, (good) PRC history is always necessarily and profoundly political, even if the trajectories of that political engagement will not necessarily end up being in line with Maoism, or even leftism.

Among PRC historians, there are some, myself included, who prefer to be more explicit about the political stakes involved as well as one's political trajectory. Even Jeremy Brown, perhaps most distant from me in terms of political position, has no problem admitting the political character of his scholarly enterprise. And that is why I think Elizabeth Perry's critique of "grassroots history," which echoes through the following pages, while valuable for sparking an important debate on methods and theories, missed the overarching intellectual and political aspects of that endeavor (Perry 2016). Actually, contra Perry, grassroots history is, like all good PRC history, eminently political. A good example is provided here by Matthew Johnson, who, in his contribution to this issue, singles out a long-standing pattern in our approach to PRC history, largely derived from the social sciences, which frames political behavior as a function of broad cultural values. Grassroots historians like Johnson and Brown (2015) instead insist on the stubborn search to recover in some way not only the experiences of "ordinary people" but also how those people made sense of those experiences and how they contributed to shape the politics of the Mao era. This radical change of perspective has coincided with a shift in methodology, made possible by the new availability of archival and "garbage" sources; but that shift also echoes a longer historical and theoretical effort, started in the sixties and, not surprisingly, under the influence of Maoism, aimed at making visible the presence and actions of the subaltern. PRC history, especially in its "grassroots" form, can at times show a certain tendency toward the sinological obsession with sources and archives—there is a certain macho pride in one's prowess in collecting garbage materials, in being the Indiana Jones of the flea markets—but the work of colleagues who specifically embrace the grassroots label has not only been consistently of the highest quality but also has invariably addressed broad, crucial historical and political questions.

There can be no sinological escape into irrelevance in PRC history, precisely because writing the history of Maoism (and post-Maoism) does not provide such a refuge. That is true of the edited volume that Perry selected as the lynchpin of her critique, *Maoism at the Grassroots*: pretty much every single one of the essays included in that volume tackles, explicitly or implicitly, issues that were central to the experience of Maoist China, its structure of governance, and our understanding of its legacy.

Yet, as I mentioned earlier, I wish we (historians of the PRC) were even more explicit about and more aware of the political stakes of this intellectual project and the challenges it poses. In their introduction to *Maoism at the Grassroots*, Brown and Johnson set for grassroots history the task of recovering the everyday life of people under Maoism, knowing what they *actually* did and how they *actually* lived. That reveals a surprising degree of positivistic optimism about the historian's ability to recover the lived experience of the past—which seems quite indefensible at this point in the history of our discipline—but, more importantly, as Alexander Day points out in his article in this issue, that also leads them, perhaps inadvertently, to reposit a duality between state and society, which is always problematic but is specifically untenable in the case of Maoism. As Day argues, everyday life is not a stable position from which to look at society; "rather, historians dialectically tack back and forth to understand emergent social categories, practices, and forms."

I want to push Day's point further here: everyday life is not only "already a structured terrain"; in Maoist China, it also was a crucial site of contestation and political struggle at all levels of society. Further from being the unadulterated repository of "real life," the everyday was at the center of the political search and the struggles of Maoist China: consumption and leisure, work and learning, social reproduction, family relationships, and the minute practices that regulated people's daily interactions were all under scrutiny during a revolution whose goal was to change not just the state but life itself. In this sense, when we focus on everyday life in Maoist China, rather than simply trying to recover whatever we can of the factual reality hidden under the rhetoric of the Party-state, we are actually engaging with one of the crucial political categories of the Maoist revolution, and, because of that, we are directly challenged to rethink what "the everyday" is, what it encompasses, what it can be, how it can change, and perhaps more importantly, how it functions both historically and in our analysis.

Maoism, especially the "high Maoism" of the Great Leap and the Cultural Revolution, represented perhaps not only one of the most radical (at times violent and disastrous) attempts at transforming society but also, because of that, it questioned and pushed to the limits the very categories that had framed the socialist state, Marxist economics, and revolutionary practices. Those categories (the everyday, the Party, class, labor, the economy, value, etc.) are also the very ones we still deploy to frame our analysis of those phenomena. Therefore, "taking Maoism seriously" also always means interrogating the concepts and intellectual frameworks that we use to analyze Maoist China. For example, once we consider how Maoism configured a very complex relationship between revolution, the leaders, and the people, culminating in a veritable attack against the Party by the people (during the Cultural Revolution), it is difficult to take the Party (or the Party-state) as any kind of stable entity, or even a fixed point of reference.[2]

Finally, "taking Maoism seriously" implies accepting that Maoism informed practices and beliefs of millions, and that those beliefs and practices left traces in the archives. In their contributions, Jeremy Brown, Sigrid Schmalzer, and Aminda Smith all urge us to place Maoism—as a complex set of desires, impositions, promises, and epistemological methods—at the center of our analysis, and to examine the sources produced in that context as an expression of that complexity.

The articles in this issue came together after years of discussion among a much wider group of scholars, all active in the PRC History Group. We are deeply indebted to that discussion, and while this issue does not do justice to the variety of voices that were involved in that long debate, we hope it will move the discussion forward, and that others will join in. One of the anonymous reviewers for this special issue intriguingly pointed out that, while we share a common sense of direction, we do not seem to grapple with the theoretical issues implied in one another's work. At first, it sounded like a strange critique, given how closely we work together, but it is probably not off the mark. Perhaps it is because "new PRC historians" end up fighting so much with other people that we do not challenge one another enough. Or perhaps it is because, while we do engage with one another's general ideas, our individual work remains siloed within our particular topics and pet projects. So maybe this special issue will offer a way for budding scholars, and especially for young PRC historians, to more clearly identify the existing theoretical fissures and to stake their own intellectual positions in the field.

The first article in this special issue, Jeremy Brown's "PRC History in Crisis and Clover," sets the stage by singling out three broad topics that will all be discussed by the other authors: ideology, sources, and politics. Brown starts by highlighting the centrality of Maoism as an aspirational framework. He argues that ideology remains crucial for understanding events and action, and we must therefore take into consideration the aspirations that Maoism engendered, first and foremost because they were shared and lived by millions. And so was the disappointment that came when the promises of Maoism were not kept and the aspirations not fulfilled.[3] Brown then addresses a series of problems that mark the practice of PRC history to this day. While we have an abundance of newly available sources, the large majority of these documents are held in private archives, which makes the task of professional verification very difficult (if not outright impossible) and resource sharing completely dependent on personal ethics. Brown reminds us that the field of PRC history suffers from an "inclusivity" crisis in terms of gender, race, ethnicity, and class, no less than academia (and society) at large but more so, especially because within China it has become much more difficult to challenge this lack of inclusion—for example, writing histories of non-Han people. And here Brown brings forth another way in which writing the history of the PRC is a political act, because it is always an act of defiance vis-à-vis the current authoritarian push of the Xi Jinping government.

The problems of dealing with sources from the PRC—what they are, how we read them, and what we can learn from them—are at the core of Sigrid Schmalzer's contribution, "Beyond Bias: Critical Analysis and Layered Reading of Mao-Era Sources." Schmalzer steps away from the trite discussion of the unredeemable "bias" of such documents and urges us instead to make visible the contexts in which our sources were produced. She exemplifies this approach with three examples: a "propaganda" report on housewives turned veterinary doctors, a recording of interviews by a visiting delegation of leftist US scientists, and a 2013 edited volume curated by a local village historian. She shows how missed connections, personal relationships, and random acquisitions might shape how we construct our stories, but also how they can illuminate specific historical questions, if we go beyond the crude dismissal of "propaganda" or even the basic notion that truth can be found by "reading against the grain."

In "Long Live the Mass Line! Errant Cadres and Post-Disillusionment PRC History" Aminda Smith connects the way we read Mao-era sources to the ideological approach that frames our understanding of Maoist politics in general. For the post-disillusionment generation, the need to prove that the Maoist state lied, that it did not do what it said it was doing, produced a mode of inquiry that privileged cadres' mistakes, mishaps, and sheer brutality. Yet, as Smith demonstrates, that narrative came directly from CCP sources, which were keen to point out cadre errors as part of the central organizational practice of the Maoist state, the mass line. Therefore, the falsification mode adopted by the previous generation of China scholars, far from constituting a counternarrative, replicates the central narrative of the Maoist state. But, more importantly, that mode also prevents us from garnering crucial insights from reports and accounts too easily dismissed as biased and, crucially, to understand under which theoretical principles and operating practices the Party-state functioned.

The contributions by Werner, Meyskens, and Johnson all address, in different ways, the ideological premises of the field. Jake Werner, in "To Confront the Totality: A Critique of Empiricism in the Historiography of the People's Republic of China," provides a cogent and thorough analysis of empiricism as the unspoken and unrecognized ideology framing the historiography of the early PRC. Like all ideologies, this too is historically specific, and Werner associates it with a (unrecognized) conception of individuality and individual interests as the supreme motor of social transformation, at the level of both civil society and the state. This conception does not emerge from the sources, but it is part of the belief structure underlying the discipline of history, solidified after the so-called "cultural turn" in the 1980s. While the "cultural turn" aimed to shift attention from the state and larger patterns of change to focus on the messy details of the everyday and was therefore meant to be an explicit and implicit critique of domination, in PRC history, the fragmentation into a myriad of unreconcilable individual stories led to the uncritical acceptance of domination through the (hidden and unchallenged) practices of neoliberalism, and to the loss of any ability and hope to explain systemic change.

In "Rethinking the Political Economy of Development in Mao's China" Covell Meyskens focuses on the Maoist economy, which, he argues, has been predominantly interpreted according to two frameworks—neoclassical and state capitalist—both assuming a specific path according to which the economy *should have* developed. Both these frameworks, while radically divergent in interpretation, are functional to shaping a narrative that precludes any alternative to the dominance of capitalism, and leads inexorably to the "end of history." Against this, Meyskens argues that the deployment of Marxist categories and programs as well as the shaping of daily lived practices (how you buy things, how you get your job, where you work and live) in the Maoist era constituted an economy that cannot be simply considered either a replication of capitalism or a pathological deviation from capitalism (the only possible and correct economic form). Meyskens instead places the development strategy of the Maoist era in the context of East Asia, where it does not appear as an aberration at all. Rather, it fit a specific historical path and geopolitical exigencies, which were in turn marked by the global context of the Cold War, often too easily removed from our evaluation of Maoism and its choices.

In his article "Foundations of Theory in PRC History: Mass Communications Research, Political Culture, and the Values Paradigm" Matthew Johnson pushes us to examine even broader and longer-standing patterns defining our field. Despite changes in theoretical approach, availability of archives, and access to sources, there is deeper continuity in how the history of the PRC has been written in US academia. Johnson traces the persistent dominance of one approach that assumes the possibility of nonviolent change in societies coming from the transformation of human cognition. This approach, which proclaims the primacy of values and privileges explanations based on political culture, was first developed in studies of psychological warfare during World War II and the Cold War. It was then adopted by the social sciences, and through area studies, came to be deployed in the explanation of the CCP success and rule. The application of mass communications theory to modeling of the Chinese Communist Party–led revolution produced analyses centered on the persistence of traditional culture and values and on the effect of media/propaganda: societies could then be controlled and changed by manipulating those levers. While most of those early studies based on this approach have since been discredited, Johnson points that the true legacy of that work is "the explanation of political behavior in terms of cultural variables," which is very much alive today.

Alexander Day forces us to reconsider the relationship between material conditions, social forms, and political categories in "Breaking with the Family Form: Historical Categories, Social Reproduction, and Everyday Life in Late 1950s Rural China." Focusing on the complex category of social reproduction, Day shows how it emerged from the late 1950s shifts in rural production, leading in turn to new social forms (outside the family) and new discursive forms in party politics, which in turn provoked further transformations in rural production. Day illustrates how everyday life does not exist outside political discourse, material conditions, and social forms, all continuously evolving and dialectically interacting. He uses this case to bring us back to Marx and the need to see social forms as well as the categories deployed to describe them, as historical products. Labor and productive labor did not exist in Maoist China under the same conditions as under capitalism, and therefore did not take the same form. Under Maoism, labor was not commodified, there was no abstract labor dominating social relations, and the result of production was not value but products, as was required under a state-regulated system.

Finally, Jan Kiely is one of the three incredibly insightful and engaged anonymous reviewers for this special issue. As he posed productive challenges, we were delighted when he graciously agreed to incorporate some of his critiques into an afterword. His contribution serves as an invitation to all in the "good left" of PRC history not to flatten our analyses into a recovery of Maoism as a reaction to our dissatisfaction with the state of the field. Rather, he invites leftist scholars to embrace the contradictions and the tensions that animated PRC history, including those political paths and avenues that Maoism itself obscured. He reminds us how Maoist epistemology was always founded on the monopoly of violence and how its explicatory power was always limited by the often simplified models it deployed. He calls on us to devise and employ theories and methods that are more responsive to complexities and differences, including the differences between us and scholars with other disciplinary backgrounds and/or from older generations.

On the whole, all the authors in this special issue challenge the fundamental ways in which the PRC was constituted as an object of investigation in anglophone scholarship (and public opinion) during the post-disillusionment era. They do so not by embracing new or old illusions about Maoist and post-Maoist China, illusions that in part marred the perspectives of scholars and activists in the long sixties and that still cloud the vision of many pro-China leftists today. What we take from the history of this young field is the need to identify our historical subjects as true political subjects, to understand their experience as one intimately enmeshed in a set of complex political ideas and practices that goes under the name of "Maoism," and finally to consider the global and long-term consequences of that experience, including for our own scholarly enterprise.

Notes

1 In the very different situation of the Soviet Union and Eastern Europe, "sinology" offered a similarly safe retreat from the dangers of political involvement. See the special issue "Doing Sinology in Former Socialist States," *China Review* 14, no. 2 (2014).

2 Gail Hershatter, Aminda Smith, and others have pointed out that "taking Maoism seriously" does not in any way mean supporting the state. If one assumes that taking Maoism seriously ends up supporting the state, one not only does a disservice to history but also does a huge disservice to millions of people (in China and abroad) who found ways to be Maoist specifically by attacking the Party-state.

3 I would also add that, for some, in minor and major ways, some aspirations were fulfilled, which in turn created other kinds of affective and political bonds to the Maoist past.

References

Bloch, Marc. 1954. *The Historian's Craft*, translated by Peter Putnam. Manchester, UK: Manchester University Press.

Brown, Jeremy, and Matthew D. Johnson, eds. 2015. *Maoism at the Grassroots: Everyday Life in China's Era of High Socialism*. Cambridge, MA: Harvard University Press.

Cusset, François. 2008. *French Theory: How Foucault, Derrida, Deleuze, & Co. Transformed the Intellectual Life of the United States*, translated by Jeff Fort. Minneapolis: University of Minnesota Press.

Fairbank, John K., and James Peck. 1970. "An Exchange." *Bulletin of Concerned Asian Scholars* 2, no. 3: 51–70.

Kelley, Robin D. G., and Betsy Esch. 1999. "Black Like Mao: Red China and Black Revolution." *Souls: A Critical Journal of Black Politics, Culture, and Society* 1, no. 4: 6–41.

Lanza, Fabio. 2017. *The End of Concern: Maoism, Activism, and Asian Studies*. Durham, NC: Duke University Press.

Perry, Elizabeth. 2016. "The Promise of PRC History." *Journal of Modern Chinese History* 10, no. 1: 113–17.

Schmalzer, Sigrid. 2016. *Red Revolution, Green Revolution: Scientific Farming in Socialist China*. Chicago: University of Chicago Press.

PRC History in Crisis and Clover

Jeremy Brown

In an introduction to a special issue of *China Quarterly* on the history of the PRC published in 2006, political scientist Julia Strauss (2006: 855) observed that "now is an enormously vibrant time for the study of the history of the People's Republic of China (PRC) in its phase of active revolution between 1949 and 1976." Strauss ended her essay with a call to action: "We are still very much in search of PRC history, and hope that others will pick up where this volume concludes" (869). In the years since 2006, PRC history has gradually acquired all the trappings of a formally recognized field of academic inquiry. These include a journal (the *PRC History Review*), an H-Net channel called H-PRC, a book series from Cambridge University Press, panels and a reception at the Association for Asian Studies annual meeting, as well as turf battles.

One promising sign of the healthy development of PRC history has been

positions 29:4   DOI 10.1215/10679847-9286662

lively arguments about scholars' theoretical frameworks, research questions, and how to find and use sources. Which theories should underpin the field? To what extent should historians build on or engage with the work of social scientists who have written about China since 1949, especially when it comes to forming research questions? Is it better to start with theories and questions, or to start with sources? How can we maximize the strengths and overcome the shortcomings of grassroots sources? I weigh in on these field-defining arguments in the first part of this article.

Vigorous scholarly debates are a sign that PRC history is in good shape, but storm clouds have accompanied the field's growth. PRC history is simultaneously flourishing and in crisis. During the year after Xi Jinping became China's top leader in 2013—the same twelve-month period when scholars outside of China launched the PRC History Group and the Cambridge book series—the Chinese Communist Party (CCP) cracked down on critical, evidence-based research about its own history and tightened access to archival sources. All scholarship is political. In the Xi Jinping era, however, researching PRC history has not only been an overt political intervention but also has become scary and dangerous. Understanding China's recent past is more important than ever in today's high-stakes environment of arbitrary detentions, censorship, internment camps, and pandemic politics. The final sections of this article argue that in response to genuine dangers that have increased since Xi Jinping took office, scholarship on China since 1949 has adapted in creative ways and will continue to flourish. A more pressing crisis for the field is addressing how the real dangers of Xi's dictatorship are exacerbating existing inequities, and finding ways for scholars in and outside of China to work toward a more inclusive field that recognizes and reflects the diversity of historians and the people they study.

PRC History Comes with Its Own Framework: Aspirational Socialism

In 2016 I asked the H-PRC discussion forum to help identify the most important and influential theoretical work in the field of PRC history. Fifteen scholars answered. Many mentioned excellent books about China that discuss or deploy theory, but that was not what I was asking for—I was wondering if there was a single theoretical work or body of work, maybe even one that did not mention China, that had most strongly influenced our field. Michael Schoenhals responded, "Whether we are its friends or members or opponents really does not matter: the fact is that it is the Chinese Communist Party that has provided us with most of the seemingly indispensable awls, edgers, and tweezers that make up the theoretical toolkits we carry along when approaching PRC history in our professional capacities. . . . An intentionally provocative alternative answer to Jeremy's question could therefore also be the *Selected Works of Mao Zedong*!" Kristin Stapleton added that the first thing that came to her mind was Marxism-Leninism–Mao Zedong Thought ("Most Important/Influential" 2016).

Schoenhals and Stapleton are correct that PRC history already comes along with the ready-made framework of Marxism-Leninism–Mao Zedong Thought. Hundreds of millions of people in China learned about and applied Maoism after 1949. Mao's interpretation of Marxism, Leninism, and Stalinism provided a road map for socialist modernization at the national policy level. It also shaped the educational curriculum, news coverage, patriotic rituals, the layout of standardized bureaucratic forms, and many other aspects of daily life in cities and villages. But in practice, Maoism was not a fixed itinerary. It shifted over time, lurching toward extremes and then overcorrecting, causing profound harm to millions and disappointment for many more. How can historians make sense of this juxtaposition between utopianism and dashed dreams?

In my research about risk, safety, and accidents after 1949, I have highlighted the Chinese Communist revolution's central promise of a safe and healthy modern society where people could go to work without being exploited and without being killed in an accident. The CCP's socialist modernization project took this promise seriously, but it fell far short of delivering on it (Brown forthcoming). When I made this point in a talk in 2017, historian Karl Gerth pointed at his midsection and said that he really wants six-pack abs and he has lots of self-help books about how to achieve perfect stomach muscles, but his desire and his bookshelf are not enough to justify calling him "Six-Pack Karl." He meant that even though China's goal during the Mao years was to achieve socialism, the gap between aspiration and reality was so large that it would be as ludicrous to call China socialist as it would to refer to Karl Gerth as Six-Pack Karl.[1]

positions 29:4   November 2021   692

Gerth is correct that "socialist China" is an inaccurate label for what sociologist Andrew Walder (1987) has referred to as "actually existing Maoism." Utopian aspirations and messy reality, however, can and should be studied simultaneously. Whether people in China studied socialist ideals because of their "intrinsic insight or value," or whether, as Walder (1987: 157) suggests, people paid attention to Mao's thought "because they had no choice," the ideals themselves were important during the Mao years and they remain relevant today. We can distinguish between Gerth's ideals—as seen on his bookshelf—versus the reality of his torso, and thereby gain a more complete understanding of him as an individual. Historians learn a lot by noticing such clues as a Bowflex machine in the corner or a Mao statue on the table. But historians should not stop there. It is also worthwhile to try to understand someone's motivation for wanting to sculpt his abdomen—does he see intrinsic value in rock-hard abs, or does he feel like he has no choice? Figuring out why someone buys *The Six-Pack Secret* or prominently displays a Mao portrait helps to understand the social context that shapes individual, family, and community choices. If historians of the People's Republic accept that the *hukou* system, class status labels, the Great Leap famine, and the Cultural Revolution significantly affected hundreds of millions of individual lives, then the starting point for PRC history projects should be an awareness of the aspirational framework that gave rise to these systems and events—Mao Zedong's road map to socialism, as conveyed in the Little Red Book, *People's Daily*, and the Stalinist *Short Course* history of the Bolshevik Party.[2]

Andrew Walder's "Actually Existing Maoism," published in 1987, reads like the product of a moment when many scholars who had previously sympathized with the stated goals of the Chinese Communist revolution suffered from embarrassed disillusionment with Maoist ideals.[3] Walder (1987: 156) writes that Maoism as a populist, egalitarian ideal was a myth, a "rationalised, heavily edited reconstruction by Western scholars, for Western consumption, designed to appeal to Western sensibilities." Focusing excessively on happy ideals, Walder argues, excludes other important aspects of Maoism, including a "paranoid political world view that sees Chinese society as riddled with hidden conspirators and traitors" and a "mentality that encourages the treatment of 'enemies' as nonhumans subjectable to any form of humiliation and torture" (158). Walder's myth-versus-reality formulation may have been a useful corrective at the time, but it presented a false dichotomy. Myth and reality were intertwined in Mao's collected works as well as in Chinese society. Anyone who has read Mao's "On the People's Democratic Dictatorship" can see how populism, egalitarianism, paranoia, and the dehumanization of enemies coexisted in a single short document. Readers of Roderick MacFarquhar and Michael Schoenhals's *Mao's Last Revolution* (2006) can find abundant evidence of how these phenomena intermingled in the everyday lives of Chinese people between 1966 and 1976.

If socialism was attempted but fell short in China, as Gerth's girth metaphor reminds us, and if mythical Maoism was different from the traumas of actually existing Maoism, as Walder noted decades ago, why should PRC historians bother mentioning socialism and Maoism? First, as Covell Meyskens argues in his article in this issue, many people in China proudly considered themselves socialists during the 1950s, 1960s, and 1970s; they found genuine inspiration in the ideas of Marx, Lenin, and Mao. To deny these identity claims is to misrepresent the lived experience of millions. Whether people memorized Mao quotations eagerly or did so under duress, their shared experience created a canon that bridged regional, ethnic, and generational divides (Leese 2011). The creation of this shared canon was part of the "real increase in social homogeneity" that Jake Werner highlights in his article in this issue.

Second, lofty socialist ideals created an existential crisis for the socialist project. The field of happiness studies claims that "HAPPINESS *equals* REALITY *minus* EXPECTATIONS" (Baucells and Sarin 2012: 49).[4] Promises about the coming of socialism in China set expectations so impossibly high that even though life expectancy, education, and health improved during the Mao years, reality fell so far short of utopia that many people were unhappy. Philosopher Ci Jiwei identified this crisis well before anyone claimed credit for inventing a happiness equation. Ci (1994: 5) calls the promise of socialist construction under Mao "sublimated hedonism." Ci writes, "had it not been for the high hopes" promised by Maoist utopianism, "the Chinese people would not have sacrificed so much and demanded so little." What happiness researchers would call unhappiness, Ci describes as "nihilism"; the Chinese term *bu manyi* 不满意 may capture the idea better than any English phrase.

In Ci's words: "At the point they expected the future to meet the present . . . nothing happened. The gap between future and present . . . which had been the locus of an energizing tension as long as people anticipated that the gap would one day be closed, became, once that anticipation evaporated through disappointment and loss of stamina, the very site of nihilism." This transition from anticipation to nihilism was palpable for some people—Chan, Madsen, and Unger ([1984] 2009: 231) identify Lin Biao's death in 1971 as a moment when questions and doubts replaced activism and hope for sentdown youth in Chen Village. "We lost faith in the system," said one sentdown youth. Another recalled, "It all seemed so hypocritical. The craze of studying Mao's work was over."

Exploring the relationship between expectations and reality has sparked path-breaking PRC history research. For example, Yiching Wu (2014) has shown how activist youth on the intellectual margins critiqued the Cultural Revolution for failing to meet socialist standards. For such thinkers as Yang Xiguang, far from being too leftist, Maoism in the 1960s and 1970s was not socialist enough. In fact, it is difficult to find a work of PRC history that does not in some way benefit from Ci Jiwei's version of the happiness equation. Even Andrew Walder, who had no use for mythical Maoism in the 1980s, comes full circle in *China under Mao: A Revolution Derailed* (2015). While Walder gives more explanatory weight to Party organization and Soviet-style political economy than to the unfulfilled promises of aspirational socialism, his book's subtitle drives home his message: the revolution must have started on track, but it went off the rails. Whatever scholars of PRC history think about socialism, practicing historical empathy means taking seriously how people in China defined, thought about, supported, or felt disappointed by socialism during the decades we are studying.

PRC History Is Not a New Field: Social Scientists Wrote the First Draft

Social scientists exploring China's recent past during the 1950s, 1960s, and 1970s were doing historical work. In fact, they founded the field of PRC history. PRC history is as old as the PRC: C. K. Yang ([1959] 1965) was doing rural fieldwork between 1948 and 1951; A. Doak Barnett (1963, 1964) saw the People's Liberation Army enter Beiping in 1949; Robert Lifton (1961) interviewed people about thought reform in 1954. In the four decades after 1949, long before historians started doing PRC history, several generations of social scientists working in area studies, political science, and sociology departments had already examined how the Communist Party was attempting to reshape China (Schurmann [1966] 1968), provincial and elite politics (Vogel 1969; MacFarquhar 1974; Teiwes 1979), communication (Liu 1971), land reform (Shue 1980), political movements (Lieberthal 1980), class stratification (Lee 1978; Rosen 1982), urban life (Whyte and Parish 1984), factory politics (Walder 1986), and many other facets of the Mao years.

After China moved on from the Mao period in the late 1970s and early 1980s, social scientists also moved on to study the changes of the reform era, leaving behind only a small handful of historically minded scholars who eventually became outliers in their own disciplines, most notably political scientists Neil Diamant and Elizabeth J. Perry and sociologists Joel Andreas and Andrew Walder. When, in the 2000s, a significant number of historians started writing about China's 1950s as history, the few social scientists still actively researching the Mao years were understandably miffed by historians' failure to cite their work and disregard for their research questions. Neil Diamant emailed me after reading *City versus Countryside in Mao's China* (2012), praising the book but noting that I had failed to cite or show how I was building on relevant political science literature about China's cellular political economy (Shue 1988), cadre corruption (Lü 2000), marriage, and veterans (Diamant 2000, 2009). Diamant was right to point out these shortcomings.

Diamant elaborates on his critique of PRC history's blindness toward earlier generations of scholarship in a review of *Revolution, Resistance, and Reform in Village China*, coauthored by political scientist Edward Friedman, historian Paul Pickowicz, and sociologist Mark Selden (2005). The book is the sequel to *Chinese Village, Socialist State* (1989). In his review Diamant (2008: 622) praises the 2005 book's coverage of rural politics but complains that the three authors disregard "most social science conventions" and "do not engage any theories, the secondary literature on rural reform, or the comparative literature on village politics."

Chinese Village, Socialist State may be the first work of PRC history that counts a trained historian among its authors. *Chinese Village, Socialist State* mentions more secondary literature than *Revolution, Resistance, and Reform* does, but its theoretical engagement remains hidden. Rather than elaborating on how it relates to theory, it gives readers its framework in the title: a local "Chinese" culture full of family complications and kinship networks clashed with a flattening socialist modernization project. This model resonates with earlier political science (Lieberthal 1980) and sociological (Schurmann [1966] 1968) works exploring the relationship between Chinese tradition and modernity during the 1950s. Friedman, Pickowicz, and Selden, however, do not belabor how their book builds on earlier work about China or how it relates to Weberian models of tradition and modernity. The authors choose to let readers make these connections for themselves. Theory is present, but it is embedded obliquely in the narrative. Hiding theory and minimizing citations of secondary literature is an explicit choice. It frustrates such critics as Diamant, but the authors must figure that they gain more than they lose by making such a choice. Scholars can see the implicit framework for themselves, while undergraduates and general readers can enjoy the accessible narrative.

Diamant does have a good point: PRC historians would benefit from reading and citing social scientists. Historians writing about China's 1950s, 1960s, and 1970s do not, however, have to accept social scientists' frameworks and questions as their own. In 2016, political scientist Elizabeth Perry (2016: 116) lamented that "many" historians of the PRC, "especially among the younger generation in the West," choose to "grub for diversity in the dustbins of grassroots society" instead of answering the "key questions that attracted but eluded an earlier generation of social scientists." Perry argues, "Fulfilling the promise of PRC history calls for rising above 'garbology' to engage seriously with the big questions posed, but necessarily left unanswered, by a previous generation of social scientists." Michael Schoenhals (2016) disagreed, writing, "The agenda of questions that attracted social scientists to the professional study of China a generation or two ago is already itself history, so let us please refrain from urging today's graduate students and assistant professors to 'revisit' it as if it were something else!"

New sources and new questions can allow historians to respect the contributions of older scholarship while explaining change over time in fresh ways that overturn timeworn or even erroneous assumptions. At the heart of this issue is the word *questions*. Perry is a pioneer in the study of the history of the People's Republic who has asked and answered many significant questions about governance in China (Perry 1994, 2005, 2012; Perry and Li 1997). Working out puzzles by looking at documents in the Shanghai Municipal Archive or other officially produced and curated sources, however, yields different results than answering questions based on such garbological materials as public security dossiers or Red Guard publications. Schoenhals has shown that rare grassroots sources can offer original answers to questions that have long interested social scientists. Inspired by Christopher Andrew and David Dilks's (1984: 1) statement that the "great danger of any missing historical dimension is that its absence may distort our understanding of other, accessible dimensions," Schoenhals (2013) has uncovered previously hidden dimensions of life in China in the 1950s and 1960s. He has asked how the presence of secret agents manipulated by public security officials affected the identification and punishment of purported counterrevolutionaries. Schoenhals (2015) has also asked how mass organizations' independently published newsletters in 1966 and 1967 call into question mistaken assumptions about the Cultural Revolution and freedom of speech in Chinese history. Grassroots sources provide new evidence about what actually happened in China during the 1950s, 1960s, and 1970s that challenges inaccurate narratives and reveals the shortcomings of officially compiled or vetted sources.

Grassroots Sources: Opportunities and a Problem

I refrained from putting "what actually happened" inside quotation marks in the previous sentence because accidents, conversations, events, fights, massacres, meetings, sexual affairs, trends, and other phenomena actually did occur in China between 1949 and the present. Different types of sources offer different ways of looking at what actually happened. If the Tianjin Municipal Archive had given me access to every document I wanted to see in 2004, I would have stayed inside its friendly and comfortable confines, playing table tennis with the staff during lunch break. But all I was allowed to see were fairly bland reports—the entire Cultural Revolution decade was off limits and personal stories and human color were few and far between.

Frustration with limited access to the official archive drove me to a boom-ing gray market that included such unofficial sources as diaries and letters but also state-created material that local representatives of the Party-state decided to discard but did not destroy (Schoenhals 2004; Brown 2010, 2019; Leese 2019). Historian Eric Hobsbawm (1985: 65–66) has lamented that scholars interested in European "history from below" initially struggled because "there simply is not a ready-made body of material about" grass-roots history:

> In most cases the grassroots historian finds only what he is looking for, not what is already waiting for him. Most sources for grassroots history have only been recognized as sources because someone has asked a ques-tion and then prospected desperately around for some way—any way—of answering it. We cannot be positivists, believing that the questions and the answers arise naturally out of the study of the material. There is generally no material until our questions have revealed it.

Hobsbawm's statement is an imperfect fit for China, where grassroots mate-rial has been ready and waiting for desperate prospectors, whether they arrive with a puzzle in mind or whether they wait for questions and answers to emerge from the sources.

Hundreds of thousands of ready-made bodies of grassroots material are stored in local Chinese archives. Some historians have been fortunate enough to gain access to these sources. Others have been shut out of official archives and have been driven to flea markets and bookstores, where sack-fuls of grassroots sources appeared in the 1990s and 2000s.[5] Scholars who already have a question in mind can find rich answers in grassroots sources. Neil Diamant (2000: 12), for example, asked what impact the marriage law of 1950 had on Chinese families. Investigation reports about marriage and divorce held at district and county archives offered many unexpected answers: "administrative bumbling" gave women "space to change their sta-tus," and the "open sexual culture" of rural areas "facilitated the sort of change envisioned" by the marriage law.

Diamant proceeded as Hobsbawm recommended: start with a question and look for answers in the sources. But scholars who do the opposite—those who, in Perry's words, "grub for diversity" in a "janitorial role" and allow new questions to emerge from their empirical findings—are advancing PRC history as well. Sinologist Michael Schoenhals (2014) has argued that fifty pages of missing persons notices (*xunren tongbao* 尋人通報) could be the starting point for an alternative narrative of China's 1960s and 1970s, a history of "lives that need not necessarily have been uneventful, but had somehow managed not to have everything about them determined by Mao Zedong's grand design." I fruitfully ignored Hobsbawm's advice when I read a dossier about a police officer accused of sexual assault. I originally bought the file because I had a question in mind about how people experienced the rural-urban divide at the grassroots. At the flea market I decided to get it because it focused on someone who had been deported from Tianjin to the countryside. Then I put it aside, used other deportation files to argue that ejecting political enemies from the city was an official program managed and funded by municipal authorities rather than an example of Red Guard–led "chaos," and forgot about it for several years. By the time I picked it up, I was no longer working on the gap between city and countryside. I read it because it was in a box waiting for me, not because I was looking for something specific.

The puzzles that emerged from the file hinged on how criminal justice functioned at the grassroots during the 1960s and 1970s. Memoirs and scholarly works commonly portray the Cultural Revolution as a lawless period characterized by false and unjust accusations. What if some accusations lodged during the Cultural Revolution were not exaggerated or fabricated, but instead revealed actual crimes? What legal avenues could victims and convicted criminals pursue? How did a shifting political climate affect how security officials investigated appeals? The answers touch on police work, sexual violence, transitional justice, and stereotypes about the Cultural Revolution (Brown 2018). A Party-state that controls access to material about the recent past while allowing discarded dossiers to circulate in flea markets has unintentionally facilitated a variety of useful approaches—some scholars have put questions first and sources second, others have started with sources and allowed questions to arise during the reading process. Original conclusions can emerge from either strategy.

One big problem with PRC history's unique source environment can be found in the footnotes, the point of which is to allow readers to assess the reliability of the writer's conclusions. This problem affects citations of sources held in official archives as well as material found in flea markets. Say I want to verify Diamant's (2000: 144, 375) claims about Yunnanese women neglecting class struggle and instead criticizing their in-laws and husbands. Diamant has helpfully provided the file and page numbers of documents held at the Chuxiong Prefectural Archive, where he enjoyed unfettered access in the 1990s. I have three ways to assess Diamant's interpretation of these sources: I could travel to the archive with file numbers in hand, I could ask a local research assistant to do the same, or I could email Diamant and ask him to dig through his photocopies and share the passage in question. Options one and two are expensive and might meet with official rejection—just because Diamant saw a source in the 1990s does not mean that archivists will let anyone see it in 2021. Option three is better, but it depends on the longevity of Diamant's storage and filing system as well as his generosity, which I know is expansive.

Garbage material discarded by the state that is now circulating in society presents an even better fourth option—sharing digitized documents—that represents a big step toward accessibility and transparency. I heard that a graduate student counted all of the sources cited in *Maoism at the Grassroots* (2015) and complained that far too many documents were held in personal collections inaccessible to readers. This critique is valid. Sixty-four of the eighty-nine footnotes in the book's "Adrift in Tianjin" chapter refer to a single diary to which only Sha Qingqing and I had access. This story about adolescent anxiety in 1976 would be more convincing if other scholars could assess our use of the source. To make this possible, I am following in the footsteps of other digitization projects[6] to make sources I have previously cited from my own collection available to other researchers through the PRC History Source Transparency Project.[7] Abandoned refuse rescued by peddlers, collectors, and historians can and should be stored and—whenever possible—shared so that as many people as possible can learn from their rich contents. Digital humanities tools can allow footnotes that include the phrase "author's collection" to be an open door rather than a dead end.

PRC History Is in Crisis, PRC History Is Flourishing

In an H-PRC discussion thread about sources cited by Frank Dikötter in *Mao's Great Famine* (2010), Sergey Radchenko defended online sharing of sources held in official archives (a category distinct from discarded refuse) on three grounds: "documents that are in the state archives are deemed to be in the public domain . . . posting select documents or portions thereof does not amount to copyright infringement . . . public interest may vastly outweigh any archival prerogative." A Chinese researcher responded that intellectual property law was not the crucial issue for Chinese scholars. Because the "Chinese government linked archive with natural security," he wrote, uploading sources, even English-language translations of them, "will probably slide people into big trouble. That's why most of Chinese scholars keep silence" ("Looking" 2015).

PRC history is not only the history of an authoritarian past but also a political intervention in an authoritarian present. This reality has created a two-tier system: scholars farther removed from the actually existing coercive organs of the People's Democratic Dictatorship (specifically, the Ministry of State Security and the Bureau to Guard Domestic Security, also known as the "First Department" of the Ministry of Public Security)[8] can make reasonable arguments about copyright, while those whose livelihoods and families are inside China legitimately fear big trouble. This divide goes deeper than how and whether scholars collect and share sources. Simply conducting research on and writing about recent Chinese history in a critical, evidence-based fashion is unacceptable by the standards of Party Center's Communique on the Current State of the Ideological Sphere of 2013 (commonly known as Document Nine).

Document Nine ("Document 9" 2013) identifies "promoting historical nihilism, trying to undermine the history of the CCP and of New China" as an approach that "is tantamount to denying the legitimacy of the CCP's long-term political dominance." Academic historians' job description is to explain change over time, not to bolster or undermine any particular political organization. Historians devoted to explaining change over time are doing a proper job if they uncover and interpret evidence that "denies the historical inevitability in China's choice of the socialist road" or that "rejects the accepted conclusions on historical events and figures." I spent years in graduate school learning how to deny historical inevitability and reject accepted conclusions. For Party Center, however, these are unacceptable expressions of historical nihilism. Document Nine considers ordinary historical research politically antagonistic, justifies closing archives and reclassifying previously accessible documents, sparks the active removal of individual historical articles from scholarly databases (Tiffert 2019), closes off publication venues, limits funding opportunities, and quashes graduate training. It makes doing PRC history an overtly political act in the here and now.

Scholars who have the privilege of holding secure academic positions outside of China can proudly violate the admonitions of Document Nine, take strong stands in favor of critical academic inquiry, and stress about whether they might encounter problems obtaining a visa, a difficulty that 5 percent of more than five hundred China scholars reported experiencing (Greitens and Truex 2020). Foreign scholars who do enter China can still visit archives and libraries, do oral history interviews, and buy books from vendors, but, as two recent cases have shown, even these innocuous acts can lead to uncomfortable interrogations or even extended detention. In 2017 in Shanghai, security agents questioned Dayton Lekner, who was working on a PhD dissertation about literary circulation during the Hundred Flowers and Anti-Rightist campaigns. The officers knew that Lekner had been interviewing elderly intellectuals about their experiences during the late 1950s. After a three-hour interrogation in a police station, the officers made Lekner promise to not release information from his interviews and to keep the interrogation secret—a pledge he proudly violated after leaving China (Lim 2017). Lekner's experience was stressful but brief. Nobu Itawani, a historian at Hokkaido University, had a longer nightmare. Itawani was detained in September 2019, apparently because he had purchased material about Kuomintang history from a used bookstore. After Prime Minister Shinzo Abe intervened, Itawani was released in November 2019, but not before he was forced to confess to "collecting inappropriate historical materials" (O'Dwyer 2019).

Historians cannot do their job properly without violating Document Nine, which can lead to unpleasant and dangerous consequences, as the experiences of Lekner and Itawani show. Restrictions on access to documents and fear of being detained seem like a crisis for PRC history research, especially compared with the pre-2013 openness of archives, conferences, flea markets, and publishing. But the crisis is not a permanent condition, nor is it all-pervasive. In 2018, 2019, and even in 2020 and 2021, as pandemic lockdowns eased in Chinese cities, I received positive reports from at least seven researchers who successfully viewed useful and interesting documents at no fewer than eight county and municipal archives throughout China. Many of those researchers also smoothly conducted oral history interviews without noticing any attention from security agents. In August 2019 I attended a workshop on PRC history at a mainland Chinese university. Professors and graduate students from Chinese institutions presented papers that included such topics as officially mandated quotas for executing counter-revolutionaries during the early 1950s, extreme starvation and violence in a single commune during the Great Leap Famine, and students assaulting their teachers during the Cultural Revolution. These edgy pieces will not be published inside China until the political situation relaxes, but workshop participants energetically debated and critiqued their arguments and use of evidence; the authors took note of the feedback they received and will wait for a more opportune political moment to share improved versions of the research.

The workshop was a welcome reminder of the extent to which post-1949 history flourished inside China during the 2000s and early 2010s. During those relatively open years a large group of Chinese experts on post-1949 history actively developed the field of *guoshi* 国史 (PRC history), a subject of inquiry that is pointedly separate from *dangshi* 党史 (Party history). Literally "history of the state"—meaning the new country that was born in 1949—*guoshi* sounds like a bland descriptor, but the term has subversive potential because it decenters the Communist Party from the study of recent Chinese history and argues for the historical validity of stories, narratives, moments, and people who operated beyond, below, around, or even in opposition to the Party. Some of the most active *guoshi* scholars work in universities (Cao 2005, 2015; Y. Li 2016; Y. Liu 2016a, 2016b; Ruan 2009; Shen 2003, 2008; Tang 2003; H. Wang 2021; K. Yang 2009, 2016; J. Zhang 2015; S. Zhang 2010). Some work in official research institutes (Chen 2003). Some are journalists (Tan 2010; J. Yang 2008, 2016), some are independent scholars who compile primary sources (D. Wang 2007) and publish such underground journals as *Bashan yeyu*, *Jiyi*, *Wangshi*, and *Zuotian*.[9] Some publish under pseudonyms (Shi 2012).

Many of the scholars at the August 2019 workshop in China expressed frustration at the increasing difficulties they face in researching and publishing on PRC history compared with the golden era of *guoshi* of the late 2000s and early 2010s. But the older professors had seen far worse, including the inside of jail cells during the 1970s and bullets flying and blood flowing in the streets of Beijing on June 3 and June 4, 1989. When viewed in comparison with previous moments of repression, the crisis facing PRC history today seems dire but not fatal. This is especially true because a multiplicity of research methods and source repositories in and outside of China are continuing to allow the field to flourish. In response to difficulties in getting access to municipal and provincial archives—and also in response to the narrow state-centered scope of the contents of documents held in these buildings—many Chinese universities have established their own archives of PRC history material, including cadre work journals, diaries, family letters, and village- and county-level dossiers. Selections from these gold mines have begun to be published outside of China (Zhang and Yan 2018; Zhang, Xi, and Yan 2018).

During the past two years nervous administrators and intrusive security agents have restricted access to or even shut down these collections. But this temporary shuttering may actually be conducive to long-term preservation: the documents are out of sight, out of mind, and ready to be revived in the future. In the meantime, researchers at the August 2019 workshop reported no restrictions on their ability to continue carrying out oral history interviews about PRC history. If doors should slam shut on doing oral history in China, other doors outside of China remain open, including the possibility of field work among recent immigrants in such communities as Vancouver as well as such valuable resources as the Michael Schoenhals Collection of Cultural Revolution materials held at Lund University and collections of grassroots sources stored at Stanford University's East Asian Library and Hoover Institution Archives. Even memoir articles written online on such blog platforms as Sina and Sohu have become revelatory sources for PRC history, as shown by Karl Gerth's most recent book—Gerth wisely used the Internet Archive's Wayback Machine to preserve blog posts before censors removed them (Gerth 2020). In other words, restrictions on conventional archival sources in China have given rise to creative and diverse research methods and have pushed researchers to unearth sources and talk to people that they might have otherwise neglected if they had been researching in a less authoritarian context. This creativity cannot help but lead to fresh topics and novel conclusions. Adaptation in response to the crisis caused by Document Nine has led to innovation. This ensures that the field of PRC history will continue to be in clover.

Making More Space for Diversity and Inclusion in PRC History

The open critical discussions and creative adaptability on display at the workshop in China in August 2019 were encouraging and energizing. But the event was not perfect. The audience seated outside of the inner table of presenters reflected the sex ratio of Chinese society—slightly more men than women, but almost even. Of the twenty-six papers presented, however, there were six female authors and twenty male authors. The leadership roles at the workshop were more skewed, more akin to the Communist Party's all-male Politburo Standing Committee. Of the workshop's sixteen discussants, fifteen were men and one was a woman. Zero of the eight panel chairs were women. Zero of the eight roundtable speakers who closed the workshop were women. During the roundtable I said that I hoped that at future workshops the inner table would look more like the audience sitting outside of it. I stopped there because I had personally contributed to the imbalance as a presenter, discussant, chair, and roundtable speaker, and also because practitioners of PRC history based outside of China have lots of work to do on diversity and inclusion issues—the maleness and whiteness of this special issue is only one small example of a broader problem that the field needs to address.

Chinese society is Han supremacist, sexist, ableist, heteronormative, and cisnormative. Where I live and work in North America is a white supremacist, sexist, ableist, heteronormative, and cisnormative society. These structures of power and oppression privilege mainstream voices and limit opportunities for marginalized groups. The field of PRC history is not immune to these structures. This observation may seem facile, but it still needs to be pointed out and openly acknowledged at conferences, editorial board meetings, seminars, and workshops—and in "state of the field" special issues like this one. The backgrounds and identities of scholars who work on PRC history may not directly determine the topics they choose, the questions they ask, the research methods they use, and the theoretical frameworks they employ. But background and identity do matter, as do unspoken social norms and assumptions that benefit privileged groups and harm marginalized ones. When conference organizers, editorial boards, and graduate mentors accept the status quo rather than actively identifying and pushing back against structures of oppression, they not only continue to harm marginalized groups and individuals but also cause suboptimal scholarly outcomes, because shutting out diverse topics, questions, methods, and frameworks means that hidden dimensions of PRC history will remain hidden.

There is no quick fix to this problem, but by recognizing it and taking it into account when organizing panels and workshops, recruiting graduate school applicants, and issuing calls for manuscripts, all scholars—especially graduate mentors and publishing gatekeepers—can push the field in more diverse and inclusive directions.[10] Repression in China under Xi Jinping, however, has created a crisis that is more difficult to address. None of the twenty-six papers presented at the workshop I attended in China in August 2019 focused on frontier regions, non-Han groups, or religious topics, let alone queer history. When I pointed out this silence during the closing roundtable, the organizers responded that these themes were truly too sensitive to be touched on at an academic workshop inside China; they said that they hoped that in the future the political situation would relax and allow coverage of today's no-go zones. This answer was heartfelt. Just look at the track record of such senior *guoshi* researchers as Wang Haiguang and Yang Kuisong, who have written empathetically and perceptively about ethnoreligious rebellion and queer history, respectively (H. Wang 2015; K. Yang 2015).

The deeper crisis facing the field of PRC history, therefore, goes beyond archival restrictions. It is an inclusivity crisis. Outside of China scholars can and must push for a field that is more inclusive of scholars and research topics that reflect the diversity of the places we study and the places where we work and live. This is a difficult, complex, long-term project, but it is achievable. Inside China, however, pushing for inclusivity and advocating for minority rights are illegal. Xi Jinping's policies exacerbate existing inequities, most notably by targeting and incarcerating Muslims in a massive forced assimilation project. As long as this coercive secularization and sinification project continues, critical historians working inside China know that the Great Leap famine and students beating up their teachers in 1966 are safer topics than frontier regions, non-Han peoples, or religion. The ongoing cultural genocide in Xinjiang, along with the repression of such marginalized voices as Marxist students at Peking University, #MeToo activists, and survivors of the Beijing massacre, among others, contributes to a gap between PRC historians in and outside of China. The many researchers inside China who actively want to advocate for diversity and inclusion—both in their scholarship and within their scholarly circles—find it difficult, if not impossible, to do so safely. This unevenness is unfair. It is a crisis for the field of PRC history.

How can scholars address this crisis? There are as many possible answers as there are scholars working on PRC history. My own answers are not meant to be prescriptions for others to follow. My own first step is to continue documenting and explaining historical change in a diverse society where people sometimes resisted or ignored state repression and violence. I happily accept Jake Werner's label of empiricism and his accurate and perceptive observation in his article in this issue that my scholarly agenda "vindicates the rights of civil society." Werner is also correct that the brand of empiricism found in my monograph and coedited volumes does not piece together events and experiences at random. It actively seeks to highlight individuals, families, communities, and narratives that have been harmed or marginalized by state repression or by scholarly blinders. This is why focusing on farmers, gay and straight factory workers, midwives, rural teachers, and women weavers was an explicitly political choice in *Dilemmas of Victory* (2007) and *Maoism at the Grassroots* (2015), as was the inclusion of chapters about Guizhou, Tibet, and Xinjiang. None of my books have come close to including every marginalized voice that has been silenced, nor did they achieve my goal of mentioning an individual person's name on at least every other page.[11] Those shortcomings can be improved on in future projects.

Step two is to continue to collaborate with scholars in China on translation projects, increasing Chinese readership of English-language scholarship, and increasing Anglophone exposure to Chinese-language scholarship. The Chinese-language edition of *Dilemmas of Victory* (2011) and chapters by Cao Shuji, Wang Haiguang, Wu Zhe, and Yang Kuisong in *Maoism at the Grassroots* (2015) are small bricks in a bridge that aims to address unevenness and unfairness in PRC history by encouraging people living, studying, and working in different political environments to listen to one another. Other more impressive bricks include the *Reading the China Dream* collaborative translation project run by David Ownby, Timothy Cheek, and Joshua Fogel, plus Geremie Barmé's prolific translations in *China Heritage*.

Chinese-to-English and English-to-Chinese language inclusion is not only an inside China/outside China problem but also a global problem. China-born scholars who are studying and working outside of China can be disadvantaged by implicit bias when admissions and hiring committees, conference organizers, and editorial boards see a name rendered in pinyin or—even in a double-blind refereeing situation—notice signs that an author's first language is not English. This then contributes to an institutional diversity problem, as the high-quality work of China-born and English as an Additional Language (EAL) scholars does not always get the recognition it deserves when it comes to graduate admissions, hiring, and publishing, leading to being overrepresented in for-profit publication venues, smaller or lesser known graduate programs, and teaching-heavy jobs. Letting nature take its course is not going to fix this problem, so I see step three toward inclusion as actively pushing back against implicit bias and valuing institutional diversity. Starting editorial reviews, graduate admissions, and hiring with this principle in mind can gradually improve the situation. A more immediate move toward institutional inclusivity would be to keep doors and gates wide open to ensure that PRC history cooperates with existing scholarly groups rather than siloing itself off as a special subfield. To what extent has the excitement of setting up a new book series, journal, and online presence blinded energetic proponents of PRC history—myself included—to the excellent work of organizations and scholars who focus on China since 1949 but might not always highlight the term "PRC history"? Chinese Historians in the United States (CHUS) and its journal *Chinese*

Historical Review, as well as the Historical Society for Twentieth-Century China (HSTCC) and its journal *Twentieth-Century China*, have long histories of inclusive field-building that can be learned from and joined.

Step four is to recognize that an inclusive approach that values diversity means practicing humility and respecting diverse viewpoints. This is what I mean when I caution against viewing my points as prescriptive. Instead of telling others to be like me, to adopt my agenda, to prioritize the grassroots sources I love or the questions I think are important, I would urge the opposite. For example, Jake Werner's approach in his piece in this issue differs from my own but is valid and important. As Werner notes, scholars need to recognize and explain how some people have benefited from state-mandated homogenization and experienced it as liberatory. To neglect or downplay this phenomenon hampers a comprehensive understanding of China's 1950s, 1960s, and 1970s. It also closes off the possibility of productive conversations with the millions of people in China today—themselves beneficiaries of homogenization—who accept Xi Jinping's defense of the need for "Vocational Education and Training Centers" in Xinjiang or who use WeChat to blithely engage in anti-Muslim bigotry and call for armed crackdowns against Hong Kong protesters. To refuse to try to understand and talk to those who voice these identity claims is as misguided as ignoring aspirational socialism.

My scholarly agenda is the product of a historical moment that celebrates civil society and that valorizes resistance against oppression. My status as a voice to listen to in the field of PRC history is the product of a historical process that has normalized white, male, straight, cis, ableist privilege. Is this so obvious that it should go without saying? Yes. Does it still need to be said? Yes. Repeatedly stating the obvious is the only way to dismantle a status quo that needs to get blown up. When I step back and recognize that voices like mine have been too loud for too long, I can make more room for voices that have been marginalized and silenced in and outside of China. This is one way to fight for inclusivity in PRC history and to allow the field to flourish even more than it already has in the years since Julia Strauss assessed the state of the field. Strauss's own search for PRC history led her to a comparative study of state formation in China and Taiwan during the 1950s (2020). Strauss's fresh approach has the potential to push the field in new directions by reminding scholars that including Taiwan in discussions of PRC history can shed light on the PRC's uniqueness while sparking imaginative and hopeful visions of alternatives and paths not taken. Taiwan, for example, shows that stepping back and making room for marginalized voices does not threaten prosperity and stability. It can do the opposite. This applies to fields of scholarly inquiry and to authoritarian dictatorships. Just look at the path of Taiwan after Chiang Ching-kuo, the heir to a violent homogenizing project parallel to the one that Xi Jinping is still pushing, stepped back and made room for voices that had been repressed for decades.

Notes

I respectfully acknowledge that this article was written on the unceded traditional territories of the Tsleil-Waututh, Kwikwetlem, Squamish, and Musqueam Nations. I am grateful to Fabio Lanza and Aminda Smith for their encouragement and patience. I thank Sigrid Schmalzer, Angela Xiao Wu, and three anonymous reviewers for their critical feedback on an earlier draft of this article. The inspiration for this article's title comes from the title of a seminar taught by Mark Halperin at Lewis and Clark College in 1999 about late imperial China "in crisis and clover."

1   Gerth (2020) elaborates on this point and presents a competing label—a form of state capitalism called "state consumerism."

2   On the impact of the *History of the Communist Party of the Soviet Union (Bolsheviks): Short Course* in China, see H. Li 2006, 2010.

3   For more on this moment, see Lanza 2017.

4   Some web pages claim that Tom Magliozzi of NPR's *Car Talk* may have uttered this phrase before Baucells and Sarin published it in a book. Google executive Mo Gawdat (2017: 26) published a more convoluted version of the formula (happiness is greater than or equal to "your perception of the events of your life" minus "your expectations of how life should behave").

5   Introductions to such sources as diaries, life stories (*zizhuan* 自傳), self-criticisms, and social intelligence reports can be found in an archived version of Lund University's Social History of China, 1949–1979, a website created in 2013 that has been removed from Lund's servers. Because the website is no longer live, the sources themselves are no longer available, but the archived essays remain quite useful (web.archive.org/web/20180515181803/http://projekt .ht.lu.se/rereso/sources).

6   Examples include the Wilson Center Digital Archive (digitalarchive.wilsoncenter.org), the Database for the History of Contemporary Chinese Political Movements (ccrd.usc.cuhk .edu.hk/Default.aspx), and the Maoist Legacy database (www.maoistlegacy.de/db/users /login). More complete listings are available at www.prchistoryresources.org.

7 PRC History Source Transparency, www.sfu.ca/prchistorytransparency.html.

8 For details on how these organizations operate, see Xu and Hua 2013.

9 The PRC History Group has archived back issues of these journals at prchistory.org /electronic-journals-archive/.

10 Pushing for diversity and inclusion is facilitated by such resources as NüVoices, which curates a directory of more than five hundred female experts on Hong Kong, Macau, mainland China, and Taiwan (nuvoices.com/experts-directory/).

11 PRC history books whose contributions have been greatly enhanced by prioritizing Chinese names and voices at the chapter, page, paragraph, and sentence levels include Andreas 2009; Eyferth 2009; Hershatter 2011; Hou 2018; Leese 2011; J. Li 2014; Schmalzer 2008, 2016; Smith 2013; and Wu 2014.

References

Andreas, Joel. 2009. *Rise of the Red Engineers: The Cultural Revolution and the Origins of China's New Class*. Stanford, CA: Stanford University Press.

Andrew, Christopher, and David Dilks. 1984. "Introduction." In *The Missing Dimension: Governments and Intelligence Communities in the Twentieth Century*, edited by Christopher Andrew and David Dilks, 1–16. Urbana: University of Illinois Press.

Barnett, A. Doak. 1963. *China on the Eve of Communist Takeover*. New York: Praeger.

Barnett, A. Doak. 1964. *Communist China: The Early Years, 1949–55*. New York: Praeger.

Baucells, Manel, and Rakesh Sarin. 2012. *Engineering Happiness: A New Approach for Building a Joyful Life*. Berkeley: University of California Press.

Brown, Jeremy. 2010. "Finding and Using Grassroots Historical Sources from the Mao Era." Dissertation Reviews, December 15. dissertationreviews.org/archives/310.

Brown, Jeremy. 2012. *City versus Countryside in Mao's China: Negotiating the Divide*. New York: Cambridge University Press.

Brown, Jeremy. 2018. "A Policeman, His Gun, and an Alleged Rape: Competing Appeals for Justice in Tianjin, 1966–1979." In *Victims, Perpetrators, and the Role of Law in Maoist China: A Case-Study Approach*, edited by Daniel Leese and Puck Engman, 127–49. Berlin: De Gruyter.

Brown, Jeremy. 2019. "Men's World." In *China Tripping: Anecdotes, Vignettes, and Reflections from Lives Lived with China*, edited by Perry Link, Jeremy Murray, and Paul G. Pickowicz, 130–33. Lanham, MD: Rowman and Littlefield.

Brown, Jeremy. Forthcoming. "Extremely Complicated Work: Sabotage and Accidents in the People's Republic of China, 1949–1973." In *Accidents and the State: Understanding Risks in the 20th Century*, edited by Peter Itzen, Birgit Metzger, and Anne Rasmussen. Bielefeld, Germany: transcript publishing.

Brown, Jeremy, and Matthew D. Johnson, eds. 2015. *Maoism at the Grassroots: Everyday Life in China's Era of High Socialism*. Cambridge, MA: Harvard University Press.

Brown, Jeremy, and Paul G. Pickowicz, eds. 2007. *Dilemmas of Victory: The Early Years of the People's Republic of China*. Cambridge, MA: Harvard University Press.

Cao, Shuji 曹樹基. 2005. *Da jihuang: 1959–1961 nian de Zhongguo renkou* 大饑荒: 1959–1961 年的中國人口 (*The Great Famine: China's Population, 1959–1961*). Hong Kong: Shidai guoji chuban youxian gongsi.

Cao, Shuji 曹樹基. 2015. "An Overt Conspiracy: Creating Rightists in Rural Henan, 1957–1958." In *Maoism at the Grassroots: Everyday Life in China's Era of High Socialism*, edited by Jeremy Brown and Matthew D. Johnson, 77–101. Cambridge, MA: Harvard University Press.

Chan, Anita, Richard Madsen, and Jonathan Unger. (1984) 2009. *Chen Village: The Recent History of a Peasant Community in Mao's China*. 3rd ed. Berkeley: University of California Press.

Chen, Donglin 陈东林. 2003. *Sanxian jianshe: Beizhan shiqi de xibu da kaifa* 三线建设: 备战 时期的西部开发 (*Third Front Construction: The Great Opening of the West during the Period of Preparing for War*). Beijing: Zhonggong zhongyang dangxiao chubanshe.

Ci, Jiwei. 1994. *Dialectic of the Chinese Revolution: From Utopianism to Hedonism*. Stanford, CA: Stanford University Press.

Diamant, Neil J. 2000. *Revolutionizing the Family: Politics, Love, and Divorce in Urban and Rural China, 1949–1968*. Berkeley: University of California Press.

Diamant, Neil J. 2008. Review of *Revolution, Resistance, and Reform in Village China*, by Edward Friedman, Paul G. Pickowicz, and Mark Selden. *Perspectives on Politics* 6, no. 3: 621–22. doi:10.1017/S1537592708081619.

Diamant, Neil J. 2009. *Embattled Glory: Veterans, Military Families, and the Politics of Patriotism in China, 1949–2007*. Lanham, MD: Rowman and Littlefield.

Dikötter, Frank. 2010. *Mao's Great Famine: The History of China's Most Devastating Catastrophe, 1958–1962*. New York: Walker and Company.

"Document 9: A ChinaFile Translation." 2013. ChinaFile, November 8. www.chinafile.com /document-9-chinafile-translation.

Eyferth, Jacob. 2009. *Eating Rice from Bamboo Roots: The Social History of a Community of Handicraft Papermakers in Rural Sichuan, 1920–2000*. Cambridge, MA: Harvard University Asia Center.

Friedman, Edward, Paul Pickowicz, and Mark Selden. 1991. *Chinese Village, Socialist State*. New Haven, CT: Yale University Press.

Friedman, Edward, Paul Pickowicz, and Mark Selden. 2005. *Revolution, Resistance, and Reform in Village China*. New Haven, CT: Yale University Press.

Gawdat, Mo. 2017. *Solve for Happy: Engineer Your Path to Joy*. New York: Gallery Books.

Gerth, Karl. 2020. *Unending Capitalism: How Consumerism Negated China's Communist Revolution*. New York: Cambridge University Press.

Greitens, Sheena Chestnut, and Rory Truex. 2020. "Repressive Experiences among China Scholars: New Evidence from Survey Data." *China Quarterly* 242: 349–75. doi:10.1017/S0305741019000365.

Hershatter, Gail. 2011. *The Gender of Memory: Rural Women and China's Collective Past*. Berkeley: University of California Press.

Hobsbawm, Eric J. 1985. "History from Below—Some Reflections." In *History from Below: Studies in Popular Protest and Popular Ideology in Honour of George Rudé*, edited by Frederick Krantz, 63–73. Montreal: Concordia University.

Hou, Li. 2018. *Building for Oil: Daqing and the Formation of the Chinese Socialist State*. Cambridge, MA: Harvard University Asia Center.

Lanza, Fabio. 2017. *The End of Concern: Maoist China, Activism, and Asian Studies*. Durham, NC: Duke University Press.

Lee, Hong Yung. 1978. *The Politics of the Chinese Cultural Revolution: A Case Study*. Berkeley: University of California Press.

Leese, Daniel. 2011. *Mao Cult: Rhetoric and Ritual in the Cultural Revolution*. Cambridge: Cambridge University Press.

Leese, Daniel. 2019. "Case Files as a Source of Alternative Memories from the Maoist Past." In *Popular Memories of the Mao Era: From Critical Debate to Reassessing History*, edited by Sebastian Veg, 199–219. Hong Kong: Hong Kong University Press.

Li, Hua-yu. 2006. *Mao and the Economic Stalinization of China, 1948–1953*. Lanham, MD: Rowman and Littlefield.

Li, Hua-yu. 2010. "Instilling Stalinism in Chinese Party Members: Absorbing Stalin's *Short Course* in the 1950s." In *China Learns from the Soviet Union*, edited by Thomas P. Bernstein and Hua-yu Li, 107–30. Lanham, MD: Lexington Books.

Li, Jie. 2014. *Shanghai Homes: Palimpsests of Private Life*. New York: Columbia University Press.

Li, Yufeng 李玉峰. 2016. "Neixiang xian jiefang hou de qingjiao 'tufei' kaoshu" 内乡县解放后的清剿 '土匪' 考述 ("Study of the CCP Eliminating 'Bandits' in Neixiang County after Liberation). *Liaocheng daxue xuebao (shehui kexue ban)* 聊城大学学报 (社会科学版) (Liaocheng University Journal [Social Science Edition]) 4: 16–24. doi.org/10.16284/j.cnki .cn37-1401/c.2016.04.003.

Lieberthal, Kenneth. 1980. *Revolution and Tradition in Tientsin, 1949–1952*. Stanford, CA: Stanford University Press.

Lifton, Robert Jay. 1961. *Thought Reform and the Psychology of Totalism: A Study of "Brain-washing" in China*. New York: W. W. Norton and Company.

Lim, Louisa. 2017. "Muzzling the Academy: Censorship Emboldened, at Home and Abroad." *Los Angeles Review of Books* China Channel, October 6. chinachannel.org/2017 /10/06/lrp-muzzling-academy.

Liu, Alan P. L. 1971. *Communications and National Integration in Communist China*. Berkeley: University of California Press.

Liu, Yajuan 刘亚娟. 2016a. "Guojia yu dushi zhi jian: Shanghai laomo xingxiang jiangou yu liubian de ge'an yanjiu (1949–1963)" 国家与都市之间: 上海劳模形象建构与流变的个案研究 ("Between State and City: A Case Study on the Construction and Changes of Shanghai Model Laborers' Images, 1949–1963"). *Zhonggong dangshi yanjiu* 中共党史研究 (CPC History Studies) 5: 68–78.

Liu, Yajuan 刘亚娟. 2016b. "Xin jiu zhi jian: Jianguo chuqi Shanghai guoying yushichang jingjiren zhidu de gaige" 新旧之间: 建国初期上海国营鱼市场经纪人制度的改革 ("Between New and Old: Reform of the Broker System in Shanghai State-Owned Fish Markets in the Early PRC"). *Shilin* 史林 (*Historical Review*) 2: 181–89.

"Looking for Great Leap 'Smoking Gun' Document." 2015. H-PRC, December 1. networks.h -net.org/node/3544/discussions/99266/looking-great-leap-smoking-gun-document.

Lü, Xiaobo. 2000. *Cadres and Corruption: The Organizational Involution of the Chinese Communist Party*. Stanford, CA: Stanford University Press.

MacFarquhar, Roderick, and Michael Schoenhals. 2006. *Mao's Last Revolution*. Cambridge, MA: Harvard University Press.

"Most Important/Influential Theoretical Work for PRC History?" 2016. H-PRC, May 12. networks.h-net.org/node/3544/discussions/124969/most-importantinfluential-theoretical -work-prc-history.

O'Dwyer, Shaun. 2019. "China's Growing Threat to Academic Freedom." *Japan Times*, November 25. www.japantimes.co.jp/opinion/2019/11/25/commentary/japan-commentary /chinas-growing-threat-academic-freedom.

Perry, Elizabeth J. 1994. "Shanghai's Strike Wave of 1957." *China Quarterly* 137: 1–27.

Perry, Elizabeth J. 2005. *Patrolling the Revolution: Worker Militias, Citizenship, and the Modern Chinese State*. Lanham, MD: Rowman and Littlefield.

Perry, Elizabeth J. 2012. *Anyuan: Mining China's Revolutionary Tradition*. Berkeley: University of California Press.

Perry, Elizabeth J. 2016. "The Promise of PRC History." *Journal of Modern Chinese History* 10, no. 1: 113–17. doi.org/10.1080/17535654.2016.1168172.

Perry, Elizabeth J., and Li Xun. 1997. *Proletarian Power: Shanghai in the Cultural Revolution*. Boulder, CO: Westview Press.

Rosen, Stanley. 1982. *Red Guard Factionalism and the Cultural Revolution in Guangzhou (Canton)*. Boulder, CO: Westview Press.

Ruan, Qinghua 阮清华. 2009. *Shanghai youmin gaizao yanjiu (1949–1958)* 上海游民改造研究 (*Research on Reforming Vagrants in Shanghai, 1949–1958*). Shanghai: Shanghai cishu chubanshe.

Schmalzer, Sigrid. 2008. *The People's Peking Man: Popular Science and Human Identity in Twentieth-Century China*. Chicago: University of Chicago Press.

Schmalzer, Sigrid. 2016. *Red Revolution, Green Revolution: Scientific Farming in Socialist China*. Chicago: University of Chicago Press.

Schoenhals, Michael. 2004. "Sinology and Historical Research on Mao's China: Some Personal Reflections." Paper presented at "Focus on Asia: Challenges in Politics and Research," University of Helsinki, January 23. portal.research.lu.se/ws/files/6336820/625480.pdf.

Schoenhals, Michael. 2013. *Spying for the People: Mao's Secret Agents, 1949–1967*. Cambridge: Cambridge University Press.

Schoenhals, Michael. 2014. "Missing Persons." ReReSo, Lunds Universitet, April 14. web.archive.org/web/20180515221827/http://projekt.ht.lu.se/rereso/sources/missing-persons/.

Schoenhals, Michael. 2015. "China's 'Great Proletarian Information Revolution' of 1966–1967." In *Maoism at the Grassroots: Everyday Life in China's Era of High Socialism*, edited by Jeremy Brown and Matthew D. Johnson, 230–58. Cambridge, MA: Harvard University Press.

Schoenhals, Michael. 2016. "Do You Have Many Contacts, Among the Lumberjacks?" PRC History Group, Document of the Month, September. prchistory.org/september-2016/.

Schurmann, Franz. (1966) 1968. *Ideology and Organization in Communist China*. 2nd ed. Berkeley: University of California Press.

Shen, Zhihua 沈志华. 2003. *Sulian zhuanjia zai Zhongguo* 苏联专家在中国 (*Soviet Experts in China*). Beijing: Zhongguo guoji guangbo chubanshe.

Shen, Zhihua 沈志华. 2008. *Zhonghua renmin gongheguo shi, di san juan, Sikao yu xuanze—Cong zhishifenzi huiyi dao fanyoupai yundong (1956–1957)* 中华人民共和国史第三卷, 思考与选择——从知识分子会议到反右派运动 (1956–1957) (*The History of the People's Republic of China*, vol. 3: *Reflections and Choices: From the Conference on Intellectuals to the Anti-Rightist Movement, [1956–1957]*). Hong Kong: Zhongwen daxue chubanshe.

Shi, Yun 史雲. 2012. *Zhang Chunqiao Yao Wenyuan shizhuan: Zizhuan, riji, gongci* 張春橋姚文元實傳: 自傳, 日記, 供詞 (*True Biography of Zhang Chunqiao and Yao Wenyuan: Autobiography, Diary, Confession*). Hong Kong: Sanlian.

Shue, Vivienne. 1980. *Peasant China in Transition: The Dynamics of Development toward Socialism, 1949–1956*. Berkeley: University of California Press.

Shue, Vivienne. 1988. *The Reach of the State: Sketches of the Chinese Body Politic*. Stanford, CA: Stanford University Press.

Smith, Aminda M. 2013. *Thought Reform and China's Dangerous Classes: Reeducation, Resistance, and the People*. Lanham, MD: Rowman and Littlefield.

Strauss, Julia. 2006. "Introduction: In Search of PRC History." *China Quarterly* 188: 855–69.

Strauss, Julia. 2020. *State Formation in China and Taiwan: Bureaucracy, Campaign, and Performance*. Cambridge: Cambridge University Press.

Tan, Hecheng 谭合成. 2010. *Xue de shenhua: Gongyuan 1967 nian Hunan Daoxian wenge da tusha jishi* 血的神话: 公元1967年湖南道县文革大屠杀纪实 (*Bloody Myth: An Account of the Cultural Revolution Massacre of 1967 in Daoxian, Hunan*). Hong Kong: Tianxingjian chubanshe.

Tang, Shaojie 唐少傑. 2003. *Yiye zhiqiu: Qinghua daxue 1968 nian "bairi da wudou"* 一葉知秋: 清華大學1968年 "百日大武鬥" (*An Episode of the Cultural Revolution: The 1968 "Hundred-Day War" at Tsinghua University*). Hong Kong: Zhongwen daxue chubanshe.

Teiwes, Frederick C. 1979. *Politics and Purges in China: Rectification and the Decline of Party Norms, 1950–1965*. Armonk, NY: M. E. Sharpe.

Tiffert, Glenn D. 2019. "Peering Down the Memory Hole: Censorship, Digitization, and the Fragility of Our Knowledge Base." *American Historical Review* 124, no. 2: 550–68.

Vogel, Ezra F. 1969. *Canton under Communism: Programs and Politics in a Provincial Capital, 1949–1968*. Cambridge, MA: Harvard University Press.

Walder, Andrew G. 1986. *Communist Neo-Traditionalism: Work and Authority in Chinese Industry*. Berkeley: University of California Press.

Walder, Andrew G. 1987. "Actually Existing Maoism." *Australian Journal of Chinese Affairs*, no. 18: 155–66. doi.org/10.2307/2158588.

Walder, Andrew G. 2015. *China under Mao: A Revolution Derailed*. Cambridge, MA: Harvard University Press.

Wang, Duanyang 王端阳. 2007. *Yige hongweibing de riji* 一个红卫兵的日记 (*Red Guard Diary*). Self-published.

Wang, Haiguang 王海光. 2015. "Radical Agricultural Collectivization and Ethnic Rebellion: The Communist Encounter with a 'New Emperor' in Guizhou's Mashan Region, 1956." In *Maoism at the Grassroots: Everyday Life in China's Era of High Socialism*, edited by Jeremy Brown and Matthew D. Johnson, 281–305. Cambridge, MA: Harvard University Press.

Wang, Haiguang 王海光. 2021. *Zhizao fan'geming: Liu Xingfu an yu wen'ge shiqi de jiceng fazhi shengtai* 制造反革命: 柳幸福案与文革时期的基层法治生态 (*Making a Counterrevolutionary: The Case of Liu Qingfu and China's Grassroots Legal System, 1949–1979*). Hong Kong: Zhongwen daxue chubanshe.

Whyte, Martin King, and William L. Parish. 1984. *Urban Life in Contemporary China*. Chicago: University of Chicago Press.

Wu, Yiching. 2014. *The Cultural Revolution at the Margins*. Cambridge, MA: Harvard University Press.

Xu, Youyu, and Hua Ze. 2013. *In the Shadow of the Rising Dragon: Stories of Repression in the New China*. New York: Palgrave Macmillan.

Yang, C. K. (1959) 1965. *Chinese Communist Society: The Family and Village*. Cambridge, MA: MIT Press.

Yang, Jisheng 楊繼繩. 2008. *Mubei: Zhongguo liushi niandai dajihuang jishi* 墓碑: 中國六十年代大饑荒紀實 (*Tombstone: A True History of the Great Famine in 1960s China*). Hong Kong: Tiandi tushu youxian gongsi.

Yang, Jisheng 楊繼繩. 2016. *Tiandi fanfu: Zhongguo wenhua da geming shi* 天地翻覆: 中國文化大革命史 (*The World Turned Upside Down: History of the Chinese Cultural Revolution*). Hong Kong: Tiandi tushu youxian gongsi.

Yang, Kuisong 杨奎松. 2009. *Zhonghua renmin gongheguo jianguo shi yanjiu* 中华人民共和国建国历史研究 (*Research on the History of the Founding of the People's Republic of China*). Vol. 1. Nanchang, China: Jiangxi renmin chubanshe.

Yang, Kuisong 杨奎松. 2015. "How a 'Bad Element' Was Made: The Discovery, Accusation, and Punishment of Zang Qiren." In *Maoism at the Grassroots: Everyday Life in China's Era of High Socialism*, edited by Jeremy Brown and Matthew D. Johnson, 19–50. Cambridge, MA: Harvard University Press.

Yang, Kuisong 杨奎松. 2016. *"Bianyuanren" jishi: Jige "wenti" xiao renwu de beiju gushi* "边缘人"纪事: 几个"问题"小人物的悲剧故事 (*A Record of "Marginal People": The Tragic Stories of Several "Problematic" Individuals*). Guangzhou, China: Guangdong renmin chubanshe.

Zhang, Jishun 张济顺. 2015. *Yuanqu de dushi: 1950 niandai de Shanghai* 远去的都市: 1950年代的上海 (*A City Displaced: Shanghai in the 1950s*). Beijing: Shehui kexue wenxian chubanshe.

Zhang, Letian, Xi Fuqun, and Yunxiang Yan, eds. 2018. *Work Journals of Zhou Shengkang, 1961–1982*. Boston: Brill.

Zhang, Letian, and Yunxiang Yan, eds. 2018. *Personal Letters between Lu Qingsheng and Jiang Zhenyuan, 1961–1986*. Boston: Brill.

Zhang, Si 张思. 2010. *Houjiaying: Yige Huabei cunzhuang de xiandai licheng* 侯家营: 一个华北村庄的现代历程 (*Houjiaying: The Modern Path of a North China Village*). Tianjin, China: Tianjin guji chubanshe.

To Confront the Totality: A Critique of Empiricism in the Historiography of the People's Republic of China

Jake Werner

> When a discovery occasions the restructuring of current ideas, this is not due exclusively to logical considerations or, more particularly, to the contradiction between the discovery and particular elements in current views. If this were the only real issue, one could always think up further hypotheses by which one could avoid changing the theory as a whole. That new views in fact win out is due to concrete historical circumstances, even if the scientist himself may be determined to change his views only by immanent motives.
> —Horkheimer (1937) 1972: 194–95

> Whenever someone gives an account of a past event, even if he is a historian, we must take into account what he unintentionally puts back into the past from the present or from some intermediate time, thus falsifying his picture of it.
> —Freud (1917) 1966: 417

positions 29:4 DOI 10.1215/10679847-9286675

Several years ago Elizabeth Perry (2016: 116) chided members of the emerging field of early PRC history for failing "to engage seriously with the big questions." According to Perry, "Intoxicated by the wealth of newly discovered sources that allow for the investigation of everyday life, they accept a division of labor in which social scientists explore the 'commanding heights' of the Chinese state and its policies, while historians grub for diversity in the dustbins of grassroots society."

This judgment may be unfair. Recent research certainly does base itself on local archival sources and grassroots documents of diverse unofficial origins. Yet there has been no shortage of significant topics explored through these materials, ranging from the contours of gender identity to the polarization between urban and rural areas to the project of reshaping individual thought and behavior.[1]

In another sense, however, Perry's complaint is well founded. Historians may address the "big questions," but they have been reluctant to venture *explanations* for the course of the history they describe. Recent studies have largely avoided the earlier debates on larger forces—totalitarianism, capitalism, imperialism, modernity—shaping the events in question. Instead they often claim an empiricist fidelity to the heterogeneity of lived experience, which is said to exceed any single framework that might offer an explanation for the full breadth of a given historical moment.

Yet what makes fragmented local sources so compelling—that they appear to be unmediated by externally established narratives or ideologies—is precisely what makes them misleading. Without a larger interpretive framework, it would be difficult to distinguish the essential from the insignificant, raising the danger that our inquiry will leave us with nothing but a mass of confused facts whose relations are unclear. On closer inspection, however, we find a different problem. Most empiricist inquiries actually are motivated by a set of structuring ideas—but those ideas remain unarticulated. Implicit theorization organizes the material through unexamined concepts whose explanatory power arises not from the sources but anachronistically, from the historian's own historically situated sensibilities. 南辕北辙:[2] the more insistently one plunges toward immediate experience, the further one moves from grasping the substance of the history.

Hardly to be preferred, however, is the reverse method so common in the social sciences: abstracting from lived reality to escape the danger of the particular case and then fitting the data that result into a crudely reified "model." As a general orientation, the historian poses the particular to deny the universal; the social scientist derives the universal through an exclusion of the particular.

While each approach imagines itself to be the opposite of the other, in truth both are founded on observations that have been conceptually disembedded from a dynamic social totality. Both approaches aim for the dream of modern scholarship, that the subjectivity of the observer would be removed to secure the objectivity of the fact. Yet the observer's subjective organization of the object is suppressed rather than overcome. Unbidden, it finds expression elsewhere and in ways that move us further from understanding the history than would bringing it to awareness and confronting it directly.

This article analyzes empiricism in the historiography of the early PRC not as an empty and neutral framework but positively, as a peculiar ideology that disclaims its own existence as ideology and thereby evades critical examination of its unstated assumptions. Hardly a novel ideology, its dominance in the discipline is nonetheless historically specific, the outcome of a particular set of social circumstances that developed over the last four decades. Originally these interpretive moves targeted the reductionisms and teleologies of an earlier empiricism. But their hegemony in the field has now foreclosed the conceptualization of a more complex relation between local and global, state and civil society, individual and collective, or economy and culture—a conceptualization that could grasp both terms in these classic oppositions as mutually constitutive, their real contradictions arising on a single but uneven social terrain shaped by a deeper set of structuring social relations.

An intentional engagement with theory, I argue, is not hostile to empirical research but would both enable and demand a closer examination of historical sources whose full richness is often diminished by the presuppositions of the reigning empiricism. I briefly pose issues at the local and global levels that cannot be addressed within the dominant framework: the reasons for the Chinese Communist Party's unprecedented success in "penetrating society" and the parallels between China and the rest of the world in the nature and timing of mass society's emergence, consolidation, and crisis. The unevenness and heterogeneity we find in our archives should not be used to deny the existence of deeper, abstract mediating processes of social life but should be understood as the end result of those processes.

While the investigation of everyday life should not be used to repudiate the idea of social structure, neither should we dismiss the mundane details of everyday life as a distraction from large historical trends. A different approach would encompass both sides of the binary, aiming to explain how daily practices themselves give rise to large structural dynamics, which in turn crystallize into a kind of objectivity that stands over and above individual historical subjects, conditioning both the reproduction of thought and practice at the grassroots and their persistent tensions.

Ultimately, I argue that the methods of historical research since the cultural turn—the focus on everyday life, the absorption in rich but messy empirical details, the close attention to the consciousness of historical actors—may be insufficient, but they remain essential to the challenge of explaining history. I build on the important advances of post–cultural turn historiography even as I critique the limits it has imposed on scholarship, pursuing the possibility of a theorization of universality that does not efface particularity but seeks to explain both terms through a structurally impelled dialectic between particular and universal.

The Structuring Binary of Contemporary Empiricism

An imbalance between the empirical and the theoretical tasks has always dogged the discipline of history. That which makes historians indispensable to the work of rich empirical description—their intense investment in the project of locating new or unique sources and their highly developed methodology for interrogating those sources—tends to become an obstacle in the work of explaining the material. Explanation requires a different set of methods: either the elaborate statistical correlation of stylized reifications in which the social sciences trade, or the methods descending from speculative philosophy that guide critical social theory. Historians' orthodoxy shrinks from both because they both require forms of abstraction that distance us from the immediate concreteness of our sources.

Since the cultural turn in the discipline, some have taken this orientation a step further, actually celebrating the neglect of explanation. Such work offers an endless procession of individual experiences, not in pursuit of a new and more complex narrative that systematically relates the actors and events of the era, but to support the claim that no such account is possible. As Jeremy Brown and Matthew Johnson (2015: 15) put it, "As voices proliferate, the credibility of a unified national narrative recedes. There is no single grassroots narrative to replace the voice of the center. Instead, we are left to ponder whether 'Mao's China' ever existed at all."

Beyond a commitment to empirical fidelity, the historiographical practice of excluding abstraction is sometimes a political commitment as well. The goal is to dissolve any coherent theoretical framework that might organize the material because such a framework threatens to do epistemic violence to the historical actors—in a way that mimics, or perhaps produces, the physical violence imposed on them by the totalizing ideology of Communism. As Wen-hsin Yeh (2000: 17) writes, "The fate of the individual in this [the twentieth] century of war and revolution has been inextricably bound to, above all, the rise of nationalism and socialism as hegemonic discourses, to the disciplining of a modern citizenship by the power of the party-state, and to the growth of a political culture of violence that these practices have spawned." The galvanizing certainties of political movements, regardless of their ideological hue, are thought to be a source of violence and domination because of their innate intolerance for dissent and difference. As Mark Selden (1995: 243) puts it, politics in China was often driven by "destructive forms of fundamentalism resting on party claims to exercise a monopoly on morality and truth." Or as William Kirby (2004: 15) writes, "It was, after all, in search of a communist ideal that China would fall under the totalitarian tyranny of Mao Zedong." For many, then, one task of historical inquiry is to break apart the connections drawn by totalizing social theory.

The presentation of an endlessly diverse set of individual experiences seems at first to presage an unmanageable chaos of facticity. Invariably, however, the empiricist does not produce a random assemblage of events and experiences; some organizing device is always employed in the presentation. To the extent it is explicitly articulated, it often appears as a purely negative framework. In the literature on the early PRC, one particularly prominent instance over the last several decades has been the project of casting doubt on the Party's claim to have initiated a thorough social transformation in China. In the Brown and Johnson volume, for example, the diversity of social life is repeatedly marshaled to prove wrong "the notion of a comprehensive post-1949 consolidation of power by the Mao-led Communist Party" (2015: 5).

The argument against absolute state control appears often, but against whom is this argument prosecuted? Curiously, the antagonists are never cited. Such a narrative has not been current among China scholars for fifty years.[3] What exactly is the impetus behind attacking a conceptual figure that no one accepts? The clues are to be found symptomatically, in the positive framework that structures these investigations. Above all, the attack against the idea of an all-powerful state vindicates the rights of civil society.

In this conceptualization, civil society is the realm of liberty: freely chosen interactions engaged for mutual gain. In Di Wang's (2018: 19) characterization, it is constituted by the "everyday habits of association that are relatively voluntary and free. That is, they are not manipulated by the needs of the state and its ruling party." Civil society is diverse, tolerant, and pragmatic, perhaps animated by a democratic ethos. In contrast, the state embodies power, coercion, ideology, uniformity, regimentation.[4] Whereas the state aims to politicize everything, to bring everything into the public realm where it can be seen and controlled, civil society under the PRC survived in "small spaces of accustomed ease and joy, beauty and indulgence, hope and faith, wit, menace, risk, or reserve" (Shue 2015: 370). Mark Selden (1993: 3) locates the distinction in "the tension between[, on the one side,] the state and the collective institutions it created, seeking to establish hegemony over household and market in defining parameters of accumulation, production, consumption, welfare, and mobility, and on the other side attempts by households and individuals to survive and flourish as autonomous economic and social units in the face of growing state power." In another common formulation, Christian Henriot (2012: 526) counterpoises an earlier era in which social conflicts played out within "an open, but fragmented society under a weak state" against developments after 1949, when "the CCP brought these tensions and contradictions under a firm grip that stifled all contestation and agency."

Under such a conceptualization, the stories found most compelling and considered most genuine are those of conflict between state and civil society, making everyday resistance a preoccupation of recent research. Shue (2015: 372–73) cites the example of a woman in Tianjin in the aftermath of the disastrous Tangshan earthquake who strategically timed her pregnancy to escape the collective obligation of relief work so she could instead pursue individual advancement by focusing on her own research and writing. Hanchao Lu (2018: 77) interprets as "everyday resistance" the determination among some of the surviving Shanghai bourgeoisie to enjoy fine clothes, expensive food, and extravagant parties: "To keep the way of life was to defend the type of character and individuality that the Communists deemed to be deviant and dissident."

A common subtheme, derived from the cultural turn's investigation into the making of meaning and the attempt to recover "hidden transcripts of resistance" slighted in earlier social movement literature (see Scott 1990), is the idea that resistance to state projects arose from the refusal of ordinary people to accept the ideological meanings demanded by the Party. Changtai Hung (2011: 6, 8), for example, contrasts the state's "system of indoctrination and control" with the "audiences [that] sometimes read, debated, and negotiated the imposed ideologies differently from the ways that the authorities intended." Barbara Mittler (2012: 5) argues that during the Cultural Revolution, "in spite of all the propagandists' efforts to deliver the one and only meaning . . . the audience responded as it did with all artistic products: everybody in his/her own way, critically as well as creatively, and most importantly, in a participatory manner."

To account for popular participation in state initiatives, scholars have exposed the state's use of manipulation and terror to generate compliance and uncovered the ways that individuals acceded to state pressure in pursuit of their own self-interest. Julia Strauss (2002), for example, describes the rollout of comprehensive labor insurance alongside the Campaign to Suppress Counterrevolutionaries as a tacitly transactional initiative in which ordinary people received material benefits in exchange for affirming the legitimacy of the new state. For Yu Liu (2010: 329), the Party's "engineering of emotions" relied on "cultivating beliefs through propagating revolutionary discourses, shaping institutional incentives through rewarding compliance and punishing defiance, exerting peer pressure through psychological manipulation, and forcing people into compliance through coercive measures." Adherence to state claims thus occurs through artifice or under duress; resistance to them is an expression of freedom.[5]

The dichotomy of state and civil society has mapped a scholarly division of labor between those who write on high politics and those who examine grassroots society. If scholars of everyday life aim to demonstrate that regular people either rejected the state's transformational vision or cynically employed it for their own ends, those writing on the highest ranks of the Party seek to show that the transformational vision, whatever its rhetoric, was in reality driven by the power interests of individual leaders. The central such individual is, of course, Mao Zedong 毛泽东, who is portrayed as an erratic and bullying autocrat fixated on imposing his own idea of a utopian society. As Michael Sheng (2011: 67) writes, "Mao's chief concern was none other than the enhancement and strengthening of the belief in his infallibility, which was the foundation of his charismatic authority."[6]

Mao's thought is generally treated as a psychological deformation, but the ideology and self-understanding of other committed Communists is routinely dismissed as well. Most work of recent decades evinces no interest in the extensive efforts that Communist leaders devoted to analyzing the social situation they found themselves within, or the struggles that many young Party members made to understand and apply the ideology. On the rare occasion it is even addressed, this aspect of consciousness is treated with a knowing cynicism, as when MacFarquhar and Schoenhals (2006: 47) dispatch the thinking behind the early moments of the Cultural Revolution as "Marxist-Leninist gobbledygook."

Differences of thought within the leadership are usually figured as a conflict between the more "pragmatic" (i.e., less "ideological") leaders such as Zhou Enlai 周恩来 and Chen Yun 陈云 and the irrational utopianism of Mao. Setting up this sort of dichotomy between reason and emotion serves to empty out the content of both intellectual positions, since the "pragmatic" side is simply in line with reality while the "ideological" side lies beyond understanding. Such a cursory treatment contrasts with an older scholarship that, even at the height of the Cold War, carefully examined Communist ideas (Schwartz 1951; Schram [1963] 1969; Wakeman 1973).[7]

To the extent that the recent historiography has attempted to explain the events of the first three decades of the PRC, it has coalesced around a narrative in which Mao's revolutionary initiatives would first set the machinery of state in motion. Deploying its range of coercive measures, the state would then force members of civil society into external expressions of enthusiasm: those targeted in the campaign would be required to confess their sins, and all the rest were required to denounce those targeted. Individuals both inside and outside the state were driven to display increasing extremes of revolutionary ardor either to avoid being targeted or to advance their own individual agendas. In the Cultural Revolution, because the state itself had fractured, members of civil society were forced to pick sides without knowing which would prevail, generating factional conflicts that ripped apart the fabric of civil society (MacFarquhar and Schoenhals 2006; Walder 2009).

Ironically, this general picture recapitulates many of the features that historians have explicitly argued against in recent decades. It is a "great men of history" account; a unidirectional top-down understanding of social dynamics; an impact–response model of the relation between state and civil society. Even as "agency" is discovered everywhere, genuine agency—the capacity to influence the movement of history—is attributed only to the powerful; everyone else can engage only in ineffectual "resistance." Yet, paradoxically, civil society ultimately triumphs over the state, not through the positive exercise of agency but because civil society is, by its very nature, impossible to subsume within the state's project of homogeneity and regimentation. Thus, even teleology sneaks back in, as when Rana Mitter (2004: 104) argues that "the disillusionment in present-day China with much of Mao's record suggests that the Chinese experience from 1949 to 1976 was a detour in China's historical path." Civil society's preferences are never explained or historicized. They stand, as it were, outside of history, and thus can never be overcome by the revolutionary's utopian delusion of transforming human nature.

The Unacknowledged Social Ontology of Contemporary Empiricism

What scholars studying both sides of the state–civil society divide have in common is the reliance on an abstract schema in which the decisions of historical actors, from the highest levels to the lowest, are interpreted as instrumental action in pursuit of individual utility. The examination centers on the "strategies" that different people in different positions utilized to advance their own "interests." These interests are, in turn, implicitly considered the real motive underneath whatever rhetoric may have been employed. Despite the sharp opposition drawn between state and civil society, then, both sides of the binary are grounded in a deeper social ontology: a universal concept of human nature in which motivation arises from *individually* defined desires, and in which the individual's relations both to other people and to ideas are constructed in an *instrumental* fashion. Individuality was initially invoked to assert the particular against the violent abstraction of the universal, but an even more abstract universality silently returns as the foundation of the account.

Methodological individualism and instrumental reason do not emerge empirically from the archive but structure a particular interpretation of it. There are, for example, multiple ways to interpret the expressions of revolutionary enthusiasm that appear regularly in the sources. Certainly these could be feigned or coerced, but they might also be authentic—expressing both genuine belief in the Party's mission and a sense of collective identity transcending any reductive individualism. The kind of direct evidence that would allow us to draw a conclusive decision one way or the other is rarely available in the archive. Perhaps, then, we can call on the retrospective judgment of the participants themselves, with due caution for the difficulties of viewing history through the constructedness of memory. Certainly many informants have attested to a purely individual motivation and instrumental relation—yet many others insist on their true belief in the cause. That we find the first group compelling while we quickly move past the latter group's "puzzling nostalgia" (Altehenger 2013) strongly suggests that our interpretive framework, rather than the material itself, is driving our conclusions.

One of the great contributions of the cultural turn has been the insistence that nothing in the archive can be read as if it discloses immediate truth. Every historical source is produced by people inhabiting a certain subject position, and what they see and report is conditioned by their cultural background, their role in the division of labor, and their location in different hierarchies of power. Historians have thus invested great care and effort in "reading sources against the grain" to unearth information that may have been distorted or contaminated in some way by those who produced it. They have been much less likely to turn these forms of critical awareness on themselves: to interrogate the kind of knowledge production that their own historical, social, and cultural embeddedness has conditioned. When historians naturalize the dominant interpretive framework of their own historical moment and social milieu as intrinsic to the human condition, not only do they lose the possibility of reflecting critically on their own assumptions, they also unwittingly read those assumptions into the sources.[8]

If the claim that humans are irreducibly individual, self-interested, and instrumentally rational does not emerge from the sources, how can we understand its widespread acceptance? To find the answer, we must historicize the historians. The deep social ontology animating the historiography has today hardened into a kind of uncritical common sense about what it is to be human, but it was not always so. The vindication of the individual against the collective, of civil society against the state, of diversity against homogeneity, of contingency against necessity, of an open-ended future against teleology, of fragmentation against totality—this was a critical intellectual project posed against an earlier historiography that rose to prominence within the discipline of history in the 1980s.

The cultural turn took aim at the increasingly evident limitations of the then-dominant modernization theory and new social history. Employing new theoretical approaches inspired by the social movements of the 1960s and 1970s, the cultural turn demonstrated how hegemonic modes of knowledge production render invisible key forms of social domination, such as those indexed in the categories gender and nation, by making them appear natural. More than shifting the perspective to neglected groups, however, the cultural turn transformed the proper object of the discipline. The existing historiography was said to subsume and efface the real substance of history, either within stereotyped social groups such as the working class, whose "objective" interests were imputed by the scholar rather than defined by the historical actors themselves, or within the arid abstraction of disembodied social forces or laws of history. The cultural turn demanded instead that history be grasped as life lived by concrete human beings inhabiting concrete historical circumstances making decisions based on the full diversity of their own ideas (Eley 2005).

By the end of the 1990s, the sensibilities cultivated within the cultural turn had established hegemony across the discipline. The prohibition on structure, necessity, and teleology—ritually invoked in each monograph—now became the premise of new work, and the aim of excavating diversity, agency, and resistance guided the choice of new topics. In the process, however, a gradual transformation of the cultural turn itself took hold. What had been a conceptually driven literature hostile to an earlier empiricism and engaging productively with gender theory, postcolonialism, and a range of poststructuralist thinkers steadily relinquished both its theoretical and critical agendas. Increasingly it was inhabited by empiricist projects on discrete thematic topics, filling gaps in the literature without advancing a larger vision. The cultural turn's preoccupations motivated these projects externally rather than shaping the inner life of the inquiries.

The achievements of the cultural turn are immense, but troubled. On the one hand, this scholarship restored to prominence elements of culture and consciousness that had been slighted in the older historiography. By investigating human beings in their concreteness, rather than as expressions of abstract forces, the cultural turn struck a devastating blow against the economic reductionism of base-superstructure theories of history, whether those of traditional Marxism or of modernization theory. It focused attention on the social margins and transnational connections, overthrowing the methodologically nationalist approach to history that anachronistically read national identity back into the ancient past and effaced or excluded those identities that failed to fit the mold. Specifically in the field of PRC history, the work of recent years has brought a previously unimaginable level of specificity to our knowledge of the uneven impact of the Party's initiatives as well as the broad range of popular responses to them.

Yet in vanquishing the one-sidedness of the old historiography, the cultural turn erected in its place the contrary one-sidedness. The unevenness and diversity of social life were asserted as general features of reality rather than conceptualized as the outcome of social processes that require explanation. Evidence of a substantial increase in social homogeneity in the middle decades of the twentieth century was sidelined because it did not fit the research priority of uncovering diversity. Concepts like nation and class were exposed as social constructs, but the reasons for their enormous plausibility and influence in the twentieth century were left unexplored. Likewise unexamined was the historical question of why nation and class, ideas once so powerful that they could be taken as natural, suddenly fell into disrepute in the closing decades of the century among both popular and academic audiences.

The Unity of Structure and Agency in Classical Social Theory

More broadly, by repudiating earlier theories that distinguished between surface appearances and deeper dynamics, the cultural turn abandoned one of the most powerful modern traditions for explaining social phenomena.[9] The classic works of social theory developed by figures like Marx, Durkheim, and Freud posited a set of structures that shaped social life but could not be directly observed; only theoretical reflection could disclose their existence. The theory's claim to truth lay in its explanatory power over observable phenomena rather than a direct quantitative confirmation or a test of its claims as falsifiable propositions.[10] Each of these theories conceptualized social structure as an intrinsically dynamic category that develops through internal tensions, rather than as a static edifice moved by external shocks or as an automatic unfolding of fixed historical laws.

Crucially, in addition to the concept of structure, these theories also maintained that our immediate experience of social life shapes forms of thought that conceal the underlying dynamics. The result was a determinate concept of misrecognition arising from the misleading forms of appearance of deeper social relations. As Durkheim ([1897] 1978: 127) put it, "Social life must be explained, not by the conception of it created by those who participate in it, but by profound causes which escape awareness." Or Marx ([1865] 1976: 37): "Scientific truth is always paradox, if judged by everyday experience, which catches only the delusive appearance of things." This idea of misrecognition plays an essential role not only in accounting for consciousness but also in theorizing the origin and reproduction of structure as well. In central concepts like value and the commodity fetish (Marx), the totem and collective effervescence (Durkheim), or repression and compensatory thinking (Freud), each maintained that while appearance certainly was different from essence, the two were related in a systematic and reciprocal way that theoretical inquiry might uncover.

In other words, the classic texts of social theory developed concepts and categories that operated on both sides of the social objectivity-subjectivity binary. This was generally not true of the dominant midcentury academic theories that claimed descent from them. Modernization theory, structural functionalism in sociology, and the Stalinist positivism that called itself Marxism or dialectical materialism portrayed a unidirectional determination of consciousness by structure, while postwar psychoanalysis tended to assume structure and look for ways to integrate maladapted consciousness into it.[11] The role that concrete individuals played in producing the abstract social forces that encompassed them was largely effaced, and the dynamism of the earlier theories was often converted into a linear teleology. A monolithic objectivity blotted out determinately multivalent subjectivity.

The cultural turn reacted against the one-dimensionality of such work not with a return to the earlier, dynamic surface-depth theories but by conflating them with later approaches and condemning them all together on the grounds that the entire notion of "depth" was an imposition of the theorist. The cultural turn ushered in the superficiality of empiricism by insisting that the surface was all that exists.

With the evacuation of structure, the goal of explaining historical development with reference to something deeper than individual decisions was left susceptible to charges of "determinism," and history was now reinterpreted as radically open to the free play of contingency. This dogma was not incidental to the project. The intellectual and political impetus behind the cultural turn can be summed up in its defining shibboleth: that the individual historical actors we study, regardless of their station, are free to make choices. History is the work of individuals rather than of abstract forces. Once this was a claim that shattered a deadening theoretical consensus. Today, having achieved hegemony, the claim is no longer critical. It does not offer explanation but forecloses it, naturalizing what would otherwise cry out for explanation—namely, what are the forces that produce and organize the diversity that we observe? Instead, the claim is asserted in rote fashion, as a sign of belonging within the discipline and an affirmation of the intellectual status quo.

But perhaps there is something deeper as well. The insistence that the individual's choices are beyond social determination may be as much a case of wish fulfillment as an intellectual commitment. To exclude understanding from the realm of individual choice not only establishes the individualist social ontology, it also preserves some sense of freedom—freedom within a world dominated by the abstract forces of commodification, competition, and the market. That form of domination is difficult to make visible because of its impersonal nature, but admitting its existence would also threaten an entire generation's political accommodation to it. The totality was not confronted; instead, awareness of it was repressed.

Such a mystification is the condition of possibility for classical liberalism as an ideology. In liberalism, methodological individualism is married to a prescription of limited government so that the invisible hand of the market can coordinate the disparate, freely determined individual desires of its subjects, thereby securing a society based solely on freedom of choice. Much of the critical purchase behind recent literature on the early PRC comes from the Party-state's violation of this principle. Chinese citizens, rather than pursuing their interests within the neutral framework of Adam Smith's system of perfect liberty, instead found the state violating at every turn their inalienable rights to life, liberty, and property.[12]

In classical liberalism, all domination is concrete and immediately visible—arising, above all, from the state—while commodification, competition, and voluntary exchange on the market are cast as the natural and unchanging framework of human life. Acceptance of this basic tenet helps us understand why features of social life that had once been open to historical inquiry and critique were suddenly shifted into civil society and the realm of freedom, placed beyond challenge or explanation. The entire conceptual impetus of the Chinese Communist Party's transformational vision was thereby rendered either illegitimate or incomprehensible. The ways in which grassroots cultural forms structured exclusion and inequality; the modes of domination arising from private property, economic exploitation, and the irrationalities of the market; the national and racial inequalities that grew from the imperialism of free trade—all of these can only be posed as political questions if civil society is denaturalized and structural forms of violence are made visible.

Classical liberalism excludes the very possibility of emancipatory politics because it casts these abstract forms of domination as an ineradicable feature of reality arising from human nature. Since a transformational politics aims to change the structures of collective life, from the standpoint of liberalism it can never be anything but violence against nature. This is why "resistance" appears in the historiography not as a political act but as a refusal of the political, and why the forms of domination targeted by the Chinese Revolution simply disappear. It is why, finally, the masses as a political subject and agent of history are supplanted by the atomized members of civil society as victims with no potential beyond victimhood (Lanza 2017: 162–64).

Historicizing the History Discipline's Empiricism

In the historical epistemology that generally accompanies empiricism, knowledge is thought to accumulate source by source and fact by fact, moving us progressively closer to the truth. A broad shift in historical understanding would be due, then, to the emergence of previously unknown facts that make prior interpretations untenable. The rethinking of the historiography of the Chinese Revolution that started in the late 1970s and provided the foundations for PRC history as a field was undoubtedly driven in part by the emergence of new information, in particular evidence of the full scale of suffering and violence in the Great Leap Forward and the Cultural Revolution. The conceptual transformation was basically complete by 1989, but the Chinese state's massacre of peacefully protesting members of civil society in that year strongly reinforced the prior trends.

Such an explanation, however, runs into the difficulty that the substance of the rethinking occurred more at the level of concepts and categories than it did at the level of new facts. In particular, the new approach rejected not just the approbation for the Party's rule that sometimes appeared in the prior historiography but also earlier historians' use of collective categories such as the people, the masses, the bourgeoisie and proletariat, or the Chinese nation (H. Wang 2016). The shift took place, moreover, well beyond the field of Chinese history, encompassing every specialization in the discipline of social history (Sewell 2005: 40–48). It took place beyond the discipline as well. Related epistemological reorientations unfolded at the same time in radically different realms—the global consolidation of antistate ideologies (ranging from Reagan-Thatcher politics to the rise of anarchism as the dominant form of leftist dissent); the new consensus in economics and development studies that free market coordination is superior to bureaucratic methods; the rise to hegemony in the social sciences of other interpretive paradigms based on methodological individualism and instrumental reason, such as game theory, public choice, and human capital. None of these transformations took place "seamlessly"; each was fiercely contested. Nonetheless, all of them proceeded ineluctably around the world and across fields and sectors.

Thus the new historiographical epistemology of the 1980s is best understood as paradigmatic in nature. In the concept developed by Thomas Kuhn ([1962] 2012), a paradigm is an intellectual framework shared by a community of scholars that defines the legitimate questions of a research agenda and the methods for conducting research within it. A successful paradigm establishes a shared sense of what the world is like and how it works, but leaves significant space for those researchers working within it to fill in the details. In this case, we know that social life is always messy, but we do not know the specifics of that mess. We know that the state will try to control and manipulate the population, to homogenize it and make it legible, but we do not know concretely what the process was like or what sorts of resistance it occasioned.

A transformation of thinking that arose contingently, from individual reasoning or experience or from a single field's new findings, would not appear as part of a systemic and global shift in subjectivity. What we are discussing requires instead a structural explanation. The hegemony of methodological individualism and a liberal political orientation in the field of social history should therefore be grounded in a broad historical restructuring of the sensibilities of historians themselves.[13]

The cultural turn arose initially as a critique of the postwar social totality of mass society, attacking the stultifying dominance of the state and other large institutions as well as the reduction of the individual to a faceless cog in a giant machine driven by abstract laws. Its vindication of the self, of civil society, and of culture and consciousness pointed in a liberatory direction. Yet as a new social totality, global in scope, was consolidated in the 1980s, this critique of one form of domination came to be embedded within a new form of domination: the unfreedom of the individual achieved not through the concrete control imposed by large bureaucracies but through the abstract control asserted by social atomization and market forces (Foucault [1978–1979] 2008; Harvey 1989; Sewell 2005: 53–62).

The cultural turn's implicit attacks on the state and social homogenization, and its explicit rejection of a concept of social structure as an explanatory strategy, continued and even intensified. Now, however, these positions expressed not a critique of domination, but an affirmation of the values and truths that arise within the highly market-mediated experience of life in neoliberal society. 忆苦思甜[14]—asserting the values of the new society by vilifying those of the old should be a familiar phenomenon for those who study the Mao era.

New Prospects: Alignment of State and Civil Society

My point is not that the findings of such investigations are wrong. Like any paradigmatic framework, the cultural turn and today's empiricism have proven productive of important new insights while simultaneously *and for the same reason* limiting our access to other insights. I have already suggested some of the facets of social life that have been illuminated within the current paradigm. But what have methodological individualism and the liberal concept of society prevented us from seeing? What courses of investigation have they closed off? Without claiming an exhaustive list, I would like to highlight three crucial limitations of the existing historiography whose overcoming would open up important new ways to understand the Mao era.

First, the focus on conflict between state and civil society has marginalized abundant evidence of alignment. While overt coercion, violence, and terror were fundamental characteristics of Communist Party rule, it does not follow that they alone were responsible for the extraordinary extent to which the state established a presence within civil society. If that were so, then it is difficult to understand the numerous examples of authoritarian regimes elsewhere in the world—and in China itself prior to Communist rule—that signally failed in similar aims despite similarly brutal methods.

The idea is not to replace empirical research exposing abuses with an apologia. The problem rather is that the current paradigm frustrates empirical investigation into the everyday foundations of the Party's authority that could help us to appreciate the broadly appealing features of the new system and to understand how its deeply oppressive practices gained consent. In other words, the question is hegemony in Gramsci's ([1929–35] 1971) sense of the concept: the kind of power, deeper than overt coercion, gained by a particular social group because that group appears to express common sense and to represent the general interest. In contrast to liberal political philosophy, the concept of hegemony does not equate the popular support for a political regime with the absence of domination. Rather than denying the legitimacy of Party rule by exaggerating the significance of those who rejected the system or by downplaying the extent of China's social transformation, such an analysis acknowledges the Party's popular legitimacy while exploring the mystified forms of coercion that produced it.

One example of this process can be seen in the formation of residents' committees in Shanghai. As Wang Zheng (2005) shows, the Party's recruitment of local housewives both to perform a wide array of services for neighborhood residents and to serve as the eyes and ears of the state at the grassroots level marked a sharp break with the prior domination of neighborhoods by gangsters. The system was newly responsive to residents' needs, as the committees worked to find jobs for the unemployed, secure adequate rations, improve sanitation and safety, and conduct literacy classes. At the same time, the committees' responsibility for neighborhood surveillance also led to conflict and repression as the Party's campaigns targeted a rising number of people.

The broad contrast of serving versus violating the residents' interests—which seems such a natural evaluative framework within the existing paradigm—is confounded in the recollections of residents. For example, Jie Li (2015) discusses the experience of her family as Shanghai was transformed after 1949. Her grandmother, who served as a residents' committee cadre in Shanghai, emphasizes the sense of liberation she gained from taking on public duties outside the home for the first time. Though her husband was victimized in the Anti-Rightist Campaign, and though this cost her the cherished position on the residents' committee, she does not question the legitimacy of the state's project: "Even in her old age, Nainai adopted the party line when speaking of this: 'Just because your *yeye* was a Rightist did not mean that I was a Rightist as well. He was the one who made the mistake, not I. My job was to help him return to the ranks of the People, to help him ideologically so that he would not make mistakes in the future'" (67). At the individual level, hegemony inheres as a structure of consciousness rather than an instrumental commitment that is simply thrown away once its use is past.

Wang identifies another powerful dynamic at play in the residents' committees. As former housewives came to embody state authority in the neighborhood, the gendered distinction of *nei-wai* (private-public) expanded with them, rendering the neighborhood a domesticated space. At one level this newly constituted presence of the state within civil society was a revolutionary challenge to prior gender norms, but at a deeper level it reconstituted gender-separated spheres in a way that also naturalized the new exercise of power.

Recognizing the popular legitimacy of the Party may be necessary to understand the course of the revolution, but merely reversing the state-society relation from conflict to cooperation will impose a new distortion on the history. Our goal should not be to marginalize the valuable findings of the last several decades revealing conflicts and tensions within the Revolution that exceeded the Party's own apprehension. Rather, historians should incorporate these findings in a larger, more complete conceptualization. In that project, the state–civil society binary may itself be a central obstacle.

In its place, a more complex and diverse set of social categories is needed to capture the lines of conflict and unity in the People's Republic. Building on the advances of the cultural turn, such categories should not be reduced to the inert "objective" terms prevalent in the social sciences or the rigid political labels that dominated the Communist Party's own discourse.[15] Yet to explain the history, we must also approach individual agency in a more critical manner and build instead on theories of collective identification and the social production of subjectivity.

Again, engaging with theory is not meant to shut down empirical investigation but to enliven it. Too often, recent scholarship has simply arranged archival findings within the pregiven paradigmatic framework, not only sacrificing explanatory power but also diminishing the specificity of the historical experience as well. What is required instead is to derive categories through a careful interrogation of the structured spaces and relations inhabited and enacted by the historical actors themselves.

In my own work, for example, I have argued that within the social regime of the factory, the Party's political narrative of liberation through submission to the collective gained credence by building on different groups' positions within the production process. On taking power, the Party launched campaigns that threw into relief the tensions intrinsic to the hierarchies of the detail division of labor. By forcing these frictions to the surface and transforming them into open conflict, the Party was able to reorient the dynamic interactions that constituted factory hierarchies in a way that subordinated existing power holders and built legitimacy for Party agents while remaking the political economy of production itself. Many campaigns in the factories portrayed in moralistic terms what was in fact a structural tension between management and rank-and-file workers. In this way, the workers' resentments were channeled against individual managers and their personal flaws, which were assimilated into politicized categories such as corruption or bureaucratism. By welcoming the active participation and initiative of the masses into these campaigns, the Party built trust among workers and gained their cooperation in holding managers accountable to Party priorities (Werner 2015: 122–204).

The aims of the campaign methodology cannot be reduced to a simple play for power or a kind of brainwashing of the workers. The success of the process was inseparable from the workers' prior experiences of injury and indignity within the production process, which the campaign made visible and charged with a particular meaning. Yet it equally arose from the successful portrayal of injury and indignity in the workplace as a product of individual abuses rather than the structural dynamics of economic growth—a misrecognition promoted both by the immediate, personalized experience of domination in the "old society" and by the emotionally intense design of the campaign mobilization.

Later mobilization campaigns in the factories built on these foundations but turned the same techniques against rank-and-file workers. In the periodic "campaigns to raise production and economize on materials" or the "socialist competitions" to meet plan quotas, those who refused to accede to the demands for an ever-longer and more intense working day were cast in moralistic terms as selfish individualists rather than proper members of the collective. A simplistic distinction between state and civil society not only fails to capture this process by which collective identification became both compelling and compulsory, it also excludes investigation into the closely connected considerations of ideology and political economy that drove the Party's fraught initiatives of simultaneously empowering and subordinating living labor.

New Prospects: Richer Perspectives on Subjectivity

A more rigorous exploration of social cooperation and conflict in the Mao era is one broad realm of inquiry that would be opened up by moving beyond the state–society binary and methodological individualism. Closely related is a second general line of inquiry: conceptualizing consciousness at both popular and elite levels in a way that does not reduce the relation between self and ideas to self-interest and instrumental rationality.

Such an approach does not preclude the idea of self-interested motivation or cynical use of ideology; instead, it demands inquiry into the conditions under which a relation between the self and its objects is rendered instrumental.[16] But capturing the true heterogeneity of belief and behavior in the Revolution requires that we recognize a wider range of motivations and self-understandings.[17] It also requires exploring the possibility that ostensibly contrasting orientations—true belief and cynical manipulation—may coexist within the same person in complex and even complementary ways. An obvious case of the latter would be high-level political leaders employing brutally instrumental means to achieve their deeply held commitment to what they considered liberatory social transformation, but such a pattern might appear at any level of the social hierarchy.

Equally important is the idea that the total social distribution of orientations toward the dominant ideology changed over time. For example, one common experience was moving from a hopeful embrace of new possibilities to disillusion at the limitations or injustices that unexpectedly arose from them. Yet such a trajectory should not be cast as a linear process: the tortuous and crosscutting paths of state policy, individual fortunes, and large-scale social transformation ensured a more complex movement. In particular, the idea that popular exhaustion with the Revolution was widespread by the mid-1960s cannot make sense of the apparently spontaneous explosion among the youth in 1966 of revolutionary enthusiasm directed against previously sacrosanct authority figures—not the result of but the necessary precondition for the success of Mao's machinations. Walder's otherwise compelling work on the formation of factions in the Cultural Revolution (2002; 2009) simply assimilates the astonishing surge of grassroots turmoil into the narrative of Mao's absolute power over Chinese people: "Municipal officials were surprised at the extent to which students and teachers targeted their leaders for criticism . . . At this point, and for several months to come, none of the participants—party officials, members of work teams, or students—could have understood the eventual scope of the campaign or *the ultimate purpose of Mao*" (2002: 444–45, emphasis added). Drawn instead to events that fit comfortably within the dominant paradigm, today's empiricism cannot even acknowledge the puzzle.[18]

Taking seriously the thinking within the Party allows us to see things we missed before. For example, if we avoid the now highly conventional language about the Party's "strategies" to suppress its "competitors" in order to "consolidate its rule," the instrumentality with which the Party treated the masses emerges as something more than cynical manipulation. It was an attempt to make the masses proper to their concept as understood in Party theory, which would in turn allow the masses to realize their historical mission. In its directive on conducting the Democratic Reform Campaign, for instance, the Shanghai Municipal Party Committee spelled out some of the techniques by which the enemies of the working class had blocked its potential:

> In places where the workers movement was more dynamic, [the bureaucratic capitalist class] adopted "divide and rule" measures such as deception, bribery, division, and intimidation to split the workers and staff and to break up unity among the workers. They also used a handful of backward elements or cultivated certain "turncoats" (*gongzei* 工贼) or "running dogs" to manage production and oppress the workers and thereby divert workers from their targets of struggle and scatter the strength of the workers (Zou 2001: 222).

Party leaders believed not that they were coercing compliance, but that they were actively remaking subjectivities—from those deformed by the "old society" into those required by a truly democratic society (Smith 2013). They thought there was a potential among the workers that had been suppressed and could be unleashed through the mass campaign.

In this process, the transformational effect of participation itself was the crucial element. A concept of static "interests" cannot capture the ways in which that form of experience actively remade workers' understanding of their own identities and how they defined their own interests. The point applies equally to those targeted by the various campaigns and those only indirectly affected by them. Subjectivity must be understood as a process of becoming within a larger field of social relations and historical dynamics rather than a fixed feature of the individual.

Considering the historical actors' ideas on their own terms deepens our analysis of what happened at the grassroots, and it also allows us to begin exploring the ideological landscape of the period as a richly contradictory formation of consciousness with real historical consequences rather than a static and schematic backdrop to agency and resistance within civil society.[19] The conceptualization of social relations and the connected vision of liberation that animated many of the Party's mobilizational campaigns were not a mask to disguise the real motivation of a lust for power, nor were they mere rhetoric to manipulate the gullible masses. For many Party members, they were the motivation for political involvement in the first place. They were also an essential factor in the popular legitimacy of Party rule, even if individuals' understandings did not always align with official textbooks.

As Max Weber ([1920] 1992: 48) argued, then, ideas are a force in history. But ideas do not become a force in history as self-subsistent substances descending through time and standing outside of social experience, imposing themselves on the minds of those who exist within history. As Durkheim ([1897] 1978: 127) put it, "Either the collective consciousness floats in a vacuum, a sort of unrepresentable absolute, or it is related to the rest of the world through the intermediary of a substratum on which it consequently depends. From another point of view, of what can this substratum be composed if not of the members of society as they are socially combined?"

This suggests a different approach from the idea that the members of civil society accepted Party propaganda because they fell prey to "manipulation." The view that whatever messages are broadcast will simply impress themselves on the people, as if the people were a blank slate, is incapable of explaining why state-controlled media (or demagogic politicians or corporate advertisers) are sometimes extraordinarily successful in their attempts at manipulation and sometimes utterly fail.

The alternative is to focus not on the scheming of those disseminating the message but on the lived circumstances of their audiences. Ideas will not take root unless they fall on fertile ground. Such an approach to the question does not involve endorsing the epistemologically and politically naïve idea that propagandists were simply peddling the truth. Instead, historians can arrive at a more sophisticated understanding of the dissemination and circulation of ideas by asking: what were people experiencing in their lives that made a certain worldview and politics plausible and compelling?[20] As Barbara Fields (1990: 110) argues,

> Ideology is best understood as the descriptive vocabulary of day-to-day existence, through which people make rough sense of the social reality that they live and create from day to day. It is the language of consciousness that suits the particular way in which people deal with their fellows. It is the interpretation in thought of the social relations through which they constantly create and re-create their collective being, in all the varied forms their collective being may assume: family, clan, tribe, nation, class, party, business enterprise, church, army, club, and so on. As such, ideologies are not delusions but real, as real as the social relations for which they stand.
>
> Ideologies are real, but it does not follow that they are scientifically accurate, or that they provide an analysis of social relations that would make sense to anyone who does not take ritual part in those social relations.

Without affirming the reductive social ontology of the Communist Party's theorists, the idea that the Party was uncovering suppressed potentials and appealing to preexisting tensions within the population offers a significantly more persuasive starting point for understanding the success of mobilizational campaigns than the idea that simply applying divisive discourse generates social conflict ex nihilo.[21]

This is not a call for a simple affirmation of the historical beliefs we endeavor to understand. As Fields suggests, one can maintain a critical perspective on the ideas while still aiming to illuminate why a particular set of historical subjects could come to find them persuasive. In fact, to understand how the wide and deep popular support for the Revolution underwent a sharp reversal in the 1970s that resulted in wide and deep popular support for the Reform period's repudiation of mass society, historical inquiry must grapple with the simultaneity of liberatory and oppressive currents within the Revolution itself (Werner 2015: 289–301). Simply reversing the one-sided neoliberal critique into a one-sided defense of mass politics and explaining the Reform-era rupture as nothing more than a power play by self-seeking elites suffers the same inadequacies as the account it means to correct (see Werner 2018: 522).

The varying approaches to misrecognition offered by Marx, Durkheim, and Freud offer fertile ground for critical investigations of consciousness. For example, each offers a starting point for theorizing how Mao came to assume such extraordinary power in Chinese society, without reducing that power to its immediately visible manifestations of institutional position or ruthless political maneuvering. From Marx's ([1843] 1978: 33–34) perspective, we could interpret the cult of personality as the fetishized apprehension of the alienated powers of society, produced by individuals but assuming a seeming autonomy over them that dominates them. For Durkheim ([1912] 1995), Mao could be seen as the totemic expression of collective life itself: society worshipping its own capacity to raise the individual above the individual's quotidian being.[22] Building on Freud, we might understand the mass adulation of Mao as the result of thwarted narcissistic impulses projected onto a figure serving as a substitute for the individual: "By making the leader his ideal he loves himself, as it were, but gets rid of the stains of frustration and discontent which mar his picture of his own empirical self" (Adorno [1951] 1991: 140).[23]

The Party cast the forms of identity it sought to engender as those that exclusively were true and rational, a claim that the historiography has rightly rejected. Yet today's skeptics too often treat the habits and beliefs targeted by the Party as privileged in their own right. Selden (1993: 14), for example, emphasizes the state's "mechanisms of coercion and control of the household sector and the market." While the planned economy undoubtedly subordinated households and the market in many ways, the force of the contrast depends on ignoring the forms of "coercion and control" that were constitutive elements of the household and the market. Naturalizing the preferences found in civil society without interrogating the constraints and compulsions that shaped them makes the motivations of those who fought against them very difficult to explain without resorting to caricature. More than that, it also casts subjectivity as something fixed, when the very instability that so fundamentally characterized the crisis of the two decades before the founding of the PRC rendered it highly fluid.

However, that fluidity was not the free play of thought and desire or the creative exploration of identity that have been such a preoccupation among historians across geographic specializations.[24] Rather, for most of the population, it was a traumatic dissolution of all those certainties required for a sense of security in the present and hope for the future, fatally undone by depression, war, hyperinflation, and the shattered legitimacy of existing elites (Werner 2017). The historiography of the PRC has largely bracketed the disastrous years before 1949, but the Communist Party's claim that it alone could put an end to the intolerable instability and extreme inequalities of the earlier period was the foundation stone of its legitimacy, which in turn became the necessary condition for integrating most of the population into a new regime of state-planned economic expansion, social leveling, and standardization of culture and social circumstances. Retrospectively, we may conclude that "the revolution was not a Liberation but (for most) was the replacement of one form of domination with another" (Esherick 1995: 48). But from the standpoint of vast numbers of the historical actors themselves, things looked quite different. The vicious competition, mutual victimization, and general chaos of the 1930s and 1940s is the background against which we might begin to understand how regimentation and homogenization could be widely experienced as liberatory.

New Prospects: Systematicity and Crisis

This brings us to the third and final realm of inquiry that could be opened by moving beyond the existing paradigm: apprehending the systematicity of society in the Mao era. This systematicity is seen domestically as a self-reproducing structure of growth, simultaneously economic and cultural, that was mediated through central planning and Party administration. It also appears internationally, with China being one of many societies impelled along a similar trajectory across the twentieth century within a common global system. The reified facts that are the raw material of empiricist projects and the reified topics that are the raw material of academic careers make it difficult to illuminate the ways in which different realms of life are systematically interconnected. Yet such a perspective is needed if we are to grasp the forces responsible for both the unprecedented success of the Party's developmentalist transformation and the inexorable accumulation of social contradictions that produced its devastating crises.

Perhaps the most persuasive evidence that systemic processes are at work in this history are the remarkable parallels in the nature and development of mass society in countries at all levels of wealth: mass society's consolidation in the immediate postwar period, the growing incorporation and homogenization of wider social constituencies that followed, the continued exclusion of certain disadvantaged populations that became increasingly restive in their demands for inclusion, the crisis and collapse of this entire form of social life across the globe in the youth rebellions of the late 1960s and the economic turmoil of the 1970s, followed by the worldwide rise of neoliberal social forms in the late 1970s.[25] Because tangible exchanges with the rest of the world became increasingly insignificant in this period, the early PRC has often been treated as if it stood outside of global history. Yet the simultaneity of developments on both sides of the Cold War divide and across the Three Worlds indicates the need for a conceptualization capable of grasping a global trajectory of change driven by structural dynamics rather than by individual decisions, concrete linkages, or historical contingency.

In contrast to most social scientists, whose methodology abstracts social phenomena away from their context within a wider system of social relations and out of their position within a larger arc of history, historians are ideally placed to inquire into the embeddedness and historicity of social life. However, empiricism's one-sided valorization of the concrete and the cultural turn's insistence on the contingency of historical events have frustrated this potential. The work of the cultural turn successfully denaturalized many of the key features of mass society, including the nation and the masses. But it has been unable to explain why these concepts came to seem natural around the world when they did or why skepticism toward them—of which the cultural turn was itself one expression—also emerged globally.

I have made use of the Régulation School's work as a starting point in conceptualizing a nonteleological and nonlinear developmental dynamic that has characterized capitalism as a global system across the twentieth century (Werner 2015). The Régulation approach, in addition to providing a persuasive macro-scale interpretation of the sharp structural reorientations in the logic of economic growth that took place in the 1940s and again in the 1970s, focuses attention on capital accumulation not simply as an economic system but as a systemically interwoven set of social relations and practices whose development and dysfunction ramify through the entire society.

However, the Régulation conceptualization is limited by the contrary one-sidedness of excessive functionalism and a failure to treat subjectivity seriously. Ultimately, what is required is a deeper theorization of modernity as a totalizing social system that nonetheless arises from everyday practices; a system both constraining on and generative of agency, structuring both social objectivity and subjectivity through the characteristic binaries of the last three centuries, riven by contradictions that drive its seemingly linear growth until they explode into the periodic general crises whose resolution involves a reversal of the foundational antinomies (Postone 1993). Returning to a concept of totality brings to awareness the essential role that the texture of social life plays in shaping consciousness and activity. Grasping this element of history as a single but variegated social terrain allows us to theorize both uniformity and difference, with neither cast as ontological but instead each arising from different locations inhabited within a larger system, and producing patterns of unevenness that themselves both perpetuate the system and create the possibility of its transformation.

Yet even without a theorization reaching to the constitutive foundations of modernity, a systematic conception of the PRC as a contradictory concatenation of social relations would open an entirely new set of possible historical investigations, exploring the system's inner dynamism rather than simply describing externally a procession of discrete events. It would, at the same time, provide a new approach to understanding the reasons that the system failed to perform as the Party expected as well as the sources of its disastrous political and economic crises—again, as generated from a systemic logic of development rather than contingently by Mao's idiosyncrasies, the deficiencies of the leadership, or exogenous shocks. Finally, it would open the possibility of a critical perspective on the history motivated not by moralistic judgment or criticism of political errors but by a structural critique: what were the historical forces that led to oppression and domination in the PRC, and how can such an inquiry shed light on the preconditions for a society in which oppression and domination would finally be overcome?

Uncovering the Relation of the Historian to History

In this article, I have emphasized the ways in which empiricism and its failure of self-reflexivity have impeded our ability to fully apprehend the richness of our sources and to use them in the construction of explanations adequate to our objects of investigation. Empiricism privileges the concrete and assumes that meaning inheres in the sources themselves (even if work needs to be done to uncover that meaning) rather than understanding meaning as a reciprocal relation between the historian (subject) and the archive (object). In so doing, it naturalizes its epistemological foundations and, by making them invisible, robs itself of the opportunity to historicize and interrogate its own ideological assumptions. Yet I have also been critical of the static and reified methods that preceded the cultural turn and that remain powerful in the social sciences. The key to an alternative that confronts both sets of problems is to restore a deep concept of relationality to our interpretive categories.

By relationality, I mean awareness of the ways in which human beings are constituted through their social connections. In the neoliberal era, such an approach has been widely forsworn in favor of conceptualizations that cast people's characteristics as ontologically given properties of the individuals or groups to which they belong. Whether apotheosizing individual will in ideologies of self-fashioning or casting it into the pit, as in neurochemical determinism or sociobiology; whether attributing group identities to an imputed essence or tradition or trauma, each of which exerts its power from outside of history—all of these otherwise varied explanatory frameworks construct individuals and groups in isolation from the larger constellation of social relations within which they exist. A relational account, by contrast, foregrounds the central forms of social mediation and the way they constitute each side of the relation. In Marx's ([1867] 1976: 149n22) example: "One man is king only because other men stand in the relation of subjects to him. They, on the other hand, imagine that they are subjects because he is king." People create their own nature, or have it imposed on them, through the social relations they inhabit. But recognition of that process after the characteristics have hardened in place can be elusive.[26]

The loss of this sense of relationality is the condition of possibility for the liberal concept of the individual: atomized and sufficient unto itself, prior to social processes. As Marx ([1857–58] 1973: 84) argues, such a concept is historically recent and itself the product of a particular set of social relations: "The more deeply we go back into history, the more does the individual, and hence also the producing individual, appear as dependent, as belonging to a greater whole . . . Only in the eighteenth century, in 'civil society,' do the various forms of social connectedness confront the individual as a mere means towards his private purposes, as external necessity."[27] The reason relationality is lost is because it is not immediately visible, but the reasons for that are fundamentally social and historically specific (Polanyi [1944] 2001). At first glance this seems counterintuitive, since the interdependence of individuals in their economic, political, and cultural exchanges is obvious— and there is nothing that liberalism celebrates more than exchange. Within a commodity society, however, those exchanges are overwhelmingly transactions rather than reciprocities (Mauss [1923–24] 1990). The social relation is constituted as a means to individual purposes rather than as an end in itself. The completed exchange dissolves the relation instead of nourishing it.

The generalization of an external and instrumental relation between subject and object is reflected in the conceptual apparatus of empiricism—not just in the designation of self-interest as the universal motivation, not just in the denial of collective forms of identification, but in the epistemology itself. As a method, empiricism imagines a sharp distinction between the observing subject and its object, namely, the stable and knowable facts the subject records. The "objectivity" of observers is defined by their refusal to find themselves in the object. In other words, empiricism is the denial of a relation in which the subject takes an active role in constituting the object and is, in turn, transformed through this relation.

For this reason, the dynamic interrelation of subject and object in history likewise escapes its grasp. We are given a basically stable conception of the self, which denies the possibility of social transformation arising from participation in historically new forms of experience. We see the opportunistic employment of ideology rather than an individual whose identity is constituted through ideology. The state and the individual members of civil society are reduced to static quantities at odds with one another; the idea that both sides of the binary might be constituted dynamically through the relation itself is lost.

The empiricist's organization of their object reifies social outcomes. It then dismisses the attempt to theorize those intangible processes responsible for social outcomes as a metaphysical post hoc imposition of the theorist. In the name of demystifying the rhetoric that people employ and of exposing the truth of self-interest and quotidian facticity, empiricism denies a deeper social logic. The result is quite at odds with the intention: such an analysis mystifies the social relations that animate everything we observe on the surface. The global structural reversals and the explosions of ideological enthusiasm that shaped the twentieth century are rendered inexplicable; so too are the obvious irrationalities and bizarre mysticisms that are also a persistent feature of modern life (Adorno 1994).

The alternative approach I have briefly sketched refuses to efface or dismiss these phenomena. In the concept of systemically induced misrecognition, it takes seriously what the historical actors believed they were doing without adopting an uncritical perspective on those claims. It sees the importance of employing concepts like social structure and large-scale historical dynamics without unmooring them from everyday life and subjectivity. In so doing it reunites immediate consciousness and abstract historical forces as a unity of opposites, each side produced within a totality whose universality is real but historically specific.

Such an approach is indeed totalizing, as its critics have maintained. The intent of totality as a category of analysis, however, is not to affirm unfreedom but to reveal it—where other approaches, both empiricist and poststructuralist, suppress awareness of it (Postone 1993: 80; 2006: 94–95). In apprehending these elements of modern social life, the critique of totality locates its standpoint neither in a hope of recuperating the past nor in a desire to affirm the present but in the determinate possibility of a future that might transcend the binary of stultifying collective and atomized individual: "Totality is what is most real. Since it is the sum of individuals' social relations which screen themselves off from individuals, it is also illusion—ideology. A liberated mankind would by no means be a totality" (Adorno [1969] 1976: 12).

Notes

My thanks to those who offered generous feedback and pushback on these ideas: Sören Brandes, Shehong Chen, Puck Engman, Jacob Eyferth, Ariel Fox, Karl Gerth, Ling Kang, Macabe Keliher, Jonathan Levy, Andrew Liu, Melissa Macauley, Kenneth Pomeranz, William Sewell, Peter Thilly, and three anonymous reviewers. Special thanks go to Fabio Lanza and Aminda Smith for organizing this issue as well as offering helpful comments. Most of all, my thanks go to the late Moishe Postone, who taught me how to think through social theory.

1 Outstanding examples include: on gender, Hershatter 2011 and Wang Zheng 2017; on the rural-urban divide, Brown 2012; on transforming the individual, Smith 2013.

2 南辕北辙 *nan yuan bei zhe*: to act at cross-purposes. The source of this *chengyu* is the story of a man who happens upon a traveler heading to the southern state of Chu. He asks: "If you are going to Chu, why are you heading north?" The traveler dismisses the objection: "But I have a good horse."

3 The totalitarian paradigm of monolithic state control over individual life was shattered when the Cultural Revolution revealed deep conflicts within the PRC to the world outside China. However, there has been a highly significant shift in scholars' delineation of the key fissures. In the Cultural Revolution era, the lines of division were understood in pro-Mao (anti-bureaucracy)/anti-Mao (pro-bureaucracy) terms, in which a popular constituency existed for both sides and there was no clear distinction between state and civil society. Since the 1980s, the state-civil society divide has been the privileged analytical prism, a development I attempt to explain below.

4 Perhaps the most prominent articulation and defense of this Enlightenment dichotomy in the current era is Scott 1998.

5 This critical posture is directed at the state as such rather than at the Communist state in particular. Those writers who address the Republican period as well are equally critical of the Guomindang state. The dominant position of the last several decades has been to emphasize continuities in state-building projects across the 1949 divide, unlike an older

historiography that focused on distinctions between the two state formations to explain the contrasting levels of success for each project or to distinguish the class constituencies each was said to serve.

6 Other studies that adopt a similar standpoint include Teiwes and Sun 1999; MacFarquhar and Schoenhals 2006; Pantsov and Levine 2015. The last is critiqued on this point in Karl 2016.

7 One welcome recent exception treating debates within the Party as a historical question is Coderre 2019.

8 For a related argument, see Smith 2014.

9 For a related discussion, see Jameson 1991: 6–16.

10 See the debates between advocates of positivism and critical theory contained in Adorno et al. (1969) 1976.

11 Important midcentury theories that sustained and deepened the explanatory sophistication of the earlier period were marginalized within academia in this period. These include the work of the Frankfurt School (Adorno, Horkheimer, Marcuse) and of French existentialism (Sartre, Beauvoir, Fanon).

12 In general, the historiography is unaware of its affinity with classical liberalism. The banishing of political economy from the field of twentieth-century Chinese history since the 1990s—in the name of combating economic determinism—has been a key reason for this general lack of awareness.

13 Lanza 2017 explores a global political shift that laid the foundations for this paradigmatic shift in the discipline: the exhaustion of the revolutionary energy that had animated many young China scholars in the late 1960s and early 1970s.

14 忆苦思甜 *yi ku si tian*: recall past bitterness to savor today's sweetness. This *chengyu* was widely used in the Mao era to describe the practice of individuals narrating the suffering they experienced before "liberation" to dramatize how wonderful life was in the present (Ho 2018: 73–76).

15 For a useful critique of positivist social science categories, see Wang Hui (2013) 2016.

16 Marx's concept of alienation ([1844] 1964: 106–19) is the best foundation on which to begin such an inquiry.

17 Although it excludes the kind of global, structural framework of social dynamics that I call for below, Hershatter 2011 remains unmatched in grasping the complexity of subjectivity in the ways I have in mind here.

18 See also MacFarquhar and Schoenhals (2006: 54), who raise and then quickly abandon the question, again placing all agency in the figure of Mao: "The process by which Mao translated high-level political intrigue into mass mobilization remains one of the many obscure issues of the Cultural Revolution." A clear statement of the inadequacies of the existing literature and a promising start toward theorizing the 1966 rupture is found in Xu 2017.

19 An outstanding example of such an approach is Wu 2014.

20 Although his conclusions depart from my own, Billeter's (1985) analysis of how class labels came to appear natural to those embedded within the PRC social regime remains an important intervention. Rather than dismissing forms of consciousness or simply describing them, he endeavors to understand how they became meaningful within a particular social context.

21 Yu Liu (2010: 336) expresses the latter position: "Depicting people as 'victims' of 'villains' provokes anger, establishing the emotional ground of struggle movements."

22 Xu (2010: 240) suggests a similar interpretation.

23 Adorno is analyzing the fascist leader in this essay, and some of his arguments do not fit the case of Mao, but there are also instructive parallels that merit further exploration.

24 In the field of Chinese history, the celebration of Jazz Age culture in 1930s Shanghai has been the principal expression of this current. See, e.g., Lee 1999; Cochran 1999.

25 For an elaboration of this point, see Werner 2012.

26 One of the most extraordinary attempts at achieving that recognition—done through the embodiment of the process itself—is Fanon (1952) 2008.

27 See also the discussion supporting this point in Fraser and Gordon 1994.

References

Adorno, Theodor W. (1951) 1991. "Freudian Theory and the Pattern of Fascist Propaganda." In *The Culture Industry: Selected Essays on Mass Culture*, edited by J. M. Bernstein, 132–57. London: Routledge.

Adorno, Theodor W. (1969) 1976. "Introduction." In *The Positivist Dispute in German Sociology*, translated by Glyn Adey and David Frisby, 1–67. New York: Harper and Row.

Adorno, Theodor W. 1994. *The Stars Down to Earth and Other Essays on the Irrational in Culture*, edited by Stephen Crook. Abingdon, UK: Routledge.

Adorno, Theodor, Hans Albert, Ralf Dahrendorf, Jürgen Habermas, Harald Pilot, and Karl R. Popper. (1969) 1976. *The Positivist Dispute in German Sociology*, translated by Glyn Adey and David Frisby. New York: Harper and Row.

Altehenger, Jennifer. 2013. "Review: *The Tragedy of Liberation: A History of the Chinese Revolution 1945–57*, by Frank Dikötter." *Times Higher Education*, October 24.

Billeter, Jean-François. 1985. "The System of 'Class Status.'" In *The Scope of State Power in China*, edited by Stuart R. Schram, 127–69. New York: St. Martin's Press.

Brown, Jeremy. 2012. *City versus Countryside in Mao's China: Negotiating the Divide*. New York: Cambridge University Press.

Brown, Jeremy, and Matthew D. Johnson, eds. 2015. *Maoism at the Grassroots: Everyday Life in China's Era of High Socialism*. Cambridge, MA: Harvard University Press.

Brown, Jeremy, and Matthew D. Johnson. 2015. "Introduction." In *Maoism at the Grassroots: Everyday Life in China's Era of High Socialism*, edited by Jeremy Brown and Matthew D. Johnson, 1–15. Cambridge, MA: Harvard University Press.

Cochran, Sherman, ed. 1999. *Inventing Nanjing Road: Commercial Culture in Shanghai, 1900–1945*. Ithaca, NY: Cornell University East Asia Program.

Coderre, Laurence. 2019. "A Necessary Evil: Conceptualizing the Socialist Commodity under Mao." *Comparative Studies in Society and History* 61, no. 1: 23–49.

Durkheim, Émile. (1897) 1978. "Review of Antonio Labriola, *Essays on the Materialist Conception of History*," translated by Mark Traugott. In *Emile Durkheim on Institutional Analysis*, edited by Mark Traugott, 123–30. Chicago: University of Chicago Press.

Durkheim, Émile. (1912) 1995. *The Elementary Forms of Religious Life*, translated by Karen E. Fields. New York: Free Press.

Eley, Geoff. 2005. *A Crooked Line: From Cultural History to the History of Society*. Ann Arbor: University of Michigan Press.

Esherick, Joseph W. 1995. "Ten Theses on the Chinese Revolution." *Modern China* 21, no. 1: 45–76.

Fanon, Frantz. (1952) 2008. *Black Skin, White Masks*, translated by Richard Philcox. New York: Grove Press.

Fields, Barbara Jeanne. 1990. "Slavery, Race, and Ideology in the United States of America." *New Left Review* 1, no. 181: 95–118.

Foucault, Michel. 2008. *The Birth of Biopolitics: Lectures at the Collège de France, 1978–1979*, translated by Graham Burchell. New York: Palgrave Macmillan.

Fraser, Nancy, and Linda Gordon. 1994. "A Genealogy of *Dependency*: Tracing a Keyword of the US Welfare State." *Signs: Journal of Women in Culture and Society* 19, no. 2: 309–36.

Freud, Sigmund. (1917) 1966. *Introductory Lectures on Psycho-Analysis*, translated by James Strachey. New York: W. W. Norton and Company.

Gramsci, Antonio. (1929–35) 1971. *Selections from the Prison Notebooks*, edited and translated by Quintin Hoare and Geoffrey Nowell Smith. New York: International Publishers.

Harvey, David. 1989. *The Condition of Postmodernity: An Enquiry into the Origins of Cultural Change*. New York: Blackwell.

Henriot, Christian. 2012. "Slums, Squats, or Hutments? Constructing and Deconstructing an In-Between Space in Modern Shanghai (1926–65)." *Frontiers of History in China* 7, no. 4: 499–528.

Hershatter, Gail. 2011. *The Gender of Memory: Rural Women and China's Collective Past*. Berkeley: University of California Press.

Ho, Denise Y. 2018. *Curating Revolution: Politics on Display in Mao's China*. Cambridge: Cambridge University Press.

Horkheimer, Max. (1937) 1972. "Traditional and Critical Theory." In *Critical Theory: Selected Essays*, translated by Matthew J. O'Connell et al., 188–243. New York: Continuum.

Hung, Chang-tai. 2011. *Mao's New World: Political Culture in the Early People's Republic*. Ithaca, NY: Cornell University Press.

Jameson, Fredric. 1991. *Postmodernism, or, the Cultural Logic of Late Capitalism*. Durham, NC: Duke University Press.

Karl, Rebecca. 2016. "Little Big Man: Review of Alexander Pantsov and Steven Levine, *Deng Xiaoping: A Revolutionary Life*." *New Left Review* 2, no. 97: 139–50.

Kirby, William C. 2004. "Introduction." In *Realms of Freedom in Modern China*, edited by William C. Kirby, 1–17. Stanford, CA: Stanford University Press.

Kuhn, Thomas S. (1962) 2012. *The Structure of Scientific Revolutions*. 4th ed. Chicago: University of Chicago Press.

Lanza, Fabio. 2017. *The End of Concern: Maoist China, Activism, and Asian Studies*. Durham, NC: Duke University Press.

Lee, Leo Ou-fan. 1999. *Shanghai Modern: The Flowering of a New Urban Culture in China, 1930–1945*. Cambridge, MA: Harvard University Press.

Li, Jie. 2015. *Shanghai Homes: Palimpsests of Private Life*. New York: Columbia University Press.

Liu, Yu. 2010. "Maoist Discourse and the Mobilization of Emotions in Revolutionary China." *Modern China* 36, no. 3: 329–62.

Lu, Hanchao. 2018. "Bourgeois Comfort under Proletarian Dictatorship: Home Life of Chinese Capitalists before the Cultural Revolution." *Journal of Social History* 52, no. 1: 74–100.

MacFarquhar, Roderick, and Michael Schoenhals. 2006. *Mao's Last Revolution*. Cambridge, MA: Belknap Press.

Marx, Karl. (1843) 1978. "On the Jewish Question." In *The Marx-Engels Reader*, 2nd ed., edited by Robert C. Tucker, 26–52. New York: W. W. Norton and Company.

Marx, Karl. (1844) 1964. *Economic and Philosophic Manuscripts of 1844*, translated by Martin Milligan. New York: International Publishers.

Marx, Karl. (1857–1858) 1973. *Grundrisse: Foundations of the Critique of Political Economy (Rough Draft)*, translated by Martin Nicolaus. New York: Penguin Books.

Marx, Karl. (1865) 1976. "Value, Price, and Profit." In *Wage-Labour and Capital and Value, Price, and Profit*, 5–62. New York: International Publishers.

Marx, Karl. (1867) 1976. *Capital: A Critique of Political Economy*, vol. 1, translated by Ben Fowkes. New York: Penguin Books.

Mauss, Marcel. (1923–24) 1990. *The Gift: The Form and Reason for Exchange in Archaic Societies*, translated by W. D. Halls. New York: W. W. Norton and Company.

Mitter, Rana. 2004. *A Bitter Revolution: China's Struggle with the Modern World*. Oxford: Oxford University Press.

Mittler, Barbara. 2012. *A Continuous Revolution: Making Sense of Cultural Revolution Culture*. Cambridge, MA: Harvard University Asia Center.

Pantsov, Alexander V., and Steven I. Levine. 2015. *Deng Xiaoping: A Revolutionary Life*. Oxford: Oxford University Press.

Perry, Elizabeth J. 2016. "The Promise of PRC History." *Journal of Modern Chinese History* 10, no. 1: 113–17.

Polanyi, Karl. (1944) 2001. *The Great Transformation: The Political and Economic Origins of Our Time*. Boston: Beacon Press.

Postone, Moishe. 1993. *Time, Labor, and Social Domination: A Reinterpretation of Marx's Critical Theory*. Cambridge: Cambridge University Press.

Postone, Moishe. 2006. "History and Helplessness: Mass Mobilization and Contemporary Forms of Anticapitalism." *Public Culture* 18, no. 1: 93–110.

Schram, Stuart R. (1963) 1969. *The Political Thought of Mao Tse-Tung*. Rev. ed. New York: Praeger.

Schwartz, Benjamin I. 1951. *Chinese Communism and the Rise of Mao*. Cambridge, MA: Harvard University Press.

Scott, James C. 1990. *Domination and the Arts of Resistance: Hidden Transcripts*. New Haven, CT: Yale University Press.

Scott, James C. 1998. *Seeing Like a State: How Certain Schemes to Improve the Human Condition Have Failed*. New Haven, CT: Yale University Press.

Selden, Mark. 1993. *The Political Economy of Chinese Development*. Armonk, NY: M. E. Sharpe.

Selden, Mark. 1995. *China in Revolution: The Yenan Way Revisited*. Armonk, NY: M. E. Sharpe.

Sewell, William H., Jr. 2005. "The Political Unconscious of Social and Cultural History, or, Confessions of a Former Quantitative Historian." In *Logics of History: Social Theory and Social Transformation*, 22–80. Chicago: University of Chicago Press.

Sheng, Michael M. 2011. "Mao and Chinese Elite Politics in the 1950s: The Gao Gang Affair Revisited." *Twentieth-Century China* 36, no. 1: 67–96.

Shue, Vivienne. 2015. "Epilogue: Mao's China—Putting Politics in Perspective." In *Maoism at the Grassroots: Everyday Life in China's Era of High Socialism*, edited by Jeremy Brown and Matthew D. Johnson, 365–79. Cambridge, MA: Harvard University Press.

Smith, Aminda M. 2013. *Thought Reform and China's Dangerous Classes: Reeducation, Resistance, and the People*. Lanham, MD: Rowman and Littlefield.

Smith, Aminda. 2014. "Lessons We Need to Learn." *PRC History Review* 1, no. 1: 17–19.

Strauss, Julia C. 2002. "Paternalist Terror: The Campaign to Suppress Counterrevolutionaries and Regime Consolidation in the People's Republic of China, 1950–1953." *Comparative Studies in Society and History* 44, no. 1: 80–105.

Teiwes, Frederick C., and Warren Sun. 1999. *China's Road to Disaster: Mao, Central Politicians, and Provincial Leaders in the Unfolding of the Great Leap Forward, 1955–1959*. Armonk, NY: M. E. Sharpe.

Wakeman, Frederic, Jr. 1973. *History and Will: Philosophical Perspectives of Mao Tse-tung's Thought*. Berkeley: University of California Press.

Walder, Andrew G. 2002. "Beijing Red Guard Factionalism: Social Interpretations Reconsidered." *Journal of Asian Studies* 61, no. 2: 437–71.

Walder, Andrew G. 2009. *Fractured Rebellion: The Beijing Red Guard Movement*. Cambridge, MA: Harvard University Press.

Wang, Di. 2018. *The Teahouse under Socialism: The Decline and Renewal of Public Life in Chengdu, 1950–2000*. Ithaca, NY: Cornell University Press.

Wang, Hui. (2013) 2016. "The Crisis of Representation and Post-Party Politics," translated by Gao Jin and Yin Zhiguang. In *China's Twentieth Century: Revolution, Retreat, and the Road to Equality*, edited by Saul Thomas, 153–78. London: Verso.

Wang, Hui. 2016. *China's Twentieth Century: Revolution, Retreat, and the Road to Equality*, edited by Saul Thomas. London: Verso.

Wang, Zheng. 2005. "Gender and Maoist Urban Reorganization." In *Gender in Motion: Divisions of Labor and Cultural Change in Late Imperial and Modern China*, edited by Bryna Goodman and Wendy Larson, 189–209. Lanham, MD: Rowman and Littlefield.

Wang, Zheng. 2017. *Finding Women in the State: A Socialist Feminist Revolution in the People's Republic of China, 1949–1964*. Oakland: University of California Press.

Weber, Max. (1920) 1992. *The Protestant Ethic and the Spirit of Capitalism*, translated by Talcott Parsons. New York: Routledge.

Werner, Jake. 2012. "Global Fordism in 1950s Urban China." *Frontiers of History in China* 7, no. 3: 415–41.

Werner, Jake. 2015. "The Making of Mass Society in Shanghai: The Socialist Transformation of Everyday Life, 1949–1958." PhD diss., University of Chicago.

Werner, Jake. 2017. "'A Vast Crucible of Electric Flame': Shanghai and the Emergence of Chinese Marxism." In *East-Asian Marxisms and Their Trajectories*, edited by Joyce C. H. Liu and Viren Murthy, 137–55. London: Routledge.

Werner, Jake. 2018. "Review of *China's Twentieth Century: Revolution, Retreat, and the Road to Equality*, by Wang Hui." *Journal of Asian Studies* 77, no. 2: 520–22.

Wu, Yiching. 2014. *The Cultural Revolution at the Margins: Chinese Socialism in Crisis*. Cambridge, MA: Harvard University Press.

Xu, Xiaohong. 2017. "Dialogic Struggle in the Becoming of the Cultural Revolution: Between Elite Conflict and Mass Mobilization." *Critical Historical Studies* 4, no. 2: 209–42.

Yeh, Wen-hsin. 2000. "Introduction: Interpreting Chinese Modernity, 1900–1950." In *Becoming Chinese: Passages to Modernity and Beyond*, edited by Wen-hsin Yeh, 1–28. Berkeley: University of California Press.

Zou, Ronggeng 邹荣庚. 2001. "Jianguo chuqi Shanghai de qiye minzhu gaige yundong" 建国初期上海的企业民主改革运动 ("Shanghai's Democratic Reform Movement in the Early PRC"). In *Lishi jubian* 历史巨变 (*A Great Historical Change*), vol. 1: 1949–1956, edited by Zou Ronggeng, 214–36. Shanghai: Shanghai shudian chubanshe.

Beyond Bias: Critical Analysis and Layered Reading of Mao-Era Sources

Sigrid Schmalzer

Undergraduate students often enter my history courses primed to identify and then dismiss sources tainted by all kinds of "bias": political bias, cultural bias, gender bias. If all else fails, the bias introduced through the process of translation threatens to disqualify any source I can offer these anglophone students. Professional historians cannot afford to be quite so picky, but they sometimes express similar attitudes. Soon after the publication of my book *Red Revolution, Green Revolution*, I had dinner with a fellow historian of the PRC. He had glanced through the bibliography and delicately shared his concern that I seemed to be relying on many unreliable sources—newspaper articles, propaganda booklets, and the like. I have heard similar cautions from other colleagues: one went so far as to suggest that a library subscription to the full-text searchable *People's Daily* would be an unwise investment since it offers little beyond government propaganda.

positions 29:4   DOI 10.1215/10679847-9286688

What then constitutes good sources for the study of PRC history? For many historians, archival documents continue to represent the gold standard (see, e.g., Dikötter 2011). Others have questioned the sanctity of the archive and instead collect materials from flea markets—or better yet, garbage piles: they identify their collecting philosophy as *garbology* and privilege what they call *grassroots archives*.[1] Still others favor oral history interviews—though how they conduct and analyze those interviews and what meaning they find therein varies so much that they arguably cannot be placed in a single category of historical scholarship.[2]

I prefer an eclectic approach to source collection and what I think of as a layered approach to source analysis. I tell my students that if we discard every flawed source we will end up with nothing at all: oral histories are shaped by current paradigms, by the effects of trauma on memory, and by the many experiences of the intervening years; archival documents reflect state priorities and collecting practices; flea markets have their own filters; and the scraps salvaged from garbage piles can be difficult to assemble into accounts that transcend individual cases.[3] Still more important, I submit that "bias" is often the most interesting aspect of a source: it helps us understand what mattered most deeply to the people we are studying. I go so far as to prohibit the use of this distracting word in my classes (except perhaps in certain senses, such as selection bias); I encourage students to think instead about the "perspectives" that sources reflect.

In other words, I argue that how we read our sources is more important than which sources we keep and which we throw away. Moreover, I emphasize the benefits of engaging directly with our sources in our narratives and analyses. We should not treat our sources as received wisdom; but neither should we adopt an attitude of seeking and destroying bias to arrive at objective facts (what Aminda Smith in this issue calls the "falsification method"). By engaging with the sources and making visible the contexts in which they were produced and have circulated, we can offer a richer understanding of their many layers of significance. To that end, I will explore some of what may be gained through a layered and self-reflexive analysis of three sources I have collected in recent years.

Not Fearing Shameful Things Like Propaganda

Historians often "fetishize" archival sources with the assumption that such materials offer a truer account than the propaganda found in published materials. When we gain access to a rich archive, that is indeed a great boon. But materials found in archives are not always better than (and sometimes not even all that different from) materials found elsewhere. And, wherever we find them, sources that smack of propaganda can be valuable on multiple levels, as evidenced in the first source I will share: an article titled "Not Fearing 'Shameful' Things, Courageously Changing the World" (1966), credited to Wu Lanxian, the vice director of the Four Sisters Veterinary Station in rural Jiangxi Province, and published by the Scientific and Technology Office in Nanyang, Henan, in an April 1966 collection that I found on the used-book website kongfz.com (Henan sheng Nanyang zhuanqu kexue jishu xiehui 1966).[4] The volume, *Collected Experiences of the National Rural Scientific Experiment Movement*, presents stories shared at a national conference held in Fujian province in March of that year. It is held together by two staples and marked on the title page as *neibu* (that is, for internal use only); the preface indicates that the recipients were intended to be political and scientific cadres at or above the commune level. The contents of such conference volumes, as it were, are frequently found in state archives throughout China and (the tantalizingly restrictive *neibu* label on this edition notwithstanding) also in properly bound books published by state presses and circulated as reading materials for general audiences, and especially for "educated youth."[5]

"Not Fearing 'Shameful' Things" is a celebratory report on a group of "housewives" (家庭妇女) *cum* peasant technicians. Their community had reportedly suffered an outbreak of swine disease in 1961. Folk veterinarians were charging high prices and failing to resolve the problem, so a local housewife, Wu Lanxian, approached the Party secretary and volunteered to study veterinary medicine herself. With his support, Wu and three other housewives received training at the county level and then returned to open the Four Sisters Veterinary Clinic. Despite the valuable services they aimed to provide, they faced much resistance from fellow villagers who mocked the notion of women engaging in science, from family members who objected to the impropriety of women handling the breeding of swine, and from local folk vets and boar keepers who resented the Four Sisters for undercutting their business.

(This is one of those points where skeptical readers might ask whether I am "relying on unreliable sources." Must I litter my writing with scare quotes or use the word *reportedly* in every sentence to demonstrate my critical lens? Or can I expect the reader to understand that I am interested in knowing what story the Science and Technology Office sought to tell? While I recognize the need to distinguish between the voices of our sources and our own authorial voices, the constant pressure to distance ourselves from our shamefully propagandistic sources bothers me: it sometimes feels not that different from the requirement in PRC publications to place every instance of the term *Cultural Revolution* in quotation marks—a perpetual reminder that it has been officially discredited, unlike, say, the term *Reform and Opening* [改革开放], which is not so marked.)

Of course, the report on the Four Sisters Veterinary Clinic is limited in many ways. It is formulaic, politically correct, and aims above all to provide an inspirational model of revolutionary technological practice. It thus cannot help demonstrate the degree to which state efforts to modernize veterinary medicine succeeded; nor can we necessarily even believe that the specific events it relates truly occurred. However, I am not ashamed of this source, for it does reveal a great deal: about state-endorsed values regarding science and modernity, about the social tensions that worried the state and without doubt produced at least some peasant resistance to new technologies, and about fundamental assumptions regarding the gendered division of labor in the countryside. The key to using this source is to analyze it as a state-produced narrative, with special attention to dialogue, and to see what emerges when we read both with and against the grain—or as Aminda Smith proposes in her contribution to this issue, when we first "map the grain" and then read against it.

Among the most frequently encountered components of stories like these are the derisive comments made by those who failed to respect the protagonists' revolutionary undertakings. Here, and in many other cases, highlighting the sexist language of conservative forces was an especially potent way of underscoring state revolutionary values. The narrator, Wu Lanxian

(1966: 19–20), told of how she "took a bamboo switch and drove the boar out the door and to the crossroads where many villagers and small children surrounded me jeering." A child shouted, "Women driving boar studs lose face and are disgraced" (妇女牵猪牯,丢脸也丢丑). A man then sarcastically added, "Liberated women can do all sorts of feats, they can drive boar studs all through the streets" (妇女翻身真能干,牵着猪牯满街串). Later, after the Four Sisters had proven themselves, the villagers' scorn changed to praise: "Women really are something, they can do anything" (妇女不简单,样样工作都能干). The story of overcoming sexist attitudes about technical knowledge linked the state's technological modernization program with the transformation of social relationships, enhancing both the revolutionary credentials of new agricultural technologies and the scientific credibility of the attack on conservative values.

The conversations in this and similar propaganda pieces may well be faked, but on another level they represent a real dialogue between the vision of socialism the state wanted to convey and the state's understandings of its audience—officials struggling to simultaneously transform both material reality and political consciousness in the rural areas. And the propaganda spinners knew what they were doing. In the original Chinese, both the insults and the praise take the form of rhyming, rhythmic couplets. The language is deliberately evocative of patterns that resonate with people throughout many regions of China, urban and rural alike.[6] And so we gain from this source an appreciation not just for the revolutionary values that state agents sought to promote, but also for the strategy they adopted in inserting those values into specific speech forms with aesthetic power.[7]

If we look below the surface rhetoric and read against the grain, we find clues as to the duties women were expected to perform in rural China. When the protagonist first began providing vet and breeding services, her mother-in-law waved her finger in her face and shouted, "If you really aim to do this work, you will never darken my door again!" But Wu Lanxian's determination won her over, and she soon changed her tune, saying, "Don't worry about the household chores. I'll cook the food and wash the clothes so you can focus on your work" (Wu 1966: 18). Here again, we do not need to believe that this conversation actually occurred, or that it hewed so closely to the classic narrative trope of tension and redemption in the relations between a woman and her mother-in-law.[8] However, and despite itself, the account reveals the diverse burdens women in Mao-era China were expected to shoulder, a form of gender imbalance that the state by no means explicitly endorsed but whose elimination this state-circulated article did not prioritize. Indeed, in falling back on such familiar discourse and narrative forms even in an account meant to contrast revolutionary and backward values, the Science and Technology Office demonstrated just how deep the assumptions about women's labor continued to run, not only in rural society but within state offices as well.

So, if we can read this source for evidence regarding state assumptions about rural divisions of labor, does it also speak at all to actual rural divisions of labor? This represents a still deeper interpretive layer—murkier, less certain, and, in some researchers' minds, of questionable value. One of the anonymous reviewers of this article when it was in draft form asked pointedly, "Why does the author so want to see in this source the 'plausibility' of reflections of social reality?" An honest question that deserves a direct answer: as much as I will defend the study of Party rhetoric as significant in its own right, I am at least as committed to learning about lived experiences. That is, I agree with Jeremy Brown (and the scholars who advised us both[9]) on the value of questions about what actually happened to Chinese people and what Chinese people actually did (see Brown's contribution to this issue). And here it is further worth noting Brown's temptation to put the phrase *what actually happened* in quotation marks and his ultimate decision not to. The pressure to distance ourselves from propaganda through the use of scare quotes is apparently mirrored by the pressure, at least in certain intellectual circles, to distance ourselves from a belief in social reality.

Fortunately, evidence from oral history testimonies can provide corroboration for the social reality of the gendered division of labor depicted in this document. However, even if I had no other sources on this subject, I would suggest that we provisionally accept the source as evidence that women were in fact performing most if not all of the cooking and cleaning labor in 1960s rural China. I would defend this interpretation based on the logic that it was not in the interest of state propaganda to emphasize the continuity of traditional and unequal gendered division of labor. This slipped into the background of the story because to present it in any other way would ring so false as to discredit the entire account.

Similarly, at this layer a picture also begins to emerge of social relationships inside and outside of the collectivist economy, and thus sheds some (albeit modest) light on what Alexander Day in his contribution to this issue calls "the emergence of categories and social forms from the real material limits and tendencies of a rapidly changing PRC society." Local resistance to gender equality and technological change was not just rhetorical, and it stemmed not just from patriarchal ideology. It also came in the form of boycotts and arose from the economic interests of marginalized people. The women in this account faced their greatest opposition from those whose business they threatened to undermine: local folk vets and boar keepers operating outside of the collectivist economy promised to terminate their relationships with any clients who tried the Four Sisters' services. Looking just at this source, should we believe that these relationships really existed? Again, I would argue provisionally yes, based on the logic of the propaganda. On the one hand, the ongoing Socialist Education Movement did provide a context that favored criticism of non-collectivized economic relationships. On the other hand, the boar keepers were not the kind of people the state would prefer to identify as class enemies: traditionally, they were poor men, often disabled, without the ability to support themselves through farming their own land (Schmalzer 2002: 14–15). In other words, if boar keepers were not presenting a real problem for state agents introducing new agricultural technologies, they would not be the best candidates for the role of villain in this story. The source thus strongly suggests that state agents had practical reasons to see their program of technological modernization as dependent on the transformation of traditional social relationships that had thus far survived the transition to collectivism.

Lost in Translation, Found in Analysis

The second source I will examine is of an entirely different type, but it similarly speaks to gendered divisions of labor and battles against patriarchy, and it similarly offers an opportunity to analyze dialogue. In 1973, a group of leftist scientists from the United States who belonged to the organization Science for the People (SftP) traveled to China to learn how science and technology worked in a socialist country. Among the artifacts from that trip is a small stack of audio cassette tapes documenting some of their many interviews with scientists, cadres, workers, and peasants. Reasons for discarding the tapes abound. To begin with, the quality of the audio is so low that many words and phrases are simply incomprehensible, and even when we can make out the words it is often unclear who is speaking. Moreover, none of the members of the delegation could speak Chinese; they relied on a translator to relay their questions and convey the responses of their interlocutors. Their itinerary was carefully planned and their visits choreographed by PRC state agents. Even with perfect acoustics, the recording would not present anything worth analyzing as a Chinese "soundscape." Unreliable? Yes. So why did I pay to have these tapes digitized, and why did I spend hours fiddling with the files, playing them repeatedly, and transcribing every possible word?

To justify this investment, I will share one of my favorite moments from the recordings. In a visit to Red Star Commune (where politically stalwart "foreign friends" Joan Hinton and Erwin Engst were then living), several members of SftP delegation had the chance to interview a peasant woman. After asking many questions about the woman's life and the material conditions of the commune (how long had they had glass windows, did all the homes have electricity, etc.), one of the women delegates asked, "What do you think still needs to be done to continue to liberate women?" The translator attempted to relay the question using the phrase "women's economic liberation" (妇女的经济解放), but the interviewee found this incomprehensible. He then turned back to the delegate, saying, "Actually, the words 'women's liberation' are not used here very often, so [chuckle] I'll keep trying."

The translator next tried the term for "equality between men and women" (男女平等). Tellingly, the woman interpreted this to relate to participation in labor. She said, "We get paid for labor the same as men. What men can do we can do by ourselves." The delegate pursued the subject further: "Do you think it's important for men to do women's work as well?" The translator laughed still more openly as he began translating. The interviewee took it in stride, but again interpreted the question in terms of women being able to do just as much of the farm work as men. To her, a liberated woman was a woman who was able to pull vegetables alongside her husband. The delegate pressed again: "What about taking care of children, cooking, cleaning . . . Should men do that as well as women?" Here at last the woman seemed to understand what the delegates wanted to hear.

> **Peasant woman:** We all take part in the labor. Whoever comes back earlier will do the cooking.
> . . .
> **SftP delegate:** What do you do when some men refuse or find it hard?
> **Peasant woman:** [spirited voice] We just criticize them [laughter] . . . If the men refuse to cook, women also will refuse to cook. [lots of laughter]
> **SftP delegate:** Women in our country have a very hard struggle to get men to help us out. We do not have day care centers and nurseries for our children, [or] as many of them.

What does this exchange capture? If we want to understand the experiences of rural Chinese women in the Mao era, the extensive oral history interviews conducted by Gail Hershatter (2011), Gao Xiaoxian (2006), Jacob Eyferth (2012), and others provide far deeper and more reliable insight. Even the "Four Sisters" propaganda piece probably offers better evidence about the actual division of domestic duties than does this portrait of rural life in a showcase commune sketched from a set of loaded, leading, and multiply translated questions.

What the SftP interview offers is something apparently quite different: a snapshot of diverse social actors with widely divergent perspectives and priorities attempting to make some type of connection. Having said that, Hershatter's admirable transparency often opens similarly revealing glimpses into the "crossings in mist" that occur when Western scholars, Chinese scholars, and Chinese rural women sit down to talk about the past.[10] Her analytical approach to oral history provides not only a fine-grained empirical understanding of the material conditions under which rural women labored but also a sophisticated analysis of the workings of memory and the dialectics of oral history practice—tools that can help us unpack meaning even from the densely wrapped package presented by SftP's interview at Red Star Commune.

Unlike the "Four Sisters" text, the SftP tape records a "real" conversation. Nonetheless, it is still bound by the scripts each participant was ready to perform. The recording thus adds to our understanding of the vision of socialism that the state sought to project to the wider world; of the language available to rural Chinese women to communicate their political knowledge and perhaps also some of their lived experiences; and of the priorities of Western leftists visiting China in the 1970s.

Nineteen seventy-three was early for American delegations to be visiting China. Science for the People's special treatment arose because the members not only possessed valuable scientific knowledge but also held explicit political commitments that made them very likely to present Cultural Revolution–era China in a good light when they returned to the United States. Chinese state agents cared deeply that these visitors appreciate what "liberation" had brought China, and they had much to say as well about improvements in the status of women since 1949. These themes and many others come through with great clarity and consistency in the book the SftP delegation wrote upon their return, and more broadly in the considerable corpus of travel literature produced by Western visitors to China during this period (Connell and Gover 1974; Schmalzer 2009). And yet, the phrase "women's liberation" produced a surprising derailment—it was close to the PRC state's own ideological commitments but still somehow off-script.

Part of the problem may have been that the SftP delegate asked what *further* needed to be done to liberate women; a truthful answer might have suggested dissatisfaction with current conditions and so posed political risks for the interviewee. But more seems to be going on here. Interviews with rural women in China today can certainly produce spirited discussion of struggles against sexism: we see a glimpse of this at the end of SftP's exchange and much more in oral history interviews by scholars and filmmakers (see, e.g., Hinton 1984). However, I suspect that most of us have experienced a phenomenon similar to what the SftP delegate encountered, in which the interviewee's preoccupation with labor and renumeration crowds out the more ideological or value-oriented concerns of the interviewer. We learn from this push-pull process the deep importance, in both material and rhetorical terms, of the work point system in the everyday lives of Mao-era peasants.

The laughter recorded on the tapes also speaks volumes. Ruth Rogaski

(2012: 588) put her finger on something important when she called on scholars to "link those giggles" recorded in Mao's speeches on birth control "to the production of science." During the 1970s, Americans traveling to China often took the laughter they encountered as evidence of widespread cheerfulness— a refutation of the grim portrayals of Chinese society dominant in the Cold War United States. In part, no doubt, their perception stemmed from an auditory version of the rose-colored glasses phenomenon, but it also betrays a lack of understanding of the cultural significance of laughter among the people they were interviewing (Schmalzer 2009: 334–45). To a researcher with experience living and working in China, the audio recordings preserved by Science for the People suggest a very different interpretation. In this and in other SftP interviews, laughter typically accompanied politically awkward moments. For example, when members of the SftP delegation interviewed insect scientist Pu Zhelong, he frequently chuckled as he discussed peasant participation in scientific decision making. Based on other sources, I am confident that Pu Zhelong in fact had a deep respect for peasant knowledge and a genuine commitment to peasant participation in science. However, the intensity of the politics surrounding peasant-scientist relations in 1973 China, combined with the uncertainties produced by transnational exchange with Western leftists (who were on the one hand partners in global struggle, and on the other hand culturally bizarre and sometimes ideologically shaky), made such topics distinctly awkward. Similarly, the laughter in the recording at Red Star Commune points to a profound sense that difficult questions were being broached across uncharted cultural and political gulfs. That said, the laughter toward the conclusion of the excerpt sounds freer, and I interpret it as a moment where both sides felt they had reached a shared political and even personal understanding.

Beyond the PRC state's interests and rural women's voices, the tapes speak most loudly to the SftP delegates' own political priorities and commitments. It is significant that the exchange ended with the SftP delegate voicing a criticism of gender relations and the splitting of household labor in the United States. While the SftP delegates had a genuine interest in Chinese people's experiences in revolution, the political context of women in the United States loomed very large, setting the terms of "liberation" and framing the significance of rural Chinese women's experiences. At the end of the day, SftP's mission in China was to bring back a story of revolution that could inspire radicals, including feminists, in the United States.

As a final layer of analysis, I have had several reasons to consider my own preoccupation with these tapes. For one thing, I am involved in the newly revitalized Science for the People movement, so anything related to the original organization is interesting for me—and this commitment grew in the Trump era, when most people seemed to be choosing between two positions that both SftP and the Mao-era state would have found untenable: either to reject science outright or to defend it as "apolitical." Moreover, while preparing a collection of diverse sources to practice analyzing with graduate students, I stumbled on another opportunity for self-reflexivity. Juxtaposing the SftP recording with an excerpt from an interview I had conducted in 2012, I could not help but notice a shared tendency to press questions of gender equity in ways that clearly did not resonate with our informants. The similar clumsiness in the SftP delegation's interview and my own was humbling to contemplate. However, that demonstrated lack of resonance (the "crossings in mist"), together with the stories our informants insisted on telling, gave me new insight into how concepts of gender and sexism do and do not translate across space and time.

Sacrifice an Archival Document before Sacrificing a Peasant-Scholar's Reprint

The third source I will share is on the surface the most mundane: it is an ordinary published book from 2013, hardly what historians usually get excited about. A still more serious apparent strike against it is its promotional nature: like many other publications of its kind, it is designed to advance local economic interests by presenting a particular community as rich in cultural heritage, and thus worthy of state and commercial investment. Biased? Yes. And yet this book has become one of the most meaningful, door-opening sources for my research on the history of agricultural terracing in Mao-era China.

In October 2016 I attended a conference on agricultural heritage in She County, Hebei, on the eastern edge of the Taihang mountains. The conference attendees had the opportunity to visit the dry-land terraces in the nearby

Figure 1 The author with Wang Linding, October 18, 2016.

village of Wangjinzhuang. As we climbed the steps of one spectacularly ter-raced hill, a local man accompanying the tour asked if he and I could become friends. He showed me a book he had coedited; we had our picture taken together (fig. 1); and we shared contact information on the social media appli-cation WeChat. I was already becoming fascinated by the landscape and local terracing culture, and I was quickly deciding to pursue the history of terrac-ing as a research project. Before the conference was over, I managed to secure a copy of the book coedited by my new friend, Wang Linding.

She County is in the midst of a deliberate attempt at transformation from an industrial economy into one focused on ecoagricultural, historical, and heritage-based tourism. The county's terraces have gained recognition at the national level as a paramount example of China's "agricultural heritage" (农业文化遗产) sites, and the county government is now pursuing similar recognition from the Food and Agriculture Organization of the United Nations. The academic community coalescing around the study of agricultural heritage represents an impressive interdisciplinarity, but the concept of "heritage" they employ has not come to terms with the significance of recent history. And for understandable reasons. The impetus to preserve "traditional" farming against the behemoth of agro-industry makes the recognition of modern developments problematic at best. And yet Mao-era history is inscribed in Wangjinzhuang's terraces (figuratively, and also literally in the form of slogans carved into the stone retaining walls). Moreover, local people and county government agents alike are enthusiastic about having this history studied and propagated.

I began my study of Wangjinzhuang with little beyond Wang Linding's volume, which he coedited with another villager and which had been published with the assistance of local officials. The book contains many interesting tidbits of local history and culture, but to my eye the most exciting inclusion is the text of a January 20, 1971, document by the She County Revolutionary Committee's Command Department for Grasping Revolution and Promoting Agriculture, originally printed in the *Study Dazhai Digest*. The article, titled "Study Dazhai, Catch up with Xiyang, the Whole County Studies Wangjinzhuang," explained that since the previous December, 576 local leaders from 167 brigades and 16 communes had come to Wangjinzhuang to receive training from the local Party secretary and labor model, Wang Quanyou. They came carrying their own food, drink, and other necessities on their backs, much like the members of the Eighth Route Army during the Anti-Japanese War. The participants studied the building of terraces and reservoirs during the day, and in the evening they listened to Wang Quanyou talk about his experience learning from Dazhai how to be self-reliant, work hard, and struggle to "transform the face" of Wangjinzhuang. Participants testified to the impact of the training on their political thought and on their ability to help their own communities make similar progress (Wang and Wang 2013).

During a subsequent trip, in July 2017, I managed to locate the original document in the She County archives—a satisfying result to be sure, especially at a time when access to Chinese archives has become more difficult. I attribute this success not only to the kindness and generosity of local administrators but also to their active interest in developing tourism by encouraging research and dissemination of local history.[11]

The archival document carries the bold red-script heading *Study Dazhai Digest* and includes inked-in additions and corrections that add to the aesthetic appeal for any historian trained to appreciate archival materials. And yet, the "authenticity" of the document and the fact that it exists in a government archive by no means diminishes the significance of the version included in Wang Linding's book. To the contrary, the 2013 version possesses layers of historical significance that the original document could not replace.

The contents of both versions testify to the Cultural Revolution–era vision of agricultural modernization through revolutionary self-reliance as exemplified by Dazhai, underscore the emphasis placed on knowledge circulation through the exchange of revolutionary experience and the emulation of labor models, and hint at the local history of the Eighth Route Army. However, the 2013 version further testifies to the meaning that recent history holds for local people and state officials today. The document appears in a chapter on the "Spirit of Quanyou," which further includes photographs of Wang Quanyou's heroic leadership when terracing the forbidding precipices of Yan'ao Gulch and moving testimonials as to his selflessness and his contributions to the "greening" of Wangjinzhuang through tree planting, water works, and soil conservation. The chapter is nestled among diverse offerings including legends about local people and geography, literature and art, descriptions of popular customs, and "red memories" (that is, accounts of Wangjinzhuang's place in revolutionary history). With respect to this last category, a historically layered analysis again proves essential, since the Eighth Route Army's achievements in She County have gained still more glory in the Reform Era because the young Deng Xiaoping was stationed there.[12]

The book must be seen as coproduced by popular and state actors: Wang Linding and his fellow coeditor would not have been able to publish it without the active interest and support of local state officials, and a team of people clearly contributed to its content. The combination of cultural heritage (including what in the Mao era would have been regarded as "superstitious" beliefs and practices), Party history, and stories about local people had to satisfy the vision that She County leaders are crafting for its future, which in turn must remain true to the larger vision dictated by the national leadership. But Wang Linding and his coeditor were responsible for collecting the core materials; their role in creating this artifact is thus highly significant. Moreover, the very fact that the state sees value in the promotion of local history and culture by "peasant-scholars" says something important about the continued (or perhaps renewed) resonance of this concept so familiar from the Mao era.

As with any source, the document as reprinted in the 2013 book is best considered not on its own, but rather in connection with other sources. The interviews I was able to conduct in July 2017 confirmed what the document strongly suggested: the far greater emphasis on political over technological education in Wang Quanyou's training sessions.[13] When I asked what kinds of terracing methods were introduced in the sessions, I consistently heard that it was the "spirit" of Wang Quanyou and Wangjinzhuang—and by extension, Chen Yonggui and Dazhai—that was imparted rather than any specific terracing technologies. Moreover, according to one informant, the political lectures that Wang Quanyou delivered each evening were memorized from a script provided the day before by a Party functionary dispatched from Handan City. If Wang Quanyou missed a beat, the Party functionary was ready at his elbow to prompt him.

And yet we should not dismiss the significance of such scripts and slogans for local people. One woman I interviewed complained about the hardship of the terracing work she performed but testified sincerely as to the inspiration she received during the noon rest period from reciting Chairman Mao's quotations: they made her feel she "was not tired anymore." Moreover, many other aspects of the interviews suggest a strong resonance between the knowledge and values handed down over generations in Wangjinzhuang and the priorities promoted through Mao-era state propaganda. I was especially struck by the shared emphasis on protecting scarce soil and water resources and the shared commitment to frugality and self-sacrifice expressed in a local saying: "Sacrifice a Communist Party member before sacrificing a single sweet-potato sprout." This ditty, a variation on a theme more widely heard in those years, resonates strongly with an older local adage collected in the 2013 volume, "Let your mother starve to death before you eat next year's seed." According to Wang Linding, this jarring reminder of the realities of scarcity and survival dates from the Daoguang reign of the Qing dynasty, when a woman actually died of starvation rather than eat the grain stored for seeding the next crop. Local culture has clearly been influenced by state priorities, and on the other side state priorities have been shaped by (or the state has actively coopted) local culture.

The 2013 source gains still further significance when we understand more about Wang Linding. Wang's moniker on WeChat, often referenced also in ordinary conversation, was, at the time I met him, 农民秀才—that is, "peasant-scholar." Wang has been passionate about local history since he was a young man, and his knowledge is genuinely respected by county-level administrators and academics alike. Based on a Republican-era handwritten genealogy he collected, supplemented by his own knowledge of village families, he has reconstructed the history of the Wang lineage in Wangjinzhuang since its founding more than twenty generations ago. He has also preserved his family's land deeds dating back to the early Qing dynasty—land his grandfather sold to support his opium addiction. In a twist of fate, these financial losses led the family to earn the favored classification of "poor peasants" in 1955: the records of the classification—including the specifics of what his grandfather owned before property was collectivized—have also made it into Wang Linding's collection of what Brown and others have termed *grassroots archives*. His preservation of such important historical records, along with his hard work publicizing Wangjinzhuang's history, is what makes Wang Linding not just a *peasant-scholar* but more specifically a *local historian*; understanding Wang Linding's role in his community and the significance the past holds for him is what makes the 1971 document as it appears in his book a richer source than the archival record offers. As the term *grassroots archives* suggests, it is not just the materials themselves (which may not be different from officially collected materials) but also the social contexts of their collection, preservation, and propagation that should matter in our analysis.

Finally, this source presents another opportunity for self-reflexivity, and specifically for recognizing the significance of the relationships that foreign scholars may form with the Chinese people whose history we study. These relationships are never simple, but rather fraught with the tensions of unequal power relations, cultural differences, and conflicting gender norms. From the first act of posing for a photograph together, possibilities for misunderstanding, objectification, and exploitation emerge. And yet, no foreign scholar (and few Chinese scholars either) gets far in China without risking these entanglements, which may go beyond "crossings in mist" into the realm of personal discomfort or danger (Schneider, Lord, and Wilczak 2020).

Wang Linding was not able to give me a copy of his book the first time we met (a member of the county Propaganda Bureau provided it to me in his stead), but the book figures prominently in the photograph taken of us on that day. As WeChat friends, he and I began sharing photographs and short notes about happenings in our families and communities. And on my second trip Wang gave me two presents. One was a Sprite bottle filled with millet he had grown on his own terraces using organic fertilizer: this is the good stuff typically grown for family and friends, for quality rather than quantity, and thus provided me with a highly material appreciation for this aspect of local agricultural history. The second was a notebook dedicated to me and inscribed with a short poem—a gift tradition that is familiar to me from the similarly inscribed notebooks (some empty, some full or half-full) that date from the Mao era, which were typically exchanged by students and scholars, and today can be purchased at flea markets. The friendship and professional relationship that Wang and I have formed is thus a part of history even as it is producing historical knowledge. It would not exist apart from the active efforts of the She County government to promote heritage tourism; it is shaped by deep, complicated, historically layered, reinvented, and renegotiated understandings of intellectual friendship across cultural contexts; and it is playing an active role in the way each of us is participating in the production of knowledge about Wangjinzhuang's recent past.

Layering, Self-Reflexivity, and the Social Production of Knowledge

What are the benefits of moving beyond bias in our approach to historical sources? The sheer number and variety of usable sources is the most immediate benefit. Libraries, bookstores, journal and newspaper databases, archives, flea markets, the bookshelves of people we are visiting (to the extent decency allows), online used book markets, blogs and other web materials, social media, interviews and casual conversations, and our own photographs and journals all become valid places to find materials for historical inquiry.

The sources themselves also become more interesting. Conducting a layered analysis of the sources means considering the contexts of their production and circulation. Explaining those contexts for every source would get in the way of our narratives. However, the contexts should at the very least inform our analysis, and in many cases sharing the contexts and our reasoning will greatly add to the richness of the stories we tell. Who produced the sources and for what audience? What did the producers intend to communicate? What linguistic, visual, formatting, or other strategies did they employ, and what is significant about those choices? Do the producers protest too much (e.g., do they reveal tensions by attempting too forcefully to deny them)? What evidence do incidental details in the sources provide about questions beyond the scope of the producers' interests? How do the sources echo earlier sources, and what echoes are found in later sources? Whose hands have the sources passed through, and what new layers of significance have they accumulated in the process? How did we find (or even help produce) the sources, and to what extent is our role significant in the meaning the sources now hold?

Once we start making a layered analysis central to our methodology, not only do we find uses for the quirkiest or most ephemeral sources, but the most apparently dry and straightforward sources gain new meaning. Statistical yearbooks become not just repositories of more- or less-reliable numbers, but also windows into the analytical categories their creators used to make sense of the world, along with clues as to institutional networks and circuits of knowledge—that is, they offer insight into what Alexander Day in this issue calls the "dialectical relationship between form and content." The signed copy of a "framework-laden doorstop devoid of footnotes" on the China Dream that Brown's colleague ceremoniously gave him becomes a source for understanding the complicated mix of academic and political pressures and opportunities facing our Chinese colleagues, along with an artifact in the history of transnational scholarly friendships.

A layered analysis also permits us to pursue, without fearing accusations of gullibility, an inquiry into what the producers of a source intended their readers to learn from it. I believe this is part of what Smith means when she says, "Before we attempt to read against the grain, we must map that grain." It is similar to the rule I ask my students to follow when interpreting propaganda sources: "I want you to *see* the source before you *see through* it." In the example I shared above, when we *see* the recurring motif of sexist villagers in propaganda narratives about the rural scientific experiment movement, we recognize the significance of the connection between science and social revolution for Party ideology. In Smith's account, when we *see* the mass line, we recognize that it always, unapologetically, contained a profoundly authoritarian rationale.

Finally, a layered approach invites, or even demands, self-reflexivity. Jake Werner (this issue) urges us to avoid succumbing to that "dream of modern scholarship, that the subjectivity of the observer would be removed to secure the objectivity of the fact," since the subjective inevitably "finds expression elsewhere and in ways that move us further from understanding the history than would bringing it to awareness and confronting it directly." I never want my writing on China to become mere navel-gazing: like Jeremy Brown, I am committed to keeping *Chinese people* at the center of Chinese history. And yet, when we adopt a self-reflexive position and make visible the dialectical processes through which researchers and historical actors produce questions, concerns, and categories, we come to clearer and more honest understandings of why certain things matter and to whom.

With self-reflexivity, and especially with feminist self-reflexivity, comes a recognition of relationships. In 1994, I was twenty-two years old in a Chinese town newly popular among backpacker-tourists. A young woman approached me offering her guide services and her friendship. My American desire to be independent and three years of Chinese language classes made me almost too proud to accept. Fortunately, I made the right choice: after a quarter century of letter writing, visits to her home, and travels together, I cannot think of a decision with more profound consequences for my connection to rural China. In 2016, when Wang Linding asked if we could become friends, I overcame my initial reluctance by reminding myself why I got into this game to begin with. Knowledge is a social product; friendships are fundamental.

Notes

1 Michael Schoenhals is widely acknowledged as the founder of the garbology school of research on Mao-era China, with Jeremy Brown as a highly regarded and widely cited spokesperson. See, e.g., Brown and Johnson 2015: 4; Brown 2010; Wang et al. 2017.

2 For a sense of the range of approaches to oral history research on PRC history, consider Friedman, Pickowicz, and Selden's *Chinese Village, Socialist State* (1991), in which interviews constitute the core source materials and are woven invisibly into a historical narrative with little explicit analytical discussion; Xiong Weimin's *Dui yu lishi, kexuejia you hua shuo* (*Scientists Have Something to Say about History*) (2017), which takes the form of direct (excerpted) transcripts of oral history interviews; and Gail Hershatter's *The Gender of Memory: Rural Women and China's Collective Past* (2011), in which the author engages directly and analytically with the interview process and transcripts to probe how people experienced the past and what shapes the ways they have (and have not) remembered it, and the ways they communicate (or do not communicate) those memories.

3 Elizabeth Perry (2016: 116) has called on historians of the PRC to "rise above" garbology and "paint their interpretations on a broad canvas."

4 I would like to be able to provide as interesting a discussion of the experience of collecting materials in China today as Craig Clunas (1999) offered in his essay on collecting posters in Beijing.

5 For an example from an archive, see Beijing shi 1965. For an example of a published "conference volume," see *Nongcun zhishi qingnian* 1974.

6 Perry Link and Kate Zhou's 2002 study of such "shunkouliu" ditties offers an academic analysis of their widespread popularity in China, and specifically how they have been used in the Reform era to criticize the state.

7 An anonymous reviewer of this article noted the distinctly different topolects spoken in the Jiangxi community where this story takes place, the Fujian community where the conference was held, and the city of Nanyang, Henan, where the volume was published. How much effort state officials put into ensuring that the dialogue in such stories would be local enough to sound authentic but generic enough to travel across diverse linguistic communities is a fascinating question for further research.

8 To my ear, the narrative echoes some of the Song-dynasty materials that Patricia Ebrey analyzed in *The Inner Quarters* (1993).

9   Jeremy Brown and I were both students of Joe Esherick and Paul Pickowicz at the University of California, San Diego, in the early 2000s.

10   Hershatter (2007) borrowed the phrase "wrinkle in time" from science fiction author Madeleine L'Engle for her analysis of rural Chinese women's memories. Here I borrow "crossings in mist" from science fiction author Ursula Le Guin's *The Lathe of Heaven* to capture the partial communication possible across the chasms that separate people with vastly differing experiences of the world.

11   Tremendous thanks to He Xianlin and Wang Liye of the She County Agricultural Bureau and to the staff at the She County Archives for all their help.

12   I encountered a similar emphasis on She County's "red culture" in the county Party secretary's remarks at the 2016 conference on Agricultural Heritage and in 2017 on a trip to a museum dedicated to the history of the 129th Regiment of the Eighth Route Army, among other places.

13   All interviews cited in this section were conducted by me with local assistants in group settings between July 11 and July 13, 2017.

References

"Beijing shi nongcun kexue shiyan xiaozu jiji fenzi huiyi wenjian" 北京市农村科学实验小组积极分子会议文件 ("Documents from the Conference of Activists in Beijing Municipal Rural Scientific Experiment Groups"). 1965. Beijing Municipal Archives, November 15, 2.22.31.

Brown, Jeremy. 2010. "Finding and Using Grassroots Historical Sources from the Mao Era." Chinese History Dissertation Reviews, December 15. dissertationreviews.wordpress.com /2010/12/15/finding-and-using-grassroots-historical-sources-from-the-mao-era-by-jeremy -brown/.

Brown, Jeremy, and Matthew D. Johnson, eds. 2015. *Maoism at the Grassroots: Everyday Life in China's Era of High Socialism*. Cambridge, MA: Harvard University Press.

Clunas, Craig. 1999. "Souvenirs of Beijing: Authority and Subjectivity in Art Historical Memory." In *Picturing Power in the People's Republic of China: Posters of the Cultural Revolution*, edited by Harriet Evans and Stephanie Donald, 47–61. Lanham, Md.: Rowman and Littlefield.

Connell, Dan, and Dan Gover, eds. 1974. *China: Science Walks on Two Legs*. New York: Avon Books.

Dikötter, Frank. 2011. *Mao's Great Famine: The History of China's Most Devastating Catastrophe, 1958–62*. New York: Walker.

Ebrey, Patricia. 1993. *The Inner Quarters: Marriage and the Lives of Chinese Women in the Sung Period*. Berkeley: University of California Press.

Eyferth, Jacob. 2012. "Women's Work and the Politics of Homespun in Socialist China, 1949–1980." *International Review of Social History* 57, no. 3: 365–91.

Friedman, Edward, Paul G. Pickowicz, and Mark Selden. 1991. *Chinese Village, Socialist State*. New Haven, CT: Yale University Press.

Gao, Xiaoxian. 2006. "'The Silver Flower Contest': Rural Women in 1950s China and the Gendered Division of Labour," translated by Yuanxi Ma. *Gender and History* 18, no. 3: 594–612.

Henan sheng Nanyang zhuanqu kexue jishu xiehui 河南省南阳专区科学技术协会, ed. 1966. *Quanguo nongye kexue shiyan yundong jingyan huiji* 全国农业科学实验运动经验汇集 (*Collection of National Experiences in the Agricultural Science Experiment Movement*). Vol. 1. N.p.

Hershatter, Gail. 2007. "Forget Remembering: Rural Women's Narratives of China's Collective Past." In *Re-envisioning the Chinese Revolution: The Politics and Poetics of Collective Memories in Reform China*, edited by Lee Ching Kwan and Yang Guobin, 69–92. Stanford, CA: Stanford University Press.

Hershatter, Gail. 2011. *The Gender of Memory: Rural Women and China's Collective Past*. Berkeley: University of California Press.

Hinton, Carma, dir. 1984. *Small Happiness: Women of a Chinese Village*. Boston: Long Bow Group.

Link, Perry, and Kate Zhou. 2002. "Shunkouliu: Popular Satirical Sayings and Popular Thought." In *Popular China: Unofficial Culture in a Globalizing Society*, edited by Perry Link, Richard P. Madsen, and Paul G. Pickowicz, 89–110. Lanham, MD: Rowman and Littlefield.

Nongcun zhishi qingnian kexue shiyan jingyan xuanbian 农村知识青年科学实验经验选编 (*Selected Experiences of Rural Educated Youth in the Scientific Experiment Movement*). 1974. Beijing: Renmin chubanshe.

Perry, Elizabeth. 2016. "The Promise of PRC History." *Journal of Modern Chinese History* 10, no. 1: 113–17.

Rogaski, Ruth. 2012. "Addicted to Science." *Historical Studies in the Natural Sciences* 42, no. 5: 581–89.

Schmalzer, Sigrid. 2002. "Breeding a Better China: Pigs, Practices, and Place in a Chinese County, 1929–1937." *Geographical Review* 92, no. 1: 1–22.

Schmalzer, Sigrid. 2009. "Speaking about China, Learning from China: Amateur China Experts in 1970s America." *Journal of American-East Asian Relations* 16, no. 4: 313–52.

Schneider, Mindi, Elizabeth Lord, and Jessica Wilczak. 2020. "We, too: Contending with the Sexual Politics of Fieldwork in China." *Gender, Place, and Culture: A Journal of Feminist Geography* 28, no. 4: 519–40. doi.org/10.1080/0966369X.2020.1781793.

Wang, Shuliang, and Wang Linding 王树梁、王林定, eds. 2013. *Wangjinzhuang* 王金庄 (*Wangjinzhuang*). Shexian, China: Shexian wenhua guangdian xinwen chubanju.

Wang, Yiwen Yvon, Michael Schoenhals, Shuji Cao, Jeremy Brown, and Daniel Leese. 2017. "Grassroots Documents and PRC History Methods: A Roundtable Discussion." Association for Asian Studies Conference, Sheraton Centre Toronto Hotel, March 17.

Wu, Lanxian 吴兰仙. 1966. "Bu pa gan 'chou' shi, ganyu huan xintian" 不怕干'丑'事,敢于换新天 ("Not Fearing 'Shameful' Things, Courageously Changing the World"). In *Quanguo nongye kexue shiyan yundong jingyan huiji* 全国农业科学实验运动经验汇集 (*Collected Experiences of the National Rural Scientific Experiment Movement*), vol. 1, edited by Henan sheng Nanyang zhuanqu kexue jishu xiehui, 17– 23. N.p.

Xiong, Weimin 熊卫民. 2017. *Dui yu lishi, kexuejia you hua shuo* 对于历史,科学家有话说 (*Scientists Have Something to Say about History*). Beijing: Dongfang chubanshe.

"Xue Dazhai, gan Xiyang, quan xian xuexi Wangjinzhuang" 学大寨,赶昔阳,全县学习王金庄 ("Study Dazhai, Catch up with Xiyang, the Whole County Studies Wangjinzhuang"). 1971. She County 涉县 Archives, Hebei Province, 68.1.3: 31–32.

Long Live the Mass Line!
Errant Cadres and Post-Disillusionment PRC History

Aminda Smith

In January 1951 a woman appeared at a People's Courthouse in Hebei Province to file suit against Chinese Communist cadres from her village, who she alleged had terrorized her husband, Guo Yuzhong, into committing suicide. According to the widow, her husband had visited a shop that was robbed the same day, and he was detained on that evidence alone. Cadres apparently interrogated Guo multiple times, beating him and subjecting him to long periods outdoors, in freezing temperatures, trying to force a confession. After a cadre threatened to detain Guo's entire family, the accused threw himself into a well and drowned (Zhang J. 1952). When the county court delayed handling her case, Guo's widow sent for her elder son, a disabled People's Liberation Army veteran, who was away working for the railroad. The younger Guo returned home and visited the district-level People's Gov-

positions 29:4   DOI 10.1215/10679847-9286701
Copyright 2021 by Duke University Press

ernment to request help. The cadres in that office, and in countless others, simply sent him away (Zhang J. 1952).

Meanwhile, crimes far more serious than Guo's alleged petty theft appeared to be going uninvestigated. That same year, a twenty-nine-year-old cart driver from Shanxi was traveling all over North China, visiting dozens of government units, all in an effort to accuse his boss of murder and fraud. The driver, Zhang Shunyou, claimed he was trying to "answer the People's Government call to enthusiastically report counterrevolutionaries" but that he could not get a single government cadre to listen to him or take his report (Zhang and Li 1952). Zhang and the Guo family were not alone. One resident of Tanglin Village had been persecuted and humiliated for ten years over a charge that was later dismissed as false. In the city of Shendong, a man had been arrested three times on allegations that were never proven. The mother of a poor railway worker in the city of Baotou accused local cadres of trumping up a corruption case against her son, but despite her pleas, no one investigated. In fact, it appears that many Party units regularly ignored citizen complaints, questions, or requests. The Tong County Party Committee had put aside and eventually lost several written complaints and suggestions from the masses under its jurisdiction. A soldier's family in Qingyuan County visited the Provincial Court 118 times to resolve a housing dispute, all to no avail. In 1952, at the Communist Party's North China Bureau alone, officials received between ten and twenty letters per day, many of which contained similar complaints about cadre malfeasance and unresponsiveness (L. Liu 1952).

Even as people encountered a seemingly cruel and/or apathetic state, the Chinese Communist Party (CCP) was publicizing a very different picture of state-society relations. Over the course of 1952, the North China Bureau and its subordinate units (which included those in the Guo family's Wuqiang County and Zhang Shunyou's village of Zhuangtou) claimed that they had indeed received many letters and visits. But the Bureau insisted, in the *People's Daily,* that this flood of correspondence revealed "a deep level of trust in the Party, and especially in Chairman Mao." According to the article, the letter writers all "demonstrated a strong sense that justice is on their side by how confidently they make criticisms and offer suggestions. They all indicate that the people's consciousness is rising; they are coming to know that the masses are truly the masters" (*Renmin ribao* 1953). These conflicting reports highlight a contradiction that historians have come to see as necessarily fundamental to analyses of the PRC: the incongruity between positive propaganda and evidence of a darker reality.

Neil Diamant (2000) has shown that government agents who were negligent, corrupt, and incompetent regularly restricted the ability of the state to exercise its full capacity for control, as is well illustrated in the case of Zhang Shunyou. Jeremy Brown (2007: 129) has added that, "in spite of its initial bumbling," the state also managed to institute near total control in some instances, terrorizing people, like Guo Yuzhong and his family, in the process. These twin motifs, bumbling cadres/brutal cadres, appear reliably in work on PRC history (including my own), which is a voyeur's delight of misbehaving officials, botched campaigns, corrupt criminal investigations, and gratuitous violence (Ho 2018; DeMare 2015; Brown and Johnson 2015; Dikötter 2013; Smith 2013; Brown and Pickowicz 2007). There is a great deal of archival evidence suggesting that the bumbling-yet-brutal state is an apt characterization, at least of the early 1950s, and especially when compared to other posited models and narratives, which as Diamant (2001: 184) argues, are far too "elegant" to "capture the all-too-common 'mess' of Chinese politics" and history.

There is nevertheless something troubling about the brutal-yet-bumbling model: it also quite elegantly reproduces the Party-state's own narrative about its governance. While the Zhang and Guo cases seem to contradict CCP rhetoric, they were, in fact, central elements in that very rhetoric. All of the stories I have included thus far are from newspapers and other published propaganda. Propagandists pulled these anecdotes from internal, classified documents; even in the state's top-secret records, tales of egregious errors were common. Indeed, one reason scholars find it relatively easy to locate examples of problems and failures is that superiors required subordinates to include discussions of "weaknesses, flaws, and mistakes" in reports. As Diamant (2010: 427) notes, internal CCP documents on Party work begin with "examples of success . . . and then shift into critique mode . . ." with the transition between the two "clearly marked by the word 'however' (*danshi* 但是)."

Thus, Party rhetoric and state narratives, from the *People's Daily* to classified memos, are chock full of lazy, negligent, and even murderous communists. If misbehaving state agents were a defining feature of CCP governance, CCP governors were acutely aware of that fact. The Guo Yuzhong and Zhang Shunyou cases read like examples of a state struggling to tame and train its own agents because that is precisely what they were designed to be. The stories were (loosely) based on true events, but the texts describing them were explicitly instructional, lessons from the core curriculum for the "Three Antis" cadre-rectification campaign. Ongoing rectification movements taught cadres to mimic these cases, and other such primers, so that virtually every situation report, survey, directive, and policy discussion produced at any level, regardless of topic, contained a similar message: Officials and superiors saw nearly every project as beset by the errant behavior of their undertrained, undermotivated, corrupt, incompetent, and capricious cadres.

This will not be a controversial claim—the first generation of social scientists observing the nascent PRC regularly noted the problems the new state had with its "middle management" (Barnett and Vogel 1967; Schurmann 1966; Teiwes 1971). Graduate students all learn that the newly victorious CCP was vexed by their mix of retained Guomindang personnel and zealous but inexperienced rural revolutionaries. Party Central launched one internal rectification movement after another in a series of ever more desperate attempts to get their massive bureaucracy to function efficiently and in line with official goals. These rectifications form the terrain of our sources and our scholarship. But we have not been sufficiently attuned to their methodological implications: Given the centrality of cadre error to the CCP's own narratives, it is hardly surprising that when we pluck cases from the official administrative record, those anecdotes show that the would-be authoritarian state was constantly impeded by its bureaucracy; such was the very argument those anecdotes were evidencing when we "recovered" them.

Once articulated, this point is obvious. Yet, there is still a prevailing tendency to see positive descriptions as rhetoric and negative depictions as rare glimpses at the reality underneath that rhetoric, even as Gail Hershatter has argued definitively against this kind of "veneer thesis" (Hershatter 2011; Smith 2014). Neil Diamant and Brian DeMare have both warned historians that reports of problems are often overstated, precisely because, as Kevin O'Brien and Li Lianjiang (2006) have shown, state agents at all levels make great use of the classic bureaucratic strategy: blame subordinates (see also Diamant 2010; DeMare 2019; O'Brien 1996). But, although they hint at deeper problems, those scholars and many others still treat negative claims as more revealing than positive ones. Diamant (2010: 427), for example, affirms that "the 'problems' section is generally closer to the truth" and that researchers should pay far more attention to the part of the document that comes after the "however." I counter, however, that there is no evidence to support that theory. Neither Diamant nor others offer concrete grounds for favoring negative claims, beyond references to "common sense" and circular reassertions of the equally suspicious suggestion that Party sources "prettify the picture" (Seymour and Anderson 1999: xiv). How, we ought to ask, is this view so compelling when we have always known that the picture the CCP painted, especially of its own cadres, was anything but pretty?

The first part of the answer is deceptively simple—we do not know the party's rhetoric as well as we think we do, and so when we see what looks like a brutal-yet-bumbling state, for instance, we do not recognize it as the Party's own understanding of its governance. The second part of the answer, the reason why we do not know CCP discourse as fully as we should, has to do with the history of our field. Much of the tenor and the tone of PRC history was set by the first generation of China scholars to encounter and study Chinese communism and by their understandable but very personal reactions to the failure of the Chinese revolution to achieve its stated aims. As Fabio Lanza has shown, many of the senior scholars who shaped emergent fields in PRC studies were themselves profoundly shaped by disillusionment (Lanza 2017). Perry Link, one of the most influential senior China scholars and a former member of the Maoist-sympathizer group, the Committee of Concerned Asian Scholars (CCAS), now repeatedly warns that the Chinese Communist Party "paints a superidealized picture that is essentially false" (Link 2007: xv).

In the post-disillusionment era, the apparent contradiction, between what the Party *said* (the onetime source of scholarly enthusiasm) and what the Party *did* (the reputed cause of scholarly disenchantment) has essentially structured the field of PRC history.[1] It has given rise to that ubiquitous formula, what we might call the post-disillusionment couplet: *CCP propaganda said* X*, but in reality, it was* Y. While the contradiction is real, and should inform our methodology, the disillusioned generation developed a zeal for falsifying Party rhetoric, which became the basis for privileging the claims that come "after the 'however'" and ignoring much of the historical record as "window dressing" (Seymour and Anderson 1999: xv).

The post-disillusionment falsification methodology often leads us to dismiss genuinely useful insights from our historical sources even as we inadvertently replicate their rhetoric. The corrective is not, however, to abandon analyses that also happen to accord with those of the Party. Rather, I argue the opposite: we need to take the state's own writing about its governance more seriously. It seems that we have yet to fully map the grain of official PRC-state sources, and thus many of our attempts to read against that grain have produced misreadings. Cutting-edge research in PRC history has begun to create more faithful cartographies of Chinese communism, which locate deep meanings we mistook for superficial rhetoric and expose fabrications we unwittingly naturalized (Hershatter 2011; Schmalzer 2016; Altehenger 2018; Ho 2018).

To map the grain of cadre error, we can begin by noting that the CCP's own discourse also emphasized the discrepancy between what the Party said and what it did. "What we say, we do" (*yao shuodao zuodao* 要说到做到) featured regularly in propaganda since at least the 1940s, as both a description of ideal cadres and a rebuke/instruction for errant cadres.[2] If reports from the people suggested that party agents were not walking the walk, state rhetoricians were among the first to point that out, because examples of hypocrisies, egregious brutalities, and the negligent misdeeds of CCP cadres went seamlessly along the grain of the Party's most important narrative in early PRC period: the mass line (*qunzhong luxian* 群众路线). Recent scholarship by political scientists has begun to reassert the importance of this fundamental concept (Liu Yu 2006; X. Chen 2012; Kennedy and Shi 2015; Tang 2016). But because the mass line has long been seen as one of the idealized claims that came "before the 'however,'" much of the anglophone historiography simply ignores it and mines descriptions of cadre error as little more than data points in the drive to debunk. If we treat the documents holistically, instead, as exchanges in a series of complex conversations about praxis, we get much better mappings of the conceptual apparatuses that shaped Chinese communism.

Cadre Error

In March 1952, Zhang Shunyou apparently stormed into the offices of the Central Committee's North China Bureau. "I've been all over Suiyuan, Chahar, and Shanxi, visiting twenty-seven offices," he ranted, "It took five months. This not only delayed production, but I also used up my savings, sold my clothes, my blankets, my pipe, and more. When I was out of money, I went behind my parents' backs and sold our household's grain to cover my travel costs. Altogether, I spent more than 240,000 yuan." Zhang further reported that he had been mistreated by government personnel, sent on wild goose chases for paperwork, and even arrested by Public Security officers, all because he was trying to participate in the mass campaign against counterrevolutionaries by reporting his employer, Song Yude (Zhang and Li 1952: 3).

Zhang's story had begun in 1951, while he was working as a cart driver for Song, a small-scale grain merchant. According to Zhang, he and his boss were working in Guisui, Inner Mongolia, when the government announced the Campaign to Suppress Counterrevolutionaries. Soon after, Zhang later reported, Song suddenly announced that he was changing his name and moving his operation to another province. Song allegedly drew up two counterfeit travel passes, and he and Zhang set off. It was around this time, Zhang said, "that I began to suspect Song Yude was not a good fellow, and I thought I should report him." Zhang shared his concerns with a cadre from his own village as well as with someone at the county-level People's Government. At the end of June 1951, Song Yude was arrested and interrogated by the district-level authorities, but he was released without charge seven days later. In July, Zhang claimed, he discovered that villagers from Song's hometown, near Datong, had accused Song of being a despotic landlord who had killed a villager. Zhang took this information to the Datong People's Government, but cadres there apparently sent Zhang away because he lacked the appropriate letter of introduction. It was then that Zhang Shunyou spent several months traversing three provinces and eventually marching into the offices of the North China Bureau (Zhang and Li 1952: 3).

The Zhang Shunyou case strikes a familiar chord. Tales of ordinary citizens seeking justice from a vast and indifferent bureaucracy abound in fiction, film, and investigative journalism. Zhang's story, and that of the Guo family, are narratively similar to the tale of He Biqiu, or Qiu Ju as she was called in Zhang Yimou's film adaptation of Chen Yuanbin's novella *The Wan Family Lawsuit*. If such narratives of state unresponsiveness were critical of the state, the CCP embraced that criticism as a key part of intra-Party discussions about its own governance. We probably only know Zhang Shunyou's story because when he thundered into the North China Bureau, Central Committee member Liu Lantao saw links between Zhang's account and ongoing efforts to discipline cadres.[3] Zhang and Guo were both featured in a cadre rectification primer, for which Liu wrote the introduction. This material was distributed to units around the country as part of the Three-Antis campaign to curb cadre errors.[4]

Zhang and Guo were instructive cases because, while there were many facets of cadre error, not paying close attention to letters and visits from ordinary people was seen as one of the most egregious, as it was directly observable by the people themselves. In 1951 Zhou Enlai and the State Administrative Council (*Zhengwuyuan*) accused subordinates across the country of ignoring the petitions and thus "alienating the masses of the people from the People's Government" ("Zhengwuyuan" 1951).

In July 1951, for example, the Beijing Municipal Government admitted that they had some problems with foot-dragging and backlogs in their handling of the people's letters. In July 1952, Beijing's Xuanwu District Government confessed that nearly everyone in their unit "had failed to take letters from the masses seriously enough on an ideological level" because cadres thought "handling letters from the masses was small stuff, that it was simply helping individual members of the masses solve problems, and that it didn't have much of an effect." As an example of the kinds of problems this attitude created, the report cited a local woman who had accused her husband of abusing her and of tax evasion: "Cadres simply transferred the letter to the tax bureau and didn't press it. During the Five Antis, [she] wrote again, this time to the mayor, saying that the government had not handled this for her" (Xuanwu qu renmin zhengfu 1952).

The Xuanwu report acknowledged they had been "bureaucratist in our work" but added, "we organized a 'Study of the Zhang Shunyou Affair' campaign, and since then, we have remedied the cadres' mistaken mindset of not taking seriously letters from the masses. They have recognized its importance" (Xuanwu qu renmin zhengfu 1952). If the report writer's optimism was genuine, however, it may have been misplaced. Zhang Shu-nyou's case had suggested that some cadres were not interested in sup-pressing counterrevolutionaries, and after a national education campaign in Zhang's name, mishandling letters continued to hinder that same work. In 1955, the Beijing Public Security Bureau claimed that since 1951 they had received 12,316 letters "accusing counterrevolutionaries or criminal ele-ments." Of those leads, the police reported, they were able to verify charges and make arrests in approximately 300 cases. The other 12,000 letters were still under consideration, having piled up for weeks before they were opened and longer still before they were registered and assigned to investigators. In the capital's Changping district, police had apparently ignored letters for so long that there were two instances in 1954 when staff did a "crash job" of handling more than 400 letters at one time, and even so, by the beginning of 1955, there were still 100 letters sitting in their offices, waiting for basic processing ("Zhonggong Beijing shiwei" 1956).

These cases certainly suggest that many cadres were bumbling and/or indifferent (sometimes brutally) to the concerns of the masses, and it might be tempting to see them as evidence of a counternarrative. But depictions of brutal and bumbling cadres were not rare lapses in the CCP's rhetoric; they were the rhetoric. And that rhetoric came straight from Party Central and the national-level ministries. Minister of Public Security Luo Ruiqing per-sonally criticized the Beijing Public Security Bureau for the "sloppy sum-maries and ambiguous ideas" in their letters-and-visits reports ("Zhonggong Beijing shiwei" 1956). He and other ministry superiors argued that incom-petence and negligence among their subordinates impeded their ability to solve cases and suggested that some cadres even purposefully mishandled letters. In 1958, for example, the ministry claimed that cadres had been intentionally intercepting mail meant for Party Central, sometimes in an effort to "block information and suppress the masses' reports about problems with grain and deaths," and other times because personnel were looking to steal the money and gifts the masses often sent, especially to Chairman Mao ("Gedi jiancha feifa jiankou xinjian de qingkuang" 1961). The Beijing Municipal Committee alleged that even noncorrupt cadres intentionally ignored letters because "cadres think that letters and visits are inconsequential, like chicken feathers and garlic skin" (鸡毛蒜皮 *jimao suanpi*) ("Shiwei guanyu" 1950). Superiors claimed it was difficult to convince cadres that, as Liu Lantao (1952) noted, "The most minute of the People's matters are the foundation of the People's major matters."

Superiors also contended that malignant apathy hampered higher-level units from handling their own letters and visits. As the Beijing Municipal Government complained, "One of the problems is that many district governments and other offices don't take letters and visits seriously enough. They drag things out, ignore letters, have bad attitudes, etc. And this is leading more and more members of the masses to take their concerns directly to the mayor or the deputy-mayor" (Beijing shi renmin zhengfu 1951). This allegation was reproduced in centrally disseminated propaganda about Party governance: Zhang and the Guo family only took their concerns to higher authorities because lower and mid-level units failed to handle their cases.

Propaganda and the Party-state's intrabureaucratic communication were all idealized, to be sure. But what was idealized was not solely, or even primarily, the claim that the CCP governed in the interest of the masses. Even the most polished propaganda agreed wholeheartedly that the Party was sometimes failing the people. What this rhetoric idealized was the apportionment of blame, which served higher officials well. As Jeffrey Kinkley (2000: 349–59) noted, the Party-state responded enthusiastically to the story about the petitioner Qiu Ju, because while Qiu encountered some mid-level government personnel who were bumbling and officious, once their superiors intervened, the Party served the people. The notion that all would be set right if the "higher-ups" (上级 *shangji*) only knew the true situation, runs through fiction, film, and journalism as well as through historical sources.[5]

O'Brien and Li have emphasized the strategic uses of accusations against cadres, noting that Chinese citizens can (potentially) level harsh criticisms about extremely sensitive topics as long as they maintain that at the level of theory and policy the Party serves the people, and violations are the fault of errant individuals (O'Brien 1996; O'Brien and Li 2006). This has not been lost on PRC historians, who have also tended to be more critical of accusations about cadre error when those accusations were made as part of cadre rectification, especially in an explicitly instructional textbook. The fact is, however, that for the CCP it was *always* about cadre rectification, even in documentation that was ostensibly about something else, because cadre error was always cast as the main impediment to the correct functioning of the mass line.

How to Read the Mass Line

Encapsulated in the shorthand phrase, "from the masses; back to the masses" (*cong qunzhong zhong lai, dao qunzhong zhong qu* 从群众中来, 到群众中去), the mass line stipulated that all correct ideas originated with the ordinary people. The role of the Party was to weed out the incorrect ideas and process the correct but "unsystematic" ideas into theoretically sound ideology and policy, while using education and propaganda to ensure that the masses recognized their own original ideas in the results. Early observers argued that the Party did endeavor to implement the mass line in the service of the people. In 1944, tasked with observing and appraising the CCP for the US government, John Service (1974: 217) argued that the Party had "a closeness to and an ability to appeal to the common people in terms which they understand." He wrote that "the widespread popular support" the CCP enjoyed must "be considered a practical indication that the policies and method of the Chinese Communists have a democratic character." In his formative study of revolutionary China, historian Mark Selden (1971) similarly argued that the mass line was "the essence" and the foundation of Party success, the means by which the CCP won mass loyalty and mobilized popular participation in state projects.

In an equally formative work, historian Chen Yung-fa (1986: 3–4) argued that Selden's claims about the mass line had overemphasized the egalitarian elements of CCP governance and suggested that Selden had been somewhat gullible about the "image projected by the Party's external publications." *New York Times* China correspondent Richard Bernstein (2010) likewise contended that John Service was "naively dazzled by the Communists." Service and many of his likeminded colleagues later recanted, after many of them were fired from the State Department and brought before the House Un-American Activities Committee. Diplomat John Davies (Williams 1989) later conceded that they had been wrong to use the term "democratic" in describing the Party's methods. In a revision, Selden (1995) also allowed that he may have overstated the democratic elements of CCP governance.

Even in his early research, however, Selden made clear that Chinese Communist conceptions of popular participation and leadership accountability were different from liberal formulations of "democracy." The mass line, as elucidated by Liu Shaoqi and then Mao, was a Leninist model for state-society relations that was in many respects a purposeful alternative to Western-style liberal democracy. As Stuart Schram ([1969] 1989: 97–98) explained in the 1960s, the mass line was developed to resolve the Leninist dilemma of how to preserve centralized power (so as to maintain the total control needed for the implementation of policies that will be fiercely opposed by "capitalists" and others), while still allowing sufficient popular participation to serve the people and maintain popular support. Efforts to implement this leadership style, Selden (1995: 243) noted, could not but reflect the difficulties inherent in combining top-down centralism with popular participation. Mao never tried to conceal what liberal observers might consider the undemocratic elements of his vision: "You are dictatorial," he imagined his detractors alleging. "You are right," he replied, "that is just what we are" (Mao 1949). Recent work on the mass line has continued to focus on how it fostered what Wenfang Tang (2016) has called "populist authoritarianism" by allowing limited forms of popular participation while maximizing the capacity for centralized control (see also X. Chen 2012; Y. Liu 2006; Kennedy and Shi 2015). As Patricia Thornton (2011) has shown, its functions, and the challenge it posed to liberal democratic modes of governance, made the mass line key to CCP success. Thus, any suggestion that the democratic claims of the mass line were more rhetorical than genuine probably indicates a conflation of Mao's Leninist conceptions of political representation with the liberal forms of democracy it critiqued. The mass line could not be a faux-democratic "whitewashing" for authoritarianism because it was always explicitly democratic *and* authoritarian.

That said, Mao and other Party leaders agreed with their critics that the reality in the PRC often failed to correspond to their ideal vision of mass-line governance. For the CCP, however, the issue was not Party policy or the leadership's will to implement it, but rather, as Mao regularly lectured, corruption, bureaucratism and other cadre errors (Chen Z. 2013). According to the Party's own historians, the five concrete practices that "fundamentally guaranteed the efficacy and implementation of the mass line" were all instructions to cadres: first, conduct grassroots surveys and investigations; second, go "squat in a spot" (*dundian* 蹲点), meaning go live and work among the people, staying in one location for an extended period of time; third, pay attention to letters and visits from the masses; fourth, participate in physical labor; and fifth, undergo regular rectification (Z. Chen 2013: 50).

The connections between cadre error and the mass line are clear in Liu Lantao's *Collected Documents on Opposing Bureaucratism*, a rectification textbook used nationwide during the Three-Antis campaign, which included the model cases of Zhang Shunyou and Guo Yuzhong. Those and other cases were also published in the *People's Daily* and numerous local and regional newspapers. When retold for public consumption, these stories were all parables about the Party losing its grassroots connection to the masses, and they suggested the fault lay with the mid-level cadres who failed to correctly implement the mass line (Zhang and Li 1952: 3). The centrality of cadre error and rectification to the Party's understanding of the mass line meant that almost without exception, discussions of work with the masses were always also discussions of cadre rectification, even if rectification was not mentioned specifically. All Party-state documents that discuss the people's opinions, the people's behavior, the people's problems, and the like were always also discussions between superiors and subordinates about how well cadres acquired, handled, and responded to that information, meaning rectification, the mass line, and the success or failure of Party-state work were all inseparable for the CCP. This is an obvious point, but it has a crucial methodological implication: bumbling and brutal cadres, wherever we find them, must always be treated as discursive elements in CCP rhetoric about cadre rectification, a rhetoric that formed the central component in the Party's defense of its commitment to mass-line work.

The brutal-yet-bumbling state was a key part of the CCP's own rhetoric, but I am not arguing that we dismiss it. On the contrary, all of the critics mentioned heretofore are surely correct about the problems of early PRC governance. But CCP leaders had correctly identified those same challenges years earlier. If we pay equally critical attention to both negative and positive archival claims, it becomes clear that cadre error was *the* narrative, instead of a counternarrative, and that mass-line rhetoric, as one of the many sets of claims that usually appear "before the 'however,'" was idealized, but not necessarily in the ways we expect. CCP hyperbole looks different when we assess it within its original discursive framework. Many of the documents that enumerate the mass line in the most detail are documents describing cadre errors, produced and circulated for rectification movements. In that context, mass-line claims do not have to be read as exaggerated statements about actual practice; they could be read as rebukes and inspirational messages to cadres. In a world where Guo Yuzhong and other members of the Party's base were committing suicide because of cadre "excesses," exhorting cadres to "remember the people are the foundation of our power" may or may not have been effective, but it was far more than a platitude.

Furthermore, brutalities such as the ones Guo suffered were cast as cadre error, but not all brutality violated the mass line, according to the CCP. The highly publicized case of Zhang Shunyou suggests that even without cadre excesses, mass-line governance, in its ideal form, was dark. Although Zhang encountered manifold difficulties in order to accuse Song Yude as a counterrevolutionary, the accusers' expenses were eventually reimbursed, according to Liu Lantao's orders, and the errant cadres who had ignored Zhang's case were disciplined. More importantly, Zhang eventually got his desired result: Song Yude was executed as a counterrevolutionary on November 26, 1952 (Y. Liu 2014: 187). CCP propaganda regularly claimed that executions and incarcerations were consistent with the mass line because "the masses demand we suppress counterrevolutionaries," and their internal discussions, together with Zhang Shunyou's own claims, suggest this assertion was sometimes true. Song's execution certainly highlights what Selden (1995: 243) called "the dark side of mobilizational politics," but it also troubles any assumption that the "dictatorship of the masses" was not at least partially supported by some members of those masses. By all accounts, Zhang Shunyou participated in governance. And without his dogged pursuit, Song Yude might have escaped the government's notice. Song's execution does not belie mass-line rhetoric; when read correctly, the case of Zhang Shunyou exemplifies the Party's ideal operation of the mass line in both its democratic and authoritarian aspects.

That idealized model of the mass line is precisely why the story of Zhang

Shunyou still appears on Party study websites, as do ideal models of unsuccessful mass-line governance, such as the case of Guo Yuzhong.[6] Brutal/bumbling cadres were not secrets the Party tried to paper over with propaganda. To paraphrase David Sedaris, one cannot claim to have "discovered" a "darker reality" when multiple high-profile websites are already sketching a comparable scene.[7] Of course, we can seek evidence to damn the state within the state's own records—such is standard historian's practice. But the role of disillusionment in the genealogy of our field has impeded our ability to do so critically.

Post-Disillusionment Epistemology in a Post-Truth Moment

One of the first scholars to defect from the early PRC-sympathizing, pro-Mao line was Pierre Ryckmans, who in 1971 wrote, under the pseudonym of Simon Leys, *The Chairman's New Clothes*. In what a biographer later called the "red-hot rant of a book," Leys advanced a scathing criticism of the CCP and was reviled for it by his as-yet Maoist colleagues and much of the international left. Ryckmans/Leys was a pioneer in the use of the post-disillusionment couplet (*CCP propaganda said X, but in reality it was Y*). For example, he described the Cultural Revolution as a "power struggle waged at the top between a handful of men and behind the smoke screen of a fictitious mass movement" (Leys [1971] 1981: 13). In the mid-1970s, Geremie Barmé, once a devoted student of Ryckmans in Australia, denounced him as a "reactionary." Barmé (2018) later admitted that, even as he wrote that accusation, from a university in Shenyang, he had "mounting misgivings" about the Chinese Communists, as "every day in the People's Republic offered grim new revelations." He soon repented for his "youthful petulance," returned to Australia, and completed a PhD under Ryckman's direction.

Others of Barmé's generation experienced analogous transformations. Political scientist Edward Friedman (2018) wrote that he and other "Maoist sympathizers" in the Committee for Concerned Asian Scholars (of which Mark Selden was also a founding member) had initially seen "the PRC through the lens of their own ideals." But, Friedman explained, observing domestic Chinese realities as well as the international relations between communist regimes in China, Vietnam, and Cambodia "disillusioned many

CCAS members and led to the swift end of the committee." In an essay titled "My Disillusionment," Perry Link (also CCAS) wrote self-critically about his initial "high hopes" for the CCP: "How wrong I was to take Mao Zedong's 'socialism' at face value." Elaborating, he recalled his first trip to China in 1973: "I had learned in graduate school that there were no flies in China after the 'Four Pests' campaign of 1958 . . . When I saw a fly on a white stone table in Suzhou, I photographed it." After a series of increasingly significant discoveries, Link's final lesson in disillusionment came in February 1989 when he and his friend Fang Lizhi had a run-in with the Chinese police. Link was shocked when he read an official Xinhua News Agency report about the encounter, which "told, in detail, a fabricated story that departed in major ways from what my own eyes had seen" (Link 2011).

Of the disillusioned, Barmé, Friedman, and Link are among the most vocal and dogmatic critics of the Mao-era CCP, whereas Selden and others seem to have retained at least a measure of their earlier sympathy. Another CCAS founder, Richard Pfeffer, was rumored to have been denied tenure for his admittedly Marxist views (Lanza 2017: 170). But scholars like Pfeffer were in the minority. Many more of their colleagues, who went on to become leading scholars in the fields of Chinese studies, have written or spoken about the way they amended their opinions of Maoism (and Marxism) when they observed realities in China that failed to correspond to the propaganda they had not only believed but also proselytized. As they became increasingly disillusioned by their discovery that "the Communist Party of China would [and did] flat-out lie," uncovering the facts that would reveal those lies became a central focus of their scholarship (Link 2011).

Of course, as this article also demonstrates, the reality of the early-PRC did indeed reveal that the Party often failed to live up to its own ideals. And critics were probably right that early observers had been somewhat "dazzled" by the Communists' idealistic rhetoric. My point is not that post-disillusionment methodology leads scholars to be overly critical of CCP claims; rather the problem occurs when the fascination with falsification leads historians to be more suspicious of positive claims about Maoism's successes and not sufficiently skeptical of negative claims that reflect poorly on the enterprise, even when both claims come from the Party-state's own archival record. All too often we are so excited by the prospect of finding a "counternarrative" that we rip cadre-error vignettes from the larger narratives within which we find them, so that they float, decontextualized, in our descriptions of the early PRC. In that context they appear as against-the-grain readings of state discourse, when, on the contrary, they were actually key features of that grain.

I have argued elsewhere that it is not quite possible to read ostensibly Maoist texts "against the grain" in a traditional sense (Smith 2013: 79–118). But in any case, effective against-the-grain readings demand a deep knowledge of the grain. Thus, I suggest we first continue to map the grain of CCP discourse, which was certainly idealized but not necessarily or "essentially" false. And while readings against *that* grain will no doubt prove revelatory, there is still plenty we can learn about PRC governance, and the experiences of the governors and the governed, by listening to what the Party-state had to say about precisely those things, by paying a bit more attention to what came "before the 'however'" and precisely how it related to what came after.

Truth and Skepticism

In a recent conversation at Harvard University, senior China scholar (and former CCAS member) Joseph Esherick (2018) reiterated his longtime defense of an empiricist mode, warning that it is dangerous, for scholarship and politics, to apply theories that suggest the instability of facts, citing in particular the dire consequences of "post-truth" politics in the Trump-era United States. While Esherick and others have valid concerns about the dangers of "alternative facts" and "fake news," the rise of such concepts cannot be pinned on scholars who have simply demanded better proof of the truth systems we are asked to accept as superior. The conspiracy theories and other features of the alleged "post-truth" mindset all rely on what Michael Lynch (2017) has called "selective uses of skepticism" to support particular political views.

In a sense, that is precisely what post-disillusionment methodology promotes: "selective skepticism." Thus, what I am advocating is not "epistemic democracy," but rather the restoration of some epistemic humility and a demand that we subject all truth claims to the same level of empirical and epistemological scrutiny. Those who advocate empiricism tend to understate the extent to which the current forms of scientific (and social scientific) empiricism *are* political theories of knowledge. Those theories were repeatedly challenged in the twentieth century but emerged victorious, in part because they were wielded in the service of the political claim, infamously intoned by Margaret Thatcher, that there are no viable alternatives to the liberal capitalist status quo (Rafael 1994). Esherick is no Thatcherite, and his fellow self-identified empiricist Geremie Barmé (2017) has insisted that we recognize both "the neo-liberal West" and the People's Republic of China as reliant on their own versions of a "post-truth bubble." But the epistemology of disillusionment did gain traction in tandem with Reaganomic/Thatcherite "no-alternative" politics, and—whether intentionally or not—scholars who write in the post-disillusionment mode abet the related assertions of liberal superiority. Given that political connection, it is significant that many of the most trenchant claims about the nature of CCP governance might not be fully supported by the sources. Unsubstantiated assumptions about what is reliable and what is unreliable, and how we know the difference, are rendering the field of PRC history both theory-poor *and* empirically unsound.

At its most extreme, the falsification drive allows dangerously reactionary claims about the evils of socialism. The apotheosis of post-disillusionment methodology can be found in Frank Dikötter's trilogy on the Mao years. Dikötter (2013) sifts out only the most horrific—and often least common—sets of examples from the vast archive of the PRC past to advance claims such as the following, rendered in a post-disillusionment couplet: "The Chinese Communist Party refers to its victory in 1949 as a 'liberation' . . . but . . . It is first and foremost a history of calculated terror and systematic violence" (xi). Scholars who work with the same archives find Dikötter's work objectionable and tend to dismiss it. As one of this issue's anonymous reviewers rightly pointed out, "PRC historians, it seems, have agreed to ignore Frank," but as the reviewer also noted, in excluding Dikötter, we might make our internecine contradictions seem starker than they are. There is, to be sure, a world of difference between Dikötter's misuse of evidence and Neil Diamant's and Brian DeMare's careful and thoughtful, if skeptical, scholarship. But the latter might inadvertently help to enable the former by suggesting that evidence reflecting poorly on the state is inherently more trustworthy than its opposite.

If we treat positive and negative evidence symmetrically, seemingly contradictory reports become conversations that informed and shaped one another, and we can rephrase the post-disillusionment couplet: *CCP sources said X as they debated and contended with Y*. Take some of Jonathan Mirsky's reminiscences, for example. The China scholar and East Asia editor of the *Times* (London) went on a 1972 CCAS trip to the PRC. Mirsky (2012: 24–28) recalls visiting the home of a "Chinese worker family," which had "brightly painted" rooms and all the amenities, plus "a radio, television," and "several shiny bicycles," unlocked, of course, because bike theft was unheard of in Communist China. The next day, however, Mirsky chanced to see a different home—"shabby, poorly painted," with "no television," and "only one well-used bicycle, which was locked." When the inhabitant of the second house told Mirsky that the first one had been a "show flat," and that in fact "there were plenty of thieves," Mirsky went from "Mao-fan to counterrevolutionary in 48 hours." Of course, Mirsky's informant was telling the truth; the PRC never managed to eradicate petty crime (Smith 2013: 181–98). Yet theft did decrease radically from pre-1949 levels, and in the early 1950s many people did have nicer living quarters than they had ever had before. Also, as Perry Link (2011) noted, the CCP has long encouraged Chinese people to be especially self-conscious of the way China might be perceived by foreigners, as foreigners and foreign governments have long disparaged China for its material conditions, even using such insults to question Chinese fitness for self-rule. Thus, it seems likely that in the earliest moments of the Cold War thaw, foreigners would be taken to the nicest apartments. None of these truths falsify the others. One does not need to dispute the inherent stability of facts to argue, as Ernest Hemingway ([1940] 1995: 23) did, that sometimes "there's no one thing that's true. It's all true."

Notes

1   Lanza (2017: 107–8) has questioned the direct causal link these scholars draw between their realization that Chinese Communism had a dark side and their turn away from Maoism.

2   As early as 1946, the Party praised the "say it, do it spirit" (shuodao zuodao jingshen 说到做到精神) of local cadres (*Renmin ribao* 1946).

3   Liu Lantao was an alternate member of the Seventh Central Committee and a full member of the Eighth.

4   For more on the campaign, see Gao 2004: 158–63.

5   Most recently, in the documentary *Shangfang* [*Petition*] (Zhao 2009). Yan Lianke (2010) plays on this theme in *Sishu*.

6   They are also archived by Marxists.org, www.marxists.org/chinese/reference-books/chinese revolution/195303/index.htm.

7   The original quote concerns rules Sedaris (2001: 154) had for potential partners, one of which was that they "could not say they had 'discovered' any shop or restaurant currently listed in the phone book."

References

Altehenger, Jennifer. 2018. *Legal Lessons: Popularizing Laws in the People's Republic of China, 1949–1989*. Cambridge, MA: Harvard University Press.

Barmé, Geremie R. 2017. "The Chairmen, Trump, and Mao." ChinaFile, January 23. www.chinafile.com/viewpoint/chairmen-trump-and-mao.

Barmé, Geremie R. 2018. "One Decent Man." *New York Review of Books*, June 28. www.nybooks.com/articles/2018/06/28/simon-leys-one-decent-man/.

Barnett, A. Doak, and Ezra Vogel. 1967. *Cadres Bureaucracy and Political Power in Communist China*. New York: Columbia University Press.

Beijing shi renmin zhengfu 北京市人民政府 (Beijing Municipal People's Government). 1951. "Guanyu 1951 nian shangbannian chuli renmin laixin he jiejian renmin de baogao" 关于1951年上半年处理人民来信和接见人民的报告 ("Report on Handling Letters and Receiving Visits from the People, First Half of 1951"). Beijing Municipal Archives 2-3-69.

Bernstein, Richard. 2010. "A Bridge to a Love for Democracy." *New York Times*, December 29.

Brown, Jeremy. 2007. "From Resisting Communists to Resisting America: Civil War and Korean War in Southwest China, 1950–51." In *Dilemmas of Victory: The Early Years of the People's Republic of China*, edited by Jeremy Brown and Paul Pickowicz, 105–29. Cambridge, MA: Harvard University Press.

Brown, Jeremy, and Matthew Johnson, eds. 2015. *Maoism at the Grassroots: Everyday Life in China's Era of High Socialism*. Cambridge, MA: Harvard University Press.

Brown, Jeremy, and Paul Pickowicz, eds. 2007. *Dilemmas of Victory: The Early Years of the People's Republic of China*. Cambridge, MA: Harvard University Press.

Chen, Xi. 2012. *Social Protest and Contentious Authoritarianism in China*. Cambridge: Cambridge University Press.

Chen, Yuanbin 陈源斌. 1992. *Wan jia susong* 万家诉讼 (*Wan Family Lawsuit*). Beijing: Zhongguo qingnian chubanshe.

Chen, Yung-fa. 1986. *Making Revolution: The Communist Movement in Eastern and Central China, 1937–1945*. Berkeley: University of California Press.

Cheng, Zhongyuan 程中原. 2013. "Xin Zhongguo chengli hou Mao Zedong guanche shishi qunzhong luxian de lilun yu shijian" 新中国成立后毛泽东贯彻实施群众路线的理论与实践 ("Mao Zedong's Implementation of Mass-Line Theory and Practice in the Early PRC"). *Dang de wenxian* 5: 49–57.

DeMare, Brian. 2015. *Mao's Cultural Army: Drama Troupes in China's Rural Revolution*. Cambridge: Cambridge University Press.

DeMare, Brian. 2019. *Land Wars: The Story of China's Agrarian Revolution*. Stanford, CA: Stanford University Press.

Diamant, Neil. 2000. *Revolutionizing the Family: Politics, Love, and Divorce in Urban and Rural China, 1949–1968*. Berkeley: University of California Press.

Diamant, Neil. 2001. "Between Martyrdom and Mischief: The Political and Social Predicament of CCP War Widows and Veterans, 1949–66." In *Scars of War: The Impact of Warfare on Modern China*, edited by Diana Lary and Stephen MacKinnon, 162–89. Vancouver: UBC Press.

Diamant, Neil. 2010. *Embattled Glory: Veterans, Military Families, and the Politics of Patriotism in China, 1949–2007*. Lanham, MD: Rowman and Littlefield.

Dikötter, Frank. 2013. *The Tragedy of Liberation: A History of the Chinese Revolution, 1945–1957*. London: Bloomsbury.

Esherick, Joseph. 2018. Remarks at the panel discussion "The End of Concern: Maoist China, Activism, and Asian Studies," Harvard Fairbank Center for Chinese Studies, Cambridge, MA, September 25. soundcloud.com/fairbank-center/the-end-of-concern-maoist -china-activism-and-asian-studies-panel-discussion.

Friedman, Edward. 2018. "Myths of Maoism." *Dissent Magazine*. November 16. www .dissentmagazine.org/online_articles/fabio-lanza-end-of-concern-review-myths-of-maoism.

Gao, James Z. 2004. *The Communist Takeover of Hangzhou: The Transformation of City and Cadre*. Honolulu: University of Hawai'i Press.

"Gedi jiancha feifa jiankou xinjian de qingkuang" 各地检查非法检扣信件的情况 ("Investigation of Illegally Confiscated Letters in Each Locality"). 1961. *Gongan gongzuo jianbao*, July 1, 3.

Hemingway, Ernest. (1940) 1995. *For Whom the Bell Tolls*. New York: Scribner.

Hershatter, Gail. 2011. *The Gender of Memory: Rural Women and China's Collective Past.* Berkeley: University of California Press.

Ho, Denise Y. 2018. *Curating Revolution: Politics on Display in Mao's China.* Cambridge: Cambridge University Press.

Kennedy, John, and Shi Yaojiang. 2015. "Rule by Virtue, the Mass Line Model, and Cadre-Mass Relations." In *East Asian Development Model: Twenty-First-Century Perspectives*, edited by Shiping Hua and Ruihua Hu, 217–33. London: Routledge.

Kinkley, Jeffrey. 2000. *Chinese Justice, the Fiction: Law and Literature in Modern China.* Stanford, CA: Stanford University Press, 2000.

Lanza, Fabio. 2017. *The End of Concern: Maoist China, Activism, and Asian Studies.* Durham, NC: Duke University Press.

Leys, Simon [Pierre Ryckmans]. (1971) 1981. *The Chairman's New Clothes: Mao and the Cultural Revolution*, translated by Carol Appleyard and Patrick Goode. London: Allison and Busby.

Link, Perry. 2007. Foreword to *Confessions of an Innocent Life in Communist China.* New York: W. W. Norton and Company.

Link, Perry. 2011. "My Disillusionment: China, 1973." *New York Review of Books*, June 22. www.nybooks.com/daily/2011/06/22/my-disillusionment-peoples-republic-1973/.

Link, Perry. 2015. "Mao's China: The Language Game." ChinaFile, May 15. www.chinafile.com/library/nyrb-china-archive/maos-china-language-game.

Liu, Lantao 刘澜涛. 1952. "Zhonggong zhongyang huabei ju di san shuji Liu Lantao zai chuli Zhang Shunyou shijian huiyi shang de jianghua" 中共中央华北局第三书记刘澜涛在处理张顺有事件会议上的讲话 ("Party Central North China Bureau Third Secretary Liu Lantao's Speech at the Conference on Handling the Zhang Shunyou Affair"). *Renmin ribao*, May 30.

Liu, Yajuan 刘亚娟. 2014. "Zhang Shunyou shijian: Yige dianxing de'shudianxing' ge an" "张顺有事件: 一个典型的 '树典型' 个案" ("The Zhang Shunyou Affair: A Model 'Cultivating Models' Case"). *Zhongyang yanjiuyuan jindai shi yanjiusuo jikan*, no. 84: 159–200.

Liu, Yu. 2006. "From the Mass Line to Mao Cult: The Production of Legitimate Dictatorship in Revolutionary China." PhD diss., Columbia University.

Lynch, Michael. 2017. "STS, Symmetry, and Post-Truth." *Social Studies of Science* 47, no. 4: 593–99.

Mao Zedong. 1949. "On the People's Democratic Dictatorship." June 30. www.marxists.org/reference/archive/mao/selected-works/volume-4/mswv4_65.htm.

Mirsky, Jonathan. 2012. "From Mao-Fan to Counterrevolutionary in 48 Hours." In *My First Trip to China: Scholars, Diplomats, and Journalists Reflect on Their First Encounters with China*, edited by Kin-ming Liu, 24–28. Hong Kong: East Slope.

O'Brien, Kevin. 1996. "Rightful Resistance." *World Politics* 49, no. 1: 31–55.

O'Brien, Kevin, and Li Lianjiang. 2006. *Rightful Resistance in Rural China*. Cambridge: Cambridge University Press.

Rafael, Vicente L. 1994. "The Cultures of Area Studies in the United States." *Social Text* 12, no. 41: 91–112.

Renmin ribao 人民日报 (*People's Daily*). 1946. "Zuoquan hongxing xiaoxue yundong" 左权红星小学运动 ("The Primary School Movement in Zuoquan, Hongxing"). August 5.

Renmin ribao 人民日报 (*People's Daily*). 1953. "Huabei diqu geji lingdao jiguan jiaqiang chuli renmin laixin he jiejian renmin gongzuo" 华北地区各级领导机关加强处理人民来信和接见人民的工作 ("Huabei Region Leadership at All Levels Strengthen the Work of Handling Letters from the People and Receiving Visits from the People"). January 29.

Schmalzer, Sigrid. 2016. *Red Revolution, Green Revolution: Scientific Farming in Socialist China*. Chicago: University of Chicago Press.

Schoenhals, Michael. 2012. *Spying for the People: Mao's Secret Agents, 1949–1967*. Cambridge: Cambridge University Press.

Schurmann, Franz. 1966. *Ideology and Organization in Communist China*. Berkeley: University of California Press.

Sedaris, David. 2001. *Me Talk Pretty One Day*. Boston: Back Bay Books.

Selden, Mark. 1971. *The Yenan Way in Revolutionary China*. Cambridge, MA: Harvard University Press.

Selden, Mark. 1995. *China in Revolution: The Yenan Way Revisited*. Armonk, NY: M. E. Sharpe.

Service, John. 1974. "The Growth of the New Fourth Army: An Example of the Popular Democratic Appeal of the Chinese Communists." In *Lost Chance in China: The World War II Dispatches of John S. Service*, edited by Joseph Esherick, 217–24. New York: Random House.

Seymour, James, and Michael Anderson. 1999. *New Ghosts, Old Ghosts: Prisons and Labor Reform Camps in China*. London: Routledge.

"Shiwei guanyu 1950 chuli renmin laixin laifang gongzuo zongjie" 市委关于. 1950. 处理人民来信来访工作总结 ("Municipal Committee on 1950 Handling Letters and Visits from the People Work Summary"). 1950. Beijing Municipal Archives 2-3-69.

Smith, Aminda M. 2013. *Thought Reform and China's Dangerous Classes: Reeducation, Resistance, and the People*. Lanham, MD: Rowman and Littlefield.

Smith, Aminda. 2014. "Lessons We Need to Learn." *PRC History Review* 1, no. 1: 17–19.

Tang, Wenfang. 2016. *Populist Authoritarianism: Chinese Political Culture and Regime Sustainability*. Oxford: Oxford University Press.

Teiwes, Frederick. 1971. *Rectification Campaigns and Purges in Communist China, 1950–61*. New York: Columbia University Press.

Thornton, Patricia. 2011. "Retrofitting the Steel Cage: From Mobilizing the Masses to Surveying the Public." In *Mao's Invisible Hand*, edited by Sebastian Heilmann and Elizabeth J. Perry, 237–68. Cambridge, MA: Harvard University Press.

Williams, Sue, dir. 1989. *China: A Century of Revolution, Part 1: China in Revolution, 1911–1949*. NY: Zeitgeist Films.

Xuanwu qu renmin zhengfu 宣武区人民政府. 1952. "Guanyu chuli renmin qunzhong laixin de zongjie baogao" 关于处理人民群众来信的总结报告 ("Summary Report on Handling Letters from the People-Masses"). Beijing Municipal Archives 2-3-69.

Yan, Lianke 阎连科. 2010. *Sishu* 四书 (*The Four Books*). Hong Kong: Mingpao chubanshe.

Zhang, Jun 张君. 1952. "Guanyu dui 'Guo Jinsheng shijian' de diaocha he chuli jueding de baogao" 关于对'郭金升事件'的调查和处理决定的报告 ("Report on the Decision Regarding the Investigation and Handling of 'the Guo Jinsheng Affair'"). *Hebei ribao*, October 23.

Zhang, Shunyou 张顺有, and Li Hengying 李恒英. 1952. "Wo jianju fangeming fenzi shi zaoyu le zhongzhong zunan" 我检举反革命分子时遭遇了种种阻难 ("The Many Obstacles I Encountered While Reporting a Counterrevolutionary"). *Renmin ribao*, May 30.

Zhang, Yimou 张艺谋, dir. 1993. *Qiu Ju da guansi* 秋菊打官司 (*The Story of Qiu Ju*). Hollywood, CA: Sony Pictures Classics.

Zhao, Liang 赵亮, dir. 2009. *Shangfang* 上访 (*Petition*). Paris: Ina, Arte France, and 3 Shadows.

"Zhengwuyuan guanyu chuli renmin laixin he jiejian renmin gongzuo de jueding" 政务院关于处理人民来信和接见人民工作的决定 ("Government Administration Council Decision on Work Handling Letters and Receiving Visits from the People"). 1951. Beijing Municipal Archives 2-3-26.

"Zhonggong Beijing shiwei bangongting guanyu chuli renmin laixin laifang gongzuo zhong cunzai de jige wenti ji gaijin yijian baogao" 中共北京市委关于处理人民来信来访中存在的几个问题 ("Beijing Municipal Party Committee Opinion on Several Problems in the Handling of Letters and Visits from the People"). 1956. Beijing Municipal Archives 1-6-1161.

Zhonggong Huabei ju bangongting chuli renmin laixin bangongshi 中共华北局办公厅处理人民来信办公室. 1953. "Jiaqiang chuli renmin laixin he jiejian renmin de gongzuo" 加强处理人民来信和接见人民的工作 ("Strengthen the Work of Handling Letters and Receiving Visits from the People"). In *Fan guanliaozhuyi wenjian ji* 反官僚主义文件集(*Collected Documents on Opposing Bureaucratism*). Beijing: Huabei renmin chubanshe. www.marxists.org /chinese/reference-books/chineserevolution/195303/index.htm.

Rethinking the Political Economy of Development in Mao's China

Covell F. Meyskens

If someone publicly declares today that China failed to develop under Mao Zedong, there is typically little need for explanation since this viewpoint accords with popular understandings of the history of state socialism in the twentieth century. In the contemporary era, a widely accepted narrative is that during the Cold War a protracted struggle took place between capitalism and socialism, and in the end capitalism won, and socialism lost. For many, capitalism's victory in the Cold War is taken as a sign of its economic superiority, and socialism's defeat is treated as definitive proof of its economic failure (Gaddis 1997; Fukuyama 1992). This same binary of success and failure frequently structures scholarly analysis of the Chinese economy in the Mao period. In the pages that follow, I do not intend to resolve the question of whether Mao's China was an economic success or failure. My aim is different. I come at the issue of the Chinese economy under Mao

positions 29:4 DOI 10.1215/10679847-9286714
Copyright 2021 by Duke University Press

from a meta-perspective, critically examining two theoretical frameworks used to evaluate Maoist economic affairs and presenting alternative explanations that I suggest more adequately explain the political economy of development in Mao's China.

Both of the theoretical frameworks that I focus on in this article presume to know what economic practices the Chinese Communist Party (CCP) should have engaged in and fault the Party for not conforming to their standards of judgment. I argue that this normative approach to analyzing Maoist development is wanting for four reasons, all of which are a result of not taking economic practices in Mao's China on their own terms. In its drive to depict China as acting in an anomalous manner, this normative standpoint insufficiently attends to the empirical specificities of economic activities of the Mao era. It does not take enough into account how China's socialist identity shaped the Communist Party's economic initiatives. Nor does it dig deep enough into how the geopolitical dynamics of the Cold War influenced Chinese development. This way of writing the history of the Mao period also overlooks similarities between China and other developmental states in Cold War East Asia.

The first theoretical framework that this article lays out and critiques is based on neoclassical economic theory. According to neoclassical economics, the fundamental issue with the CCP's approach to development was its inefficiency. A major source of inefficiency was the Party's decision to repress markets and not prioritize growth in light industry—the economic sector for which China's large population provided a comparative advantage. If the Party had pursued this policy direction, the theory goes that then domestic growth and consumption would have been higher. Instead of adhering to this comparative advantage-conforming policy line, the CCP concentrated on heavy industrial growth and implemented a policy of import substitution.

While supporters of the neoclassical framework criticize the CCP for contravening the principle of comparative advantage, proponents of the second framework think that the problem with Mao's China was that it never broke completely with capitalist practices and never truly turned into a socialist country. Still entrenched in capitalist logics, the CCP made China into a state capitalist regime. Theoretical claims of this sort come in two different varieties. The first variety maintains that China was state capitalist, because markets were not entirely liquidated, and the government took on a superintendent role in economic affairs. The second variety holds that China maintained a capitalist economy under Mao, since surplus value continued to be extracted from labor and channeled into capital accumulation. The only difference was that, rather than private actors exploiting workers, it was state agents running a countrywide bureaucracy who oversaw the mining of surplus value from Chinese labor to increase national capital and be internationally competitive.

I argue here that neither the neoclassical nor the state capitalist framework gives a sufficient assessment of the political economy of development in Mao's China. The neoclassical framework falls short in two regards. First, neoclassical analysis portrays the CCP's economic policies as abnormal. However, many of the developmental techniques implemented in China were practiced by other East Asian states that also sought to avoid overreliance on more advanced industrial countries and strengthen their geopolitical position. Second, while the CCP did not funnel its big rural population into light industry, government administrators did mobilize large quantities of rural labor for another purpose. The Maoist state routinely made up for scarce domestic machinery by routing masses of rural workers into labor-intensive infrastructure construction projects.

The state capitalist framework, on the other hand, errs in not sufficiently considering the seminal effects that the CCP's identification of China as a socialist country had on its economic course. As students of Marxist-Leninism, CCP leaders followed central pieces of its narrative of how to liberate China from feudalism and capitalism. Following Marxist-Leninism's stagist view of history, Party officials sought to have China progress first to a socialist developmental phase before reaching history's finale and morphing into a communist industrial nation. To attain this end, the Party undertook a series of policies to contain economic practices and actors that were viewed to be in the way of China's progress toward the end of history. Markets and private property were suppressed. The population was classified into political categories that structured their life chances and differentiated their value to socialist development. People in turn came to see their class status not based on their socioeconomic position as Marxism argues is the case in a capitalist system, but rather in terms of their state-assigned political category.

In line with the Soviet model of development, the Communist Party also gave first priority to heavy industrial growth, underfunded rural development, and treated labor exploitation as nonexistent in a socialist system, thereby delegitimating demands by laborers for better working conditions as contrary to the objectives of socialist developmentalism. As a result of the underdevelopment of the countryside, the money-commodity-money relationship, which Marx asserted was characteristic of capitalism, became largely nonoperative in rural areas, as the Party demonetized them to bolster urban industrialization. Cash became very scarce in the urban economy too, as many items were only obtainable with state-issued ration coupons. China's geopolitical standing as a socialist country also significantly impacted its developmental trajectory. Beset by fears that the United States and the Soviet Union might militarily challenge China, Party leaders militarized China's developmental strategy and sanctioned the criticism of anyone who advocated alternative developmental methods as supporting bourgeois capitalist, Soviet, or counterrevolutionary policies that conflicted with the Party's project of building socialism in China.

The Neoclassical Framework

When scholars assess the political economy of Mao's China according to neoclassical principles, the most frequent problem that they cite is its inefficiency (Branstetter and Lardy 2008: 634; Deng and Shen 2019; Lin 2003: 70–90; Lin 2012: 71, 78; Naughton 2007: 80–82). Yet the question is inefficient in comparison to what? The answer is that the Chinese economy was inefficient in comparison to what neoclassical theory assumes to be optimal conduct (Marshall 1890). What the Chinese Communist Party should have done, following neoclassical norms, is favor markets and invest in economic sectors in which it had a comparative advantage (Ricardo 1817). This was not what the Communist Party did. It instituted a planned economy in which government personnel regularly flouted the principle of comparative advantage and tried to keep market activity to a minimum.

According to neoclassical ideas of correct economic behavior, the Communist Party should have recognized that the most efficient method of achieving economic growth was channeling resources toward labor-intensive industries because China was short on capital and had a big population. The Chinese government did not follow this developmental policy. It ignored the comparative advantage that its huge labor force gave it in the labor-intensive light-industrial sector. Instead, it promoted heavy industrial development and pursued import substitution. The latter policy caused the prices of domestic goods to be higher than on international markets, and it enabled Chinese companies to remain inefficient, since they were not subject to foreign pressures to innovate, increase quality control, and improve production methods. Prioritizing heavy industrial development led to inefficiencies too, as start-up costs for projects were higher not only because China had a small existing capital base but also because building heavy industry required larger initial outlays than light industry.

Development in Cold War East Asia

Examined through the lens of neoclassical theory, Chinese developmental policy appears to have irrationally broken with universally valid economic truths. However, when the same policies are placed in regional perspective, Chinese industrial strategy appears not to be unreasonable but rather to be cut from a similar cloth as the economic practices of other East Asian states during the Cold War. In Taiwan, Japan, and the two Koreas, state elites implemented policies of industrial growth that while not exactly the same as China's still had significant overlap. As Bruce Cumings (1999: 88–92) has illustrated, government administrators in all four countries fostered development by nationalizing industries or forming cartels, shielding domestic industry from international competition, intentionally setting high prices for producer goods and low prices for consumer goods, backing import substitution, maximizing the extraction of agricultural resources, suppressing consumption, and maintaining a tight lid on labor politics. Every one of these policies also found favor in Mao's China.

Seen in this light, Chinese economic statecraft was not an aberrant deviation from a presumed neoclassical norm. It was part of a regional trend of East Asian states supervising development to establish a domestic industrial base that prevented national dependency on foreign industrial goods and shored up the country's geopolitical condition. By drawing attention to points of resemblance between the developmental strategies of Mao's China and other states in East Asia, I do not mean to imply that they were identical in every respect. They were most definitely not. There were, however, structural commonalities in how East Asian governments on both sides of the Cold War divide handled national development. They all treated the creation of a robust industrial apparatus as a vital national affair that could not be left to the vicissitudes of domestic or international markets. Central government administrators had to take a leading role in overcoming the nation's underdeveloped state and constructing a new industrial future (Amsden 1989; Johnson 1982; Wade 1990).

Labor-Intensive Infrastructure Construction

Neoclassical interpretations of the Chinese economy under Mao also overlook the central role that labor-intensive methods of economic development played in the CCP's drive to transform China into an industrial nation. As Sigrid Schmalzer (2014: 79) has demonstrated, the CCP had leaned on the mass mobilization of labor as a means of development since the 1930s when it had to make do with the scant resources present in the impoverished mountains of inland China where its revolutionary base areas were located. The form that labor-intensive development assumed after the People's Republic of China's (PRC) establishment in 1949 was not the light-industrial sort that neoclassical economists take China to task for disregarding. It involved Chinese government representatives marshaling large quantities of labor to build economic infrastructure.

Like the CCP's statist approach to development, this strategy of bolstering China's infrastructural foundation was not an economic anomaly only found in socialist China. Its basic method bore a striking resemblance to the policy proposals of developmental economist W. Arthur Lewis. In his landmark 1954 paper "Economic Development with Unlimited Supplies of Labour," Lewis contended that if a country had very little in the way of industrial resources but had a large agricultural population, then one way that the government could bring about industrialization relatively quickly was to restrict consumption and direct idle rural labor toward the construction of infrastructure (Eisenman 2018: 7–8). The CCP pursued an analogous developmental strategy right from the beginning of the PRC, marshaling a hundred thousand rural workers in the early 1950s to build the first railroad executed under CCP rule—the Chengdu-Kunming Line (Chengyu tielu 1953).

In subsequent years, economic planners continued to count on the muscle power of rural labor to complete other railroad projects (Meyskens 2015). The same labor-intensive construction techniques were utilized to erect dams, set up oilfields, reclaim land, put up buildings, fell forests, dig irrigation networks, and construct other pieces of infrastructure (Hershatter 2011: 241; Li 2009: 239–41; Pietz 2015: 174–82, 187–229, 238–51; "Shiyou shiren" 2000; Zhou 2018: 69–86). In all these economic endeavors, government representatives routinely made up for a lack of adequate industrial machinery by mustering a large rural labor force and assigning its members to perform labor-intensive construction work. The Communist Party thus did not ignore its comparative advantage in undertaking economic activities that required a sizable number of workers. Labor-intensive development was indeed central to the Party's approach to building China into a socialist industrial society, just not in the manner prescribed by neoclassical economics.

The State Capitalism Framework

For neoclassical analysts, the principal defect of the political economy of Mao's China was its inefficiency. On the opposite end of the political spectrum, scholars inspired by Marx and his progenitors have dealt with the issue of Chinese development from a rather different perspective. They question whether it is even correct to characterize China during the Mao era as a socialist economy. They argue that the PRC is more appropriately categorized as a form of state capitalism. This line of argumentation has taken two different forms. The first variety bases its claim that Mao's China was a form of state capitalism on the continuing existence of markets and the state's attempt to control market activities. According to this line of reasoning, if markets are operating in a given time and place, and state agents are heavily involved in administering economic relations, then that economic system is rightly classified as an instance of state capitalism.

This line of argumentation has not yet become a well-established histo-riographic position in studies of the Mao period (Gerth 2020; Zhao 2018: 13). It is, however, a well-worn theme in Marxist studies of the Soviet Union and East European states (van der Linden 2007: 59–62, 107–25, 180–92, 258–79). Given the amount of ink that has been spilled determining whether the persistence of markets disqualified the Soviet Union and East European countries as socialist states and made them into state capitalist regimes, it seems likely that this genre of argument will gain more prominence in PRC studies in years to come.

In a recent edited volume (Liu and Murthy 2017), Viren Murthy has argued from a very different theoretical perspective that state capitalism was the dominant politico-economic form in Mao's China. His claim is rooted in the work of Marxist historian Moishe Postone. According to Postone (2017: 44), countries like the Soviet Union and Mao's China were not socialist. They were statist regimes pursuing, in Postone's words, "alternative forms of capitalist accumulation." Postone (2017: 32, 34) comes to this conclusion based on a set of theoretical assumptions. He maintains that "traditional Marxism" has wrongly assumed that a regime is socialist if a proletarian movement forms a political regime that abolishes private property and mar-kets and founds "a new form of society, characterized by collective owner-ship of the means of production and economic planning."

Postone is of the opinion that this view of socialism derives from a faulty interpretation of Marx's analysis of capitalism. According to Postone, the essential characteristics of a capitalist society are not the presence of private property and the market. Rather, the key determining attribute of capital-ism is economic agents exploiting labor through the extraction of surplus value which is reinvested into the production process to increase the accu-mulation of capital. Postone (2017: 40) deduces from this argument that putatively socialist regimes were really state capitalist in character since they constructed elaborate administrative structures to extort surplus value from labor and plough it back into capital accumulation.

Postone is not alone in opining that states in the twentieth century that declared themselves socialist were actually state capitalist. In the history of Western Marxism, many scholars have taken this position (e.g., van der Lin-den 2007). The theoretician who comes closest to encompassing Postone's arguments is Friedrich Pollock. A member of the Frankfurt School, Pollock (1982: 75–78) averred that a governmental regime was state capitalist if it met the following conditions: the replacement of autonomous markets with a governmental regime that manages the entire nation as if it were one huge capitalist factory. Under state capitalism, the whole nation becomes a signal corporation in which different economic sectors are treated like the workshops of a factory whose coordination the state orchestrates to augment the accumulation of national capital. To this end, members of the economic bureaucracy formulate wide-ranging economic plans that designate desired levels of "production, consumption, savings, . . . [and] investments." Prices are set by government fiat. "The profit interests of individuals and groups are subordinated to the general plan," and the national economy is run through a "scientifically-based management" system. All of these governmental activities are undertaken with the aim of boosting the economic resources that the state is able to draw on and deploy to push forward the process of capital accumulation.

Absent from the above analyses of state capitalism is a consideration of international affairs. Since the next part of this paper will consider China's position in the international order, let us consider one final Marxist explanation of why the Soviet Union was state capitalist that could be extended to China. This theory was promulgated by Tony Cliff in the 1970s. Similar to Pollock, Cliff ([1974] 2018) viewed the state in the Soviet Union as transforming the nation into one gigantic capitalist corporation. This nation-corporation was not like a private corporation. It did not take its competitors to be private or public companies striving to obtain more market share. Its competition was other states vying for influence in the global economy. Moreover, since capitalist states were hostile toward the existence of socialist countries, they had to strive to not just economically outcompete capitalist states but also develop defense capabilities that enabled them to survive in an antagonistic world (see also Gerth 2020).

Building Socialism with Marxist-Leninist Characteristics

It is my view that Mao's China was not capitalist but socialist. Behind the Communist Party's claim that China was socialist, there was not, as Postone implies, a solid capitalist core waiting to be uncovered by critical analysis. Nor was China's self-presentation as a socialist regime an act of false consciousness. The Party did not dupe the Chinese public into believing that it was building socialism when in fact China was capitalist all along. People who lived through the Mao era knew what kind of country they experienced— a country that took constructing a socialist economy as a driving political goal.

In making this assertion, I do not intend to deny that Mao's China had markets and that industrial workers were paid a wage. I even accept that work-points given to rural labor were a kind of wage. I also do not debate that the economic system erected during the Mao era was exploitative. It undoubtedly was. Even though Chinese political economy had all these attributes, I still disagree that Mao's China was a state capitalist regime. The logic behind my critique of the state capitalist framework can be summarized with a four-word phrase: China's socialist identity mattered. It informed how the Chinese state managed the economy. It impacted how the Party approached labor exploitation, and it shaped how foreign states related to the People's Republic. Scholars that claim that China in the Mao era was state capitalist do not adequately account for how China's socialist identity was embedded into its domestic and international affairs. Particularly consequential was how the Party leadership's self-perception as carrying forward the political lineage of Marxist-Leninism affected their understanding of the economic norms that the Chinese government had to enforce in the present and pursue in the future to advance China's transformation into a socialist country.

For lifelong communist revolutionaries like Mao Zedong and his comrades in arms, it would have made no sense to argue, as Postone does, that the Party's seizure of state power to execute a proletarian revolution was not a crucial feature of building a socialist country. Quite to the contrary, CCP leaders subscribed, like other Marxist-Leninist state builders, to what Jean-François Lyotard (1984: 32) has called a grand "narrative of emancipation." Years of revolutionary struggle had forged in top CCP members a strongly held belief that their historic purpose was to train "the 'people,' under the name of the 'nation' in order to point them down the path of progress." For CCP elites, history's dialectical arrow did not point toward state capitalism. It was headed toward a future in which the Party had unshackled the Chinese nation from imperialist subjection and removed the remnants of capitalism and feudalism from the Chinese polity (Apter and Saich 1994: 90–95, 115–21; Chen 2001: 7–8).

When Party leaders tried to move the Chinese economy in this progressive direction, the policies that they implemented were rooted in the Marxist-Leninist idea that China had to pass through distinct economic phases, with each phase being more advanced than the last, from feudalism and capitalism to socialism and finally communism. Party leaders' adherence to this historical schema profoundly impacted how they administered economic affairs, as Marxist-Leninism marked off some economic actors and practices as conducive to moving history toward its inevitable communist climax, while other economic activities and agents were tarred as illegitimate holdovers of an oppressive feudal and capitalist system that had to be brought under control and eventually expunged from the political order for the country to experience historical progress (Fitzpatrick 1993; Golfo, 2003: 17; Lenin 1932: 70–75, 78–85). This ideological understanding of what counted as legitimate economic behavior had very practical consequences for the course of Chinese development, as it structured the kinds of resources that the CCP endeavored to accumulate, curb, and jettison.

When the Party founded the PRC, it quickly moved to root out what it perceived to be feudal and capitalist elements within the national economy. Viewing landlords and rich peasants to be relics of a feudal and capitalist past, officials stripped them of their power and property and slotted them into the lower stratum of the social order (Lee and Selden 2009: 29). The Party then reassigned their landholdings to lower and middle peasants, who were entrusted with power over local society (DeMare 2019; Hinton 1966; Selden 1971). Over the course of the 1950s, lower and middle peasants lost their land too, as ownership of land was socialized and transferred to collective institutions (Li 2009: 23–80). Despite this shift in ownership, the political classifications attributed to individuals during land reform continued to structure power relations in rural areas (Wu 2014: 39–40).

People classified as rich peasants and landlords remained in a position of structural inferiority, and people labeled as lower and middle peasants retained positions of authority. Factional conflicts notwithstanding, this political arrangement lasted until the Party annulled the political classification system in the early 1980s. The political labels that the state ascribed to people in the countryside became particularly consequential during the Great Leap Forward when rural cadres used their political connections to provide scarce food to their family members and associates (Cao and Yang 2016). During the other years of the Mao era, leading local rural cadres used their power to give jobs to their close contacts which earned more workpoints and required less physical labor (Li 2009: 133). Political categories were such an enduring feature of social life in the Mao period that people came to develop a sense of class consciousness that was defined not by their relationship to the means of production, as Marxist scholars argue occurs under capitalism (Elster 1986: 29–34). Rather, the "classes" that individuals conceived themselves and others to be members of were none other than the political classifications that government officials assigned them to during land reform (Wemheuer 2019: 29–31; Fitzpatrick 1993).

The reorganization of the rural economy through land reform was only one part of China's transition to socialism according to Marxist-Leninism's eschatological narrative. The CCP had also to eliminate private business in cities and make state-owned and collective enterprises the core building blocks of the urban economy. In parallel to the remaking of the political economy of urban and rural areas, central planning agencies were established to implement governmental policies about what economic resources should be produced and consumed. Only with state control over the means of production institutionally cemented could the Party not only check the private accumulation of wealth through property ownership and the exploitation of labor that prevailed in a capitalist economic system but also orchestrate the building of China into a socialist society (Selden and Lippit 1982; Wemheuer 2019: 17). To ensure that China's transition to socialism had a favorable social environment, urban officials engaged in the same governmental practice as their rural counterparts: they classified members of the urban population in different categories based on whether they were perceived to be integral to constructing socialism in China. Placed atop the political order were revolutionary cadres, industrial workers, and family members of revolutionary martyrs, while capitalists, counterrevolutionaries, and later rightists were relegated to an inferior political status (Wemheuer 2019: 29).

The CCP's stratification of Chinese society into politically suspect and favored categories of people had significant effects on China's developmental path. People deemed dangerous to the regime had to undergo thought reform and were sent to labor camps, where many stayed for decades. Isolated from the larger body politic, these marked people usually could not apply their technical and administrative skills to developmental efforts that matched their educational background and work experience because of the political threat that they were perceived to pose to building socialism in China (Smith 2012; Wang 2017). Although some individuals with bad class labels were still allowed to partake in economic activities that were more closely aligned with their skill set—most notably for projects related to national security—the politics of class status still operated as an important factor structuring the development of Mao's China and the life chances of individuals (Feigenbaum 2003: 72). For example, Zhaojin Zeng and Joshua Eisenman (2018) have demonstrated how attacks on scientists, technicians, and intellectuals during the Anti-Rightist campaign contributed to the subsequent depression of economic growth. Additionally, Andrew Walder and his colleagues have shown that people with a good class status tended to obtain more economic advantages and positions of administrative power than those with negative political classifications, a phenomenon that persisted even after the end of the Mao era (Treiman and Walder 2019; Walder, Li, and Treiman 2000: 191–209).

Socialist Development and Its Limits

The CCP's differentiation of legitimate and illegitimate behavior also led to the devaluation and suppression of economic practices thought to be bourgeois, rightist, or counterrevolutionary, while economic conduct considered by the state to be socialist was thought of positively and encouraged. If a given economic practice was characterized by the state as being socialist, it was politically incorrect to consider it to be exploitative since socialist practices were by definition not exploitative. The Party's politicization of exploitation in this way meant that social groups that sought to challenge economic inequities could be delegitimized by categorizing their demands as bourgeois, rightist, or counterrevolutionary concerns that contradicted the collective aims that the CCP deemed necessary for advancing the construction of socialist China (Shearer 2009). Criticisms of this sort were used by the Party to disempower political movements advocating higher wages or expanding comprehensive welfare benefits beyond the narrow economic realm occupied by state-owned enterprises, whether it was the strike wave in 1957 during the Hundred Flowers Campaign or industrial worker protests in the late 1960s during the Cultural Revolution (Dillon 2015: 157–228; Perry and Xun 1997: 97–117; Wemheuer 2019: 235, 241–42).

The CCP did not constrain the growth of wages and welfare outlays in pursuit of the profit motive, as would have been the case with a capitalist enterprise. Rather, as Alexander Day has detailed in his article for this issue, economic governance in Mao's China was centered on channeling resources toward the production of specific economic resources considered critical to building Chinese socialism. Most consequential on a structural level was the ideological view inherited from the Soviet Union that economic endeavors linked to consumption were "non-productive," closely connected to capitalism, and thus less worthy of development (Golfo 2003: 17; Li and Xia 2018: 75–78).

Imprinted with these negative political associations, the consumer sector was sapped of state investment, as raising consumption was not taken as a political priority but as a capitalist practice that had to be repressed. Central planners poured resources, instead, into the generation of economic goods categorized as "productive" and thereby more integral to the socialist developmental project. Included within this domain were heavy industrial items—such as coal, iron, and machinery—that were part of the aptly named producer goods sector, whose output, rather than serving as consumables, was funneled back into the production process to increase the total production capacity of heavy industry and the amount of economic resources, especially of the heavy industrial sort, available to China's socialist regime (Selden 1992: 113, 121–25, 129–30, 134–35).

In tandem, rural prices and living standards were kept at a minimalistic level, and very few resources were allotted to modernizing agriculture. Funding for rural areas was so low that it became nearly demonetized. Rural residents were principally remunerated for their labor in work-points, earning on average only 11–15 RMB per year in cash (*Nongye* jingji 1983:

516–17). This fiscal situation meant that the money-commodity-money rela-tionship that Karl Marx maintained was a defining feature of a capitalist economy did not hold for the countryside in socialist China (Marx 1909: 168–73). This result was in part a result of cash and commodities being so scarce in rural areas that residents had no money to purchase commodities and even when they did there was little that they could buy. It was also a consequence of how work-points operated. Work-points could not like cash be exchanged for any commodity at any location that recognized the value of the currency used. Work-points were only exchangeable for grain and only at the local work-unit where they were earned (Wemheuer 2019: 24). Similarly in urban areas, a ration coupons regime covered 80 percent of basic consumer goods. Only with ration coupons could workers acquire staple goods such as cloth, grain, milk, eggs, tofu, and oil. Like work-points in rural areas, these coupons were only usable at specific workplaces or only in particular cities or provinces. Very few people were issued ration coupons that were valid throughout the country (Wu 2014: 153).

Instituting work-points in rural areas was partially a way for the Com-munist Party to limit the formation of new rural classes, since all rural resi-dents were treated as agricultural laborers who were paid roughly the same amount in work-points (Wemheuer 2019: 100–101). It was also a way for the government to constrict rural consumption, so that more resources could be directed toward urban industrial development. Though this policy system-atically disadvantaged rural areas, it could not be legitimately called exploit-ative since the Party had officially eliminated exploitation from the Chinese economy. Party leaders pushed the extraction of rural resources for the sake of urban industrialization into high gear in the late 1950s after the CCP determined that China had completed its conversion to the socialist phase of history (meaning the elimination of private ownership of means of produc-tion). As with earlier policy initiatives, Party officials proceeded to embrace a Marxist-Leninist developmental script and debated when the PRC would be ready to reach history's culmination and become a communist society. At Mao's urging, the Party launched the Great Leap to effectuate this penulti-mate move in China's economic trajectory (Walder 2015: 153–57).

If the CCP had thought of the PRC as a capitalist state, it would have never embarked on the Great Leap, since capitalist states do not hold the

Marxist-Leninist view that there is a historical stage after capitalism. Within the political logic of capitalism, there is no future phase of economic history that has to be achieved for historical progress to occur. All that the future holds is more capitalism. While capitalist regimes do acknowledge that a country might become socialist or fascist, this shift in character is not conceived as a historical step forward but as falling backward in history since capitalism is the only politico-economic formation recognized as progressive. If Mao's China had been a capitalist country, there would have therefore been no impetus to engage in a utopian movement like the Great Leap, which aimed to rapidly reach history's developmental end point, since the end of history had already come, and its name was capitalism (Buck-Morss 2000).

Socialist Insecurity and Capitalist Antagonism

The Communist Party's drive to bring China to a higher stage of development was profoundly shaped by its subordinate position within a global capitalist system dominated by the United States, which sought during the Cold War to prevent communist countries from expanding their foreign influence and eventually eliminating communist governments from the world economy, so that only capitalist regimes were left in the international order (Gaddis 1982; Leffler 2007; Westad 2007: 8–38). China's international status as a socialist state imparted Chinese development with a pronounced military bent as it faced off against a hostile capitalist world. This effect was visible from the PRC's very first years.

In 1950, Beijing decided to participate in the Korean War to consolidate control over the national economy and strengthen its alliance with the Soviet Union against the American-led capitalist camp (Garver 2016: 60–62). During the war, roughly 40 percent of state investment went into national defense. After hostilities subsided, while state investment in military industries declined, it remained a significant part of the national budget, as the United States stationed tens of thousands of troops in South Korea, Japan, and the Philippines to contain socialist expansion in East Asia at the hands of Mao's China and the Soviet Union. The breakdown of Sino-Soviet relations in the late 1950s further intensified Beijing's security concerns, as Moscow bivouacked hundreds of thousands of troops on China's northern border and engaged in border skirmishes (Li and Xia 2018: 94). Troubled by the prospect that the United States or the Soviet Union might wage war against China, the Communist Party dedicated an average of 20 percent of the state budget to bolstering its military power from the early 1950s into the early 1970s (Fravel 2019: 72–138, 236–69; Mulvenon 2001: 36–37).

In this regard, the PRC was akin to the Soviet Union, which invested heavily in expanding its military industrial base out of concern that capitalist states might one day attack (Davies 1994: 143; Hanson 2003: 30–34). The PRC also adopted the Soviet Union's policy of prioritizing heavy industry over all other economic sectors, because China shared the Soviet view that heavy industry was critical to maintaining international security in a global environment in which the American-led capitalist world was endeavoring to contain socialist regimes and one day in the future do away with them entirely. In the face of capitalist animosity, Chinese economic planners severely limited investment in the consumer sector and made every effort to ensure that socialist China acquired a heavy industrial apparatus that could overcome enemy forces in the event that war broke out (Lardy 1985: 5). Strategic development choices were thus not simply based on theoretical or ideological frameworks: they were determined and defined by the Cold War imbalance of power, which was heavily tilted in favor of the US and Soviet armed forces, and fostered the very real fears that China's leaders had of their country's weakness.

The Party's apprehension about military threats to Chinese socialism grew even higher in the late 1960s and early '70s. The cause of the Party's trepidation was mounting tensions with the United States and its former-friend-turned-bitter-enemy, the Soviet Union. The CCP leadership worried that the United States might bring its fight against a socialist insurgency in Vietnam onto Chinese soil, and that the Soviet Union might take intensifying border friction as a pretext for a full-scale assault on Chinese territory. To guarantee that socialist China was properly prepared for a Sino-American or Sino-Soviet war, economic planners allocated nearly 40 percent of the capital construction budget to enhance China's military capabilities between 1964 and 1980 in a project called the Third Front (Chen 2003: 235; Garver 2016: 189–91).

When the Third Front campaign was at its height between 1964 and 1972, the central government de-emphasized development in China's industrial heartlands along the coast and in the northeast, since the Party center thought that the United States or the Soviet Union could easily bombard them with air raids or nuclear strikes and reduce coastal industry to rubble. Granted economic priority, the Chinese interior received roughly 50 percent of capital construction investment. Industrial projects were not placed in large cities in inland China because they were also judged to be vulnerable to aerial attacks. They were instead hidden in mountains and scattered over large areas, so that they would be harder for Soviet or American aircraft to find and bomb (Naughton 1988: 354–55). The Communist Party did not undertake this mammoth project to safeguard state capitalism in China. It did so to guarantee that Chinese socialism had sufficient military industrial power to meet the challenge of security threats emanating from Washington and Moscow.

The construction strategies behind the Third Front campaign also bore the imprint of Cold War tensions between the socialist and capitalist world. Concerned that war might break out at any moment, the Party center urged Third Front administrators to race against time to build up the country's military industrial defenses before the United States or the Soviet Union launched an attack (Shapiro 2001: 70–75). According to government orders, this rush to construct an industrial war machine could not principally rely on machinery, machine-made goods, and technically skilled personnel, which were all in short supply. Project administrators had to instead implement what the Party considered to be the socialist way of industrial development. Masses of workers needed to be mobilized to make up for industrial shortages, with manual labor and hand tools replacing machines, and handicrafts substituting for factory-made products. When Third Front participants questioned whether it was feasible to exchange manpower for machinery and technical expertise, the binary politics of the Cold War came into play. Party officials quashed critics by claiming that they were betraying the developmental ways of socialist China and supporting the bourgeois economic methods of the capitalist world and the revisionist techniques of the Soviet Union (Meyskens 2020: 122–64).

The Party's hostility toward the developmental policies of its Cold War enemies were also stamped into the economic practices of everyday life in Mao's China. In the countryside, if someone expressed too much concern in village meetings about how many work-points they were attributed for their labor, there was a serious risk during the Cultural Revolution that they would be charged with being a "capitalist roader" who was disloyal to China's project of building a socialist country in which people were indifferent to receiving personal material rewards for their labor. Others opened themselves up to similar attacks if they advocated higher wages or giving more of the grain harvest to local residents to consume instead of selling it to the state or stockpiling it as reserves (Oi 1989: 150–51). Rural cadres were susceptible to the same kind of criticism if they overly favored their family members and other close relations (Li 2009: 133).

This built-in tendency for calls for more material wealth to be delegitimized in the Mao era played a vital role in economic differentiation being fairly flat within a given rural area and within a given urban area despite the massive economic divide between the city and the countryside. This tendency toward socioeconomic leveling was further reinforced in the urban realm when the Party condemned constructing cities with extensive non-productive facilities as following bourgeois capitalist and Soviet models. For the Chinese to be socialist, urban planners had to reduce the construction of nonproductive buildings—such as administrative offices, cultural centers, and housing—as well as make buildings out of local resources, such as rammed earth or local vegetation, instead of scarce materials, such as cement and iron (Li 2018: 95–134). In this way, socialist China's international conflict with capitalists in the White House and revisionists in the Kremlin became woven into the fabric of everyday life in cities across Cold War China.

Conclusion

When scholars talk about the political economy of the Mao era, they often focus on its faults. In this article, I have evaluated two theoretical approaches, both of which take a narrative of failure as their analytical starting point. Neoclassical economists, on the one hand, criticize Mao's China for not being sufficiently capitalist, maximizing efficiency, and following the principle of comparative advantage. Advocates of the state capitalist paradigm, on the other hand, censure the CCP for not completely purging China of markets, wage labor, and the extraction of surplus value. In both cases, the presumption that Maoist economics was lacking is rooted in a firm conviction of knowing what policies should have been pursued instead of the ones that the CCP implemented. This sense of epistemological certainty leads to analyses that have significant blind spots.

The neoclassical paradigm, for instance, argues that Chinese developmental strategy made the mistake of not complying with universally applicable economic principles. However, from a regional standpoint, it is not Chinese developmental strategy that is out of place in East Asia. It is the neoclassical assumption that comparative advantage defying state-led industrialization was atypical at a time when all East Asian governments sought to administer the growth of a national industrial apparatus that increased their geopolitical and economic power. The neoclassical assertion that Mao's China neglected its comparative advantage in labor-intensive pursuits is equally flawed in that it does not notice the central position that mass mobilization played in the building of state socialism in China.

The theoretical presuppositions underlying the state capitalist framework also make its supporters blind to key features of Maoist development. Convinced that Mao's China was capitalist, adherents of this interpretation fail to consider the structural influence that the PRC's socialist identity had on both domestic policy formation and China's position in the global Cold War. As I have shown, the CCP leadership's subscription to socialism yielded a distinct vision of historical progress that pervaded its developmental policies. The Party's understanding of history's direction came through in the state structures built to develop the economy, the practices the regime endeavored to eradicate, and how state agents utilized resources.

The Party's self-identification as a socialist regime was also apparent in its claim that exploitation had disappeared from the national landscape, how it handled labor discontent, and how it classified the population. The political categories that the CCP used to differentiate Chinese society in turn came to influence people's life chances and led many people in China to understand class through the political labels that the state imputed to the national population, not in terms of their relationship to the means of production. China's placement on the socialist side on the Bamboo Curtain also greatly affected its developmental arc. Apprehensive of nearly constant threats by the United States and the Soviet Union, the Party prioritized holding down consumption, so that the country could maintain a large military budget and invest massive amounts of resources into the expansion of heavy industrial sectors linked to national defense. The Party center assailed as favoring the developmental techniques of bourgeois capitalism or the Soviet Union anyone who came out against the labor-intensive, fast-paced building strategies that the Party center regarded as essential to quickly augmenting China's military industrial complex before Cold War frictions erupted in war. People were likewise castigated as cavorting with China's Cold War opponents for speaking out in favor of raising wages, extending welfare benefits, or lifting consumption standards.

For the field of PRC studies to gain a firmer grasp on the political economy of development in Mao's China, I contend that historians should follow a methodological approach that does not begin with the assumption that Mao's China was an economic failure. As demonstrated in this article, narratives of failure tend to result in explanations that see the Chinese economy not for what it was in practice, but as it could have been if only the Chinese government had put policies into action that were more in line with the analyst's theoretical biases. I call on historians to adopt a different approach to the study of Chinese development and scour available documentation with the aim of comprehending economic practices on their own terms. Achieving this analytical task will require a thorough examination of the logics behind policies advocated by the central leadership and how they were executed. It will also necessitate paying careful attention to state and nonstate actors all the way down to the grassroots, whose economic activities both conformed to and broke with officially sanctioned practices. Only then will it be possible to not flatten out the complexity of how political economy worked under Maoism.

References

Amsden, Alice. 1989. *Asia's Next Giant: South Korea and Late Industrialization*. New York: Oxford University Press.

Apter, David E., and Tony Saich. 1994. *Revolutionary Discourse in Mao's Republic*. Cambridge, MA: Harvard University Press.

Branstetter, Lee, and Nicholas R. Lardy. 2008. "China's Embrace of Globalization." In *China's Great Economic Transformation*, edited by Loren Brandt and Thomas G. Rawski, 633–82. Cambridge: Cambridge University Press.

Buck-Morss, Susan. 2000. *Dream World and Catastrophe: The Passing of Mass Utopia in East and West*. Cambridge, MA: MIT Press.

Cao, Shuji, and Bin Yang. 2016. "Cadres, Grain, and Sexual Abuse in Wuwei County, Mao's China." *Journal of Women's History* 28, no. 2: 33–57.

Chen, Donglin 陈东林. 2003. *Sanxian jianshe:* Beizhan shiqi de xibu da kaifa 三线建设：备战时期的西部大开发 (*The Third Front: Opening the West Campaign of the War Preparation Era*). Beijing: Zhonggong zhongyang dangxiao chubanshe.

Chen, Jian. 2001. *Mao's China and the Cold War*. Chapel Hill: University of North Carolina Press.

Chengyu tielu gongcheng zongjie bianjie weiyuanhui bian 成渝铁路工程总结委员会编. 1953. *Chengyu tielu gongcheng zongjie* 成渝铁路工程总结 (*A Summary of the Chengdu-Chongqing Railroad Project*). Chengdu, China: Tielu bu di er gongchengju yinshuasuo.

Cliff, Tony. (1974) 2018. *State Capitalism in Russia*. Chicago: Haymarket Books.

Cumings, Bruce. 1999. *Parallax Visions: Making Sense of American-East Asian Relations at the End of the Century*. Durham, NC: Duke University Press.

Davies, R. W. 1994. "Industry." In *The Economic Transformation of the Soviet Union, 1913–1945*, edited by R. W. Davies, Mark Harrison, and S. G. Wheatcroft, 131–57. New York: Cambridge University Press.

Demare, Brian. 2019. *Land Wars: The Story of China's Agrarian Revolution*. Stanford, CA: Stanford University Press.

Deng, Kent, and Jim H. Shen. 2019. "From State Resource Allocation to a 'Low Level Equilibrium Trap': Re-evaluation of Economic Performance of Mao's China, 1949–78." London School of Economics and Political Science, Economic History Working Paper No. 298, July. eprints.lse.ac.uk/101127/1/Deng_from_state_resource_allocation_published.pdf.

Dillon, Nara. 2015. *Radical Inequalities: China's Revolutionary Welfare State in Comparative Perspective*. Cambridge, MA: Harvard University Asia Center.

Eisenman, Joshua. 2018. "Commune Kabuki: Development and Productivity Growth under Maoist China's Rural Collectives." *Development and Change* 49, no. 6: 1553–79.

Elster, Jon. 1986. *An Introduction to Karl Marx*. Cambridge: Cambridge University Press.

Feigenbaum, Evan. 2003. *China's Techno-Warriors: National Security and Strategic Competition from the Nuclear to the Information Age*. Stanford, CA: Stanford University Press.

Fitzpatrick, Sheila. 1993. "Ascribing Class: The Construction of Social Identity in Soviet Russia." *Journal of Modern History* 65, no. 4: 745–70.

Fravel, M. Taylor. 2019. *Active Defense: China's Military Strategy since 1949*. Princeton, NJ: Princeton University Press.

Fukuyama, Francis. 1992. *The End of History and the Last Man*. New York: Free Press.

Gaddis, John Lewis. 1982. *Strategies of Containment: A Critical Appraisal of Postwar American National Security Policy*. New York: Oxford University Press.

Gaddis, John Lewis. 1997. *We Now Know: Rethinking Cold War History*. New York: Oxford University Press.

Garver, John W. 2016. *China's Quest: The History of the Foreign Relations of the People's Republic of China*. Oxford: Oxford University Press.

Gerth, Karl. 2020. *Unending Capitalism: How Consumerism Negated China's Communist Revolution*. Cambridge: Cambridge University Press.

Golfo, Alexopoulos. 2003. *Stalin's Outcasts: Aliens, Citizens, and the Soviet State, 1926–1936*. Ithaca, NY: Cornell University Press.

Hanson, Philip. 2003. *The Rise and Fall of the Soviet Economy: An Economic History of the USSR from 1945*. London: Pearson Education.

Hershatter, Gail. 2011. *The Gender of Memory: Rural Women and China's Collective Past*. Berkeley: University of California Press.

Hinton, William. 1966. *Fanshen: A Documentary of Revolution in a Chinese Village*. New York: Monthly Review Press.

Johnson, Chalmers. 1982. *MITI and the Japanese Miracle: The Growth of Industrial Policy, 1925–1975*. Stanford, CA: Stanford University Press.

Lardy, Nicholas R. 1985. *Agriculture in China's Modern Economic Development*. New York: Cambridge University Press.

Lee, Ching Kwan, and Mark Selden. 2009. "Inequality and Its Enemies in Revolutionary and Reform China." *Economic and Political Weekly* 43, no. 52: 27–36.

Leffler, Melvyn P. 2007. *For the Soul of Mankind: The United States, the Soviet Union, and the Cold War*. New York: Hill and Wang.

Lenin, V. I. 1932. *State and Revolution*. New York: International Publishers.

Lewis, W. Arthur. 1954. "Economic Development with Unlimited Supplies of Labour." *Manchester School* 22, no. 2: 139–91.

Li, Huaiyin. 2009. *Village China under Socialism and Reform: A Micro-History, 1948–2008*. Stanford, CA: Stanford University Press.

Li Danhui and Yafeng Xia. 2018. *Mao and the Sino-Soviet Split, 1959–1973*. Lanham, MD: Rowman and Littlefield.

Lin, Yifu Justin. 2003. *The Chinese Miracle: Development Strategy and Economic Reform*. Hong Kong: Chinese University Press.

Lin, Yifu Justin. 2012. *Demystifying the Chinese Economy*. Cambridge: Cambridge University Press.

Liu, Joyce C. H., and Viren Murthy, eds. 2017. *East-Asian Marxisms and Their Trajectories*. London: Routledge.

Lyotard, Jean-François. 1984. *The Postmodern Condition: A Report on Knowledge*. Minneapolis: University of Minnesota Press.

Marshall, Alfred. 1890. *Principles of Economics*. London: Macmillan.

Marx, Karl. 1909. *Capital: A Critique of Political Economy. Volume I: The Process of Capitalist Production*. Chicago: Charles H. Kerr and Company.

Meyskens, Covell. 2015. "Third Front Railroads and Industrial Modernity in Late Maoist China." *Twentieth Century China* 40, no. 3: 238–60.

Meyskens, Covell. 2020. *Mao's Third Front: The Militarization of Cold War China*. New York: Cambridge University Press.

Mulvenon, James. 2001. *Soldiers of Fortune: The Rise and Fall of the Chinese Military-Business Complex, 1978–1998*. Armonk, NY: M.E. Sharpe.

Naughton, Barry. 1988. "The Third Front: Defence Industrialization in Chinese Interior." *China Quarterly* 115: 351–86.

Naughton, Barry. 2007. *The Chinese Economy: Transitions and Growth*. Cambridge, MA: MIT Press.

Nong mu yu ye bu jihua si. 1983. *Nongye jingji ziliao, 1949–1983*. Beijing: Nong mu yu ye bu jihua si.

Oi, Jean C. 1989. *State and Peasant in Contemporary China: The Political Economy of Village Government*. Berkeley: University of California Press.

Perry, Elizabeth J., and Li Xun. 1997. *Proletarian Power: Shanghai in the Cultural Revolution*. Boulder, CO: Westview Press.

Pietz, David A. 2015. *The Yellow River: The Problem of Water in Modern China*. Cambridge, MA: Harvard University Press.

Pollock, Friedrich. 1982. "State Capitalism." In *The Essential Frankfurt School Reader*, edited by Andrew Arato and Eike Gebhardt, 71–94. New York: Continuum.

Postone, Moishe. 2017. "Marx, Temporality, and Modernity." In *East-Asian Marxisms and Their Trajectories*, edited by Joyce C. H. Liu and Viren Murthy, 29–48. London: Routledge.

Ricardo, David. 1817. *On the Principles of Political Economy and Taxation*. London: John Murray.

Schmalzer, Sigrid. 2014. "Self-Reliant Science: The Impact of the Cold War on Science in Socialist China." In *Science and Technology in the Global Cold War*, edited by Naomi Oreskes and John Krige, 75–106. Cambridge, MA: MIT Press.

Selden, Mark. 1971. *The Yenan Way in Revolutionary China*. Cambridge, MA: Harvard University Press.

Selden, Mark. 1992. *The Political Economy of Chinese Development*. London: Routledge.

Selden, Mark, and Victor Lippit, eds. 1982. *The Transition to Socialism in China*. Armonk, NY: M. E. Sharpe.

Shapiro, Judith. 2001. *Mao's War Against Nature: Politics and the Environment in Revolutionary China*. New York: Cambridge University Press.

Shearer, David R. 2009. *Policing Stalin's Socialism: Repression and Social Order in the Soviet Union, 1924–1953*. New Haven, CT: Yale University Press.

"Shiyou shiren" Changqing youtian bianweihui 石油师人 长庆油田编委会. 2000. "*Shiyou shiren": Zai Changqing youtian jishi* 石油师人: 在长庆油田纪实 (*"Oil Soldiers": On-the-Spot Record of the Changqing Oilfield*). Beijing: Shiyou gongye chubanshe.

Smith, Aminda M. 2012. *Thought Reform and China's Dangerous Classes: Reeducation, Resistance, and the People*. Lanham, MD: Rowman and Littlefield.

Treiman, Donald J., and Andrew G. Walder. 2019. "The Impact of Class Labels on Life Chances in China." *American Journal of Sociology* 124, no. 4: 1125–63.

van der Linden, Marcel. 2007. *Western Marxism and the Soviet Union: A Survey of Critical Theories and Debates since 1917*. Leiden, Netherlands: Brill.

Wade, Robert. 1990. *Governing the Market: Economic Theory and the Role of Government in Taiwan's Industrialization*. Princeton, NJ: Princeton University Press.

Walder, Andrew G. 2015. *China under Mao: A Revolution Derailed*. Cambridge, MA: Harvard University Press.

Walder, Andrew G., Bobai Li, and Donald J. Treiman. 2000. "Politics and Life Chances in a State Socialist Regime: Dual Career Paths into the Urban Chinese Elite, 1949 to 1996." *American Sociological Review* 65, no. 2: 191–209.

Wang, Ning. 2017. *Banished to the Great Northern Wilderness: Political Exile and Re-education in Mao's China*. Ithaca, NY: Cornell University Press.

Wemheuer, Felix. 2019. *A Social History of Maoist China: Conflict and Change, 1949–1976*. Cambridge, MA: Cambridge University Press.

Westad, Odd Arne. 2007. *The Global Cold War: Third World Interventions and the Making of Our Times*. Cambridge: Cambridge University Press.

Wu, Yiching. 2014. *The Cultural Revolution at the Margins: Chinese Socialism in Crisis*. Cambridge, MA: Harvard University Press.

Zeng, Zhaojin, and Joshua Eisenman. 2018. "The Price of Persecution: The Long-Term Effects of the Anti-Rightist Campaign on Economic Performance in Post-Mao China." *World Development* 109: 249–60.

Zhao, Mi. 2018. "State Capitalism and Entertainment Markets: The Socialist Transformation of Quyi in Tianjin, 1949–1964." *Modern China* 44, no. 5: 525–56.

Zhou, Shuxuan. 2018. "We Planted All These Trees Decades Ago: Elder Activism against Devaluing Women's Labour." In *Gender Dynamics, Feminist Activism, and Social Transformation*, edited by Wu Guoguang, Feng Yuan, and Helen Lansdowne, 69–86. London: Routledge.

Foundations of Theory in PRC History:

Mass Communications Research, Political Culture, and the Values Paradigm

Matthew D. Johnson

In fact, today, research on China's contemporary history is already situated in this process of rapid change: First, from reform and opening onward, contemporary history has already been incorporated into the content of university history teaching. Second, in 1987 the People's Congress passed the Archive Law, which includes the article that international conventions stipulate declassification of government archives after thirty years; although the degree of archival openness varies by location, most have implemented this law, and have carried out declassification work year by year. Third, following the post-1949 establishment of the Chinese mainland work unit personnel file system and its reform and opening, [now that] a large number of lower-level units no longer exist, individual, work unit, and other nongovernmental (*minjian*) historical materials have appeared everywhere, creating plentiful research conditions for the study of microhistory, individual history, and social history. Fourth, within the past ten years, scholars of history who originally rejected research on contemporary history—in particular our colleagues—have

positions 29:4 DOI 10.1215/10679847-9286727
Copyright 2021 by Duke University Press

now increasingly begun to set foot into this field, especially with regard to micro-history and social history, where a good-sized contingent of researchers is already in the midst of forming, and moreover a considerable number of scholarly achievements have begun to accumulate. Although all of this can only be called the start (*qibu*) of Chinese mainland contemporary history research, the foundation of this start is sturdy and steeped in hope.
—Yang 2012: 149

This passage written by historian Yang Kuisong provides a succinct introduction to the conditions and methods that have created the field of the history of the People's Republic of China (PRC). The essay from which it is drawn, titled "The Start and Significance of Historical Research on Contemporary China," was published as the introduction to a special section of the May 2012 issue of the Shanghai Academy of Social Sciences' *Journal of Social Sciences* (*Shehui kexue*). Shanghai has a reputation for intellectual openness compared with other major cities in China. Its former foreign concessions also testify to China's history of colonization at the hands of stronger countries—empires of "the West" and Japan.

The collective assessment of PRC historiography introduced by Yang's essay can be seen as reflecting some of Shanghai's openness. Several essays for the section titled "A Written Conversation on 'Building the Discipline of China's Contemporary History'" ("Zhongguo dangdai shi xueke jianshe" *bitan*) criticize what they depict as orthodox frameworks and categories of historical interpretation. Their authors are after something new. As the passage from Yang's essay suggests, these historians want to write histories of individuals and local societies, not of political movements, and not of glorious leaders and their achievements. Their history is not "Party history." Instead, "starting" to write the history of contemporary China (by which is meant China after 1949) involves creating an entirely new historical discipline, in the sense that history is now written from the perspective of smaller social units and more localized narratives. This is history "from below."

Several of the essays also reflect the lessons of Shanghai's postcolonial experience—legacies that also infuse the official historiography of the PRC and, at least to a degree, the politics of the history profession generally. Bottom-up history must also be made national in method as well as subject. Foreign scholars are described (with frustration) as already possessing a "notable advantage" in producing research about important recent events such as the Cultural Revolution (Jin 2012: 160–61). Imported terminology, viewpoints, and discursive systems are described as threatening to "colonize" China's intellectual culture (Jiang 2012: 156). These manifestations of historiographical invasion prompt further questions, such as whether theory derived from the experiences of other societies—the example chosen was French sociologist Pierre Bourdieu's theory of cultural capital—was really applicable to China's particularities and unique trajectory (Yang and Cao 2012: 166–69). This is history in which empiricism holds the key to constructing theory that is novel, independent, and yet still grounded in a sense of collective truth.

Both the reconstruction of history as a break from existing narratives and the reconstruction of history as collective and political act, are issues that are familiar to most writers of history. Historical writing in China, as elsewhere, is informed by internal debates concerning which conceptual frameworks should be applied to understanding and interpreting the past for others—these frameworks of interpretation are what is meant by "theory." To some, microhistory, individual history, and social history are the most relevant theories to apply to new archival sources and interviews, as expressed in the passage from Yang Kuisong's essay. For others, more specific theoretical tools are needed to elucidate interrelationships between various parts of the total social order that might be harder to name or perceive at first glance: for example, the role of cultural capital in determining which ideologies had the greatest influence among twentieth-century revolutionary intellectuals. Another, more encompassing view would describe even the most abstraction-free statements of fact as theory-laden, the construction of particular kinds of knowledge around particular peoples and areas (Schwartz [1980] 1996: 103). Inevitably, writing about the past involves questions of whether theory is applicable, whose theory is applicable, and how power dynamics affect the description of past experience. No matter how we write history, we engage with theory.

Or maybe it is the other way around—that theory engages with us. This article describes the origins of the PRC history field in the United States as one way of addressing the question posed by the editors of this special issue:

how PRC history is written and should be written. Its starting point is how PRC history *has* been written. Unlike Yang Kuisong's account, the conditions I begin with are not archives, memories, or other reminders of the past, but instead what I call the *values paradigm* of social change. Like "theory, "paradigm" is a somewhat amorphous metaphor for ways or systems of thinking. The way it is used in this article is to indicate a normalized and enduring scholarly practice through which researchers interpreting the society of the PRC have organized their observations as knowledge (T. S. Kuhn 1962: 1–20; Heilbron 1998). My argument concerning the values paradigm is that research on PRC history is widely derived from an approach to knowledge that predates area studies: the theory that societies can be controlled and changed through the transformation of human cognition—referred to as "public opinion," "values," "culture," "political culture," "tradition," or "belief"—by nonviolent means.[1] A separate, but related argument is that this paradigm has proven more important than the availability or content of new sources in determining how PRC history has been written.

My goal in making these arguments is twofold: to highlight the intellectual debt (or burden) that links PRC history, via area studies, to policy science; and to elucidate other ways of guiding research in place of the increasingly exhausted values paradigm–based approach. The first section of the article therefore addresses the beginnings of mass communications research in the United States, and in particular the impact of war on experimental science, which created the institutional and theoretical basis for studying change in external societies and its susceptibility to media influence. This was the "revolution" from which the values paradigm emerged. Next, the article addresses how concepts of communications and culture, including political culture, became embedded within area studies, and how they were subsequently accepted by the scholarly community within area studies that sought to observe the process of China's post-1949 politics and formulate explanations for the apparent efficacy of Communist Party rule. During roughly the period between the Cultural Revolution (1966–76) and availability of new sources and archives (1980s–90s), the China field as a whole began to show more signs of theoretical completion. However, as the article's third section shows, the revival of Chinese political culture as an explanatory variable in modeling and predicting political behavior returned as "neoculturalism," which posited a familiar relationship between state and society based on shared repertoires of symbols and values—while, at the same time, jettisoning the normative assumption that state-society relations in China would evolve in the direction of liberal democracy. In the final section, the article details how neoculturalism's efficient, if narrow, argument for the explanatory primacy of values over structures has further evolved into a theory of cultural governance, or cultural control, that posits the Party-state as the most important variable in explaining social change and individual behavior.

Hidden political commitments of intellectuals are part of the chief lore of scholarly research communities. Such mysteries, as well as the "fears, expectations, desires, and repressed elements" signaled by theoretical allegiances (Ankersmit 2001: 1), lie beyond the scope of analysis here; intellectual history is what remains. Several contributors to this special issue argue for theoretical allegiance to Maoism or "left PRC history." Their starting point is that we should "take Maoism seriously" and critically interrogate "positivistic empiricism." I can think of no historian of the PRC, left or otherwise, who does not think that Maoism was important, or who would not admit that methods and categories of historiographical writing can obscure as much as they illuminate. In *Maoism at the Grassroots: Everyday Life in China's Era of High Socialism* (Brown and Johnson 2015), a book I coedited, historians from around the world grappled with the question of what we could learn about PRC history from the perspective of new sources, using methods that privileged narrating history from the bottom up rather than the top down. What we found was that Maoism—which I would define (no doubt naively to some) as veneration of the figure of Mao Zedong, acceptance and use of "Mao Zedong Thought," and Party-state orchestration of mass mobilization carried out in Mao's name—was not ubiquitous in PRC society. We also found that the state-society dichotomy did not capture the historical change that we were seeing at the individual and local level, and we argued instead for the importance of particularism and "the presence of individual and collective responses to centralizing, hegemonic forms of state power" (Brown and Johnson 2015: 5). Important to what? In our view, important to understanding the forces and changes that shaped everyday existence. Social scientists had admitted to the existence of particularism, but their view of change was top-down and ultimately rested on two flawed methodological assumptions: that the Party-state behaved the same everywhere (it didn't), and that resistance to the "Party Center," including from within the Chinese Communist Party (CCP) itself, was Mao-led and only widespread during the Cultural Revolution (we saw it occurring earlier, and as an intrinsic feature of everyday life).

What this means for PRC history is, and should be, up for debate. Part of the answer will depend on how theoretical frameworks impact our organization and interpretation of the empirical. In the introduction to *Maoism at the Grassroots*, and in the conclusion to this article, I have suggested that the narrower debate over whether Maoism is important for understanding the experience of everyday life sidesteps the Party-state's use of violence and other forms of coercion to compel behavior that conforms with "Maoist logics."[2] My point is that we need a theory, and especially a theory of the process by which societies become totalistically politicized, that can accommodate the obvious fact of coercion in creating and reproducing new forms of social order, whether in China or elsewhere. I also think that present-day politics demand we point to this coercion without valorizing it. Does this mean "attempting to erase any positive aspects of the socialist project," as argued against in this special issue's introduction? Maybe, but that accusation misses another point, which is that the socialist project was demonstrably contested in its own time. And so to take as a starting point the assumption that narrating China's past requires accepting the universality of Maoist consciousness, mass-line "praxis," and so on may be good for "left" politics, but it is not good for historical understanding. Which gets to the real core of what this article is about—how historical and social scientific explanations of political change in China have become intellectually dependent on the abstraction of mass consciousness, and how this abstraction has been used to paper over Maoism's endemic violence.

Engineering Values:
The Policy Science of Mass Communications and Social Change

Before there were area studies and Chinese studies, American communications researchers put the question of how societies could be managed through media at the center of scholarly inquiry in the social sciences. World War I had taught thinkers and policymakers that mass communication technology could serve strategic needs by mobilizing, or demoralizing, populations psychologically. After World War I, attention turned to the underpinnings of political behavior, in particular the "management of opinion" by governments and the emerging fields of professional public relations and advertising (Mattelart [1991] 1994: 64–66). Another behavioral theory to emerge from the study of social psychology, "mass culture," attributed integration in both capitalist and noncapitalist societies to the role of media technologies in homogenizing popular values (Bell 1997: 112). What these experimental approaches had in common was their search for a theory of how human behavior could be modified through the use of media. Through them, social change became conceptually linked to the organization of individuals into communities sharing common attitudes and worldviews.

Harold D. Lasswell was a figure of considerable consequence in further distilling wartime experience into the emerging policy science of mass communications. During World War I, Lasswell had worked with University of Chicago political scientist Edward Mirriam while the latter was chief American war propagandist in Rome. Under Mirriam's guidance, Lasswell wrote a doctoral dissertation later published as *Propaganda Technique in the World War* (1927), which combined content analysis with psychological theory (Almond 1987: 252). Lasswell (1927: 2–10) sought to explain the phenomenon of propaganda: the control of public opinion and the impact of opinion on world politics. The bedrock of his research consisted of the assumptions that propaganda was effective in mobilizing populations to act and that its effects could be further refined and improved through technical study. During the 1930s, Lasswell sought to further identify the national symbols and mentalities that impacted attitudes toward international relations, resulting in monographs such as *World Politics and Personal Insecurity* (1935). Lasswell's work as a political scientist was notable for its emphasis on value patterns in society as the basis for how political power was exercised; change occurred as a result of the definition and distribution of dominant social values by and among elites. Within this framework, opinion management connected elite values to society. The journal *Public Opinion* served as a forum in which Laswell and other researchers reported new findings concerning the impact of persuasive communication on groups within American society. Much of this new research was underwritten by the Rockefeller Foundation, whose trustees sought "democratic prophylaxis" against the effects of Soviet and Axis propaganda on America's immigrant population (Simpson 1994: 22).

The primacy of values change and its operational derivative, opinion management, in political study became further consolidated during World War II, when mass communications research fed directly into psychological warfare. The interwar period had given rise to a cluster of institutional projects focused on the engineering of mass consent: Lasswell at the Library of Congress; public opinion analyst Hadley Cantril's Princeton Public Opinion Research Project; and mathematician-turned-psychologist Paul Lazarsfeld's Office of Radio Research at Columbia University (Simpson 1994: 22). During World War II, Lasswell worked with the Library of Congress and Department of Justice to pioneer media content analysis on a world scale, while also serving as a consultant for the Office of War Information (OWI), the Office of Strategic Services (OSS), the Federal Communications Commission Foreign Broadcast Monitoring Service, and the US Army's Psychological Warfare Branch. Communications researchers were not the only academics to assist in formulating and implementing wartime political communication policies; area studies scholars also supported US propaganda and intelligence agencies such as the OWI and OSS (Cumings 1999: 173). As a result, the World War II period considerably intensified fusion between mass communications research and international affairs.

Communications-centered theories of social change focused on the relationship between elites, symbols, and mass society at the national and international levels. In the context of the Cold War, international communication research was particularly valued for its relevance to the global political struggle between the United States and the USSR (Mattelart [1991] 1994: 90–93). Media content analysis was used by Lasswell and a new cohort of researchers, including sociologist Daniel Lerner and political scientist Ithiel de Sola Pool, to produce insights into foreign elite behavior and public opinion; Lerner and Pool went on to shape the activities of important new centers such as the Hoover Institution (and its Carnegie Corporation–funded Revolution and the Development of International Relations [RADIR] Project) and Center for International Studies (CENIS) at the Massachusetts

Institute of Technology. Post–World War II studies differed from earlier mass communications research in terms of the examination of wider processes of social change, such as modernization and democratization, and by incorporating a wider range of factors in explaining human behavior.[3] Culture and "national character" were measured and analyzed as environmental determinants believed to shape political thought, feeling, and actions (McGuire 2004: 23–27). Research moved beyond support for war and into the realm of international development policy, where American policymakers sought to legitimate nonviolent forms of global intervention through appeals to the predictive power of social science (Gilman 2007).

The seemingly effective use of mass communication technology for war during the first half of the twentieth century created new theories of social change and intellectual tools to analyze them. As a result, communication became understood as a powerful interface between elites and societies, and between the United States and other countries. Post–World War II social science scholarship thus came to view change in terms of both elite management and preexisting environmental conditions such as culture within area studies–defined regions. Analysis of symbols and media content doubled as insight into elite and popular values; theory that posited communications as the key link between political systems and society was further validated by systems-theoretical thinking, or "system sciences," which treated political systems as machines for control (Eriksson 2011: 131). The new field of cybernetics, combining social science with information science—and, increasingly, biology and neuroscience—dominated the policy-research nexus and aligned theory with the conceptual territory of bureaucratic management (Pooley 2008: 45).

China's Politics:
Communication and Culture as Explanations of Political Behavior

In the eyes of policymakers, post–World War II industrial society was characterized not by a restoration of order but by a control crisis. State institutions cultivated and leveraged intellectuals to provide policy advice on issues ranging from domestic political integration to the coordination of overseas markets (Beniger 1986: 11). The Social Science Research Council (SSRC) and American Council of Learned Societies (ACLS), already enlisted as sources for recruitment of "academic advisors" during World War II, were put to the task of producing policy-relevant research suited to the purpose of global competition under Cold War conditions (Cumings 1999: 176; Engerman 2009). In the words of one SSRC report, what was needed from area specialists was "research knowledge about every region" to inform the strategies of decision-makers (Bennett 1951: 4–5). Mass communications research was linked to new goals defined by modernization theory and development—specifically, the integration of foreign countries into the US-planned global industrial economy (Escobar 1995; Engerman et al. 2003). Daniel Lerner, in particular, placed media at the center of American policy discussions concerning how "traditional" peoples could be motivated and influenced to become modern (Lerner 1958; Shah 2011).

Research on China was impacted by all of these developments, perhaps none more than the application of mass communications theory to modeling of the CCP-led revolution. Studies of Communist Party and Nationalist Party elites by Ithiel de Sola Pool and political scientist Robert North showed continuity with earlier mass communications research by focusing on the relationship between values and political change (North and Pool 1952). However, a new paradigm began to emerge in 1955 as a result of the SSRC's Committee on Comparative Politics and Committee on Political Behavior sponsorship of conferences meant to foster interdisciplinary theories of foreign political systems that would supersede narrower area studies–based models (Almond and Coleman 1960: vii). Publication of *The Politics of Developing Areas* (1960), edited by political scientists Gabriel A. Almond and James S. Coleman, marked the emergence of regional political behavior as a discrete object of study: "If we are to improve our capacity for explaining and predicting the directions of political change and, in particular, the prospects of democratic modernization in these areas, it is more important to analyze their traditional cultures, the impact of Western and other influences on them, their political socialization and recruitment practices, and their political 'infrastructures'—interest groups, political parties, and media of communication" (Almond and Coleman 1960: viii). China was not a major concern of the volume's authors, though a chapter on the politics of Southeast Asia was written by Lucien W. Pye, who had worked with both Almond and Harold Lasswell when writing a doctoral dissertation on China's warlord politics during the 1920s. Where the volume belied its debt to mass communications approaches, however, was in its treatment of ideas and emotions—including those inherited from "traditional culture"—as key variables in the explanation of political behavior. Cultural change, along with the increasingly mass nature of politics and political organizations, represented critical links in the causal chain that shaped politics' "behavioral base" (Almond and Coleman 1960: 3–4, 149–50).

Cultural explanations for national behavior were common within area studies if not social science. If anything, social scientists like Pye injected a more dynamic view of social experience into the discussion by portraying political change as the outcome of interactions between elite-driven modernization processes and preexisting cultural values. In *Communications and Political Development* (1963), edited by Pye with an introduction from Almond, communications research was cited approvingly for having illustrated the importance of mass communications in political development—a reference to democratization—and the "complex process by which cultural values are transmitted" within societies (Pye 1963: ix). Pye credited communications with "pressure" leading to the downfall of traditional societies and with the success, or failure, of subsequent nation-building efforts. The "flow of information and control of messages" was thus key to shaping the political process of modernization—a theory that was linked directly with cybernetics and organization theory (Pye 1963: 3–5). Tension existed between the achievement of nation-statehood and the "particularistic character of each nation as it reflects its cultural and social history" or the "psychological and cultural character of [its] people" (Pye 1963: 12–20). Communications research brought to light "essential dynamics of the original traditional society . . . most important in determining the ability of the society to accept and reject specific qualities of the world culture" (Pye 1963: 19–20). Understanding aspirations, values, standards, needs, ideas, expectations, and other cognitive foundations of social behavior were matters central to political and social analysis. However, Pye was also quick to return the discussion to policy-relevant questions of how to "preserve community" and manage conflict between values while moving societies toward an end state of democratic modernity.

Focus on communications and, increasingly, culture as explanations for political behavior in the "developing areas" of the world had a direct and visible impact on the China field in the 1960s and 1970s. Analysis of CCP governance reflected a focus on values and beliefs as primary drivers of change. The paradigm had both positive and negative variants. On the positive side, political scientist Franklin S. Houn argued that propaganda, as a form of communication, was essential to postrevolutionary control over China's society, due to the Communists' ability to engineer ideological conformity through the mass media (Houn 1961). This theory was pursued further by Frederick T. C. Yu (1964) and, later, Alan P. L. Liu (1971). Liu's *Communications and National Integration in Communist China*, which began as a dissertation directed by Ithiel de Sola Pool and Lucian Pye, further argued that the importance of communication to Communist leaders was related both to their totalitarian political ideology and China's status as a developing nation; in addition to serving purposes of social control, mass media and other forms of "agitation" contributed to national integration and economic development (Liu 1971: 1–2). Communications-based studies argued that the CCP's creation of new values and beliefs had produced a transformation of China's entire social structure (Chu 1977), while other scholars expanded the scope of inquiry beyond propaganda and media to ask how distinctive forms of Communist organization, such as the small group (*xiaozu*), were used to create a new "empire" through thought reform and attitudinal reorientation (Whyte 1974: 1–2).

According to researchers who espoused the negative impact of culture under the values paradigm, it was preexisting traditional beliefs—termed "political culture"—that controlled and distorted the developing world's transition toward modernity. Described as the "embedded . . . pattern of orientation to political actions" within a society, political culture marked a return to studies of national character while claiming to offer more illuminating perspectives on differences between political systems and the individual psychology of populations (Pye 1965: 7, 8–11). The concept, developed by Gabriel Almond and political scientist Sidney Verba, was adopted by policy-focused Asia experts such as Lucien Pye for the purpose of comparing patterns of national development and identifying methods for "best produc[ing] desired changes in a nation's politics" (Pye 1965: 11). Grounded in the assumption that social change, and political development in particular, was rooted in beliefs about politics, Pye and others looked for "constants" in Chinese culture that would explain the CCP's emergence and the apparent success of its authoritarian political system (Pye 1966; Pye 1971).

Studies in the political culture mold reopened inquiry into the sources of social values through the analysis of individual and group dynamics, kinship structure, and canonical texts—a move that suggested, though did not directly acknowledge, legacies of the "culture and personality" paradigm within anthropology, represented by figures such as Clyde Kluckhohn, Margaret Mead, and Ruth Benedict.[4] Society was understood as a culturally bound system, an assumption that further linked the political culture approach, like the communications-based studies with which it overlapped, to systems sciences and cybernetics.[5] Political culture researchers were distinguished by their adoption of the vocabulary of psychology: Lucien Pye's *The Spirit of Chinese Politics: A Psychocultural Study of the Authority Crisis in Political Development* (1968) was a signal work in this regard, as was Richard Solomon's *Mao's Revolution and the Chinese Political Culture* (1971). Solomon was Pye's student. What further connected both scholars was their shared effort to explain the disorder and failure of China's Great Proletarian Cultural Revolution as arising from the modernization process. Culture, and its manifestation through psychology, was the source of this disorder, in particular the dependency on authority taught by Confucian tradition. While such views appear largely discredited within the field of China studies today, their major legacy was the explanation of political behavior in terms of cultural variables.

Political culture was a refinement rather than a break with the interpretation of tradition and premodern political structures in modernization theory-based social science. In early formulations, political culture—"rooted in the native genius of each nation"—was treated as the key determinant of "orientation to political actions" throughout national societies (Pye 1965: 3–4). Political development unfolded, or was inhibited, according to how cultural traditions impacted ideologically differing versions of modernization (Pye 1963). However, instead of positing an abstract collision between modernity and tradition, political culture researchers sought to demonstrate how the specific characteristics of comparative political systems arose from the distinctive, culturally embedded psychologies of both leaders and the led.

What political culture did not do was simply subsume the other major theoretical strand to emerge from the values paradigm, which posited that political change in China was driven primarily by the organizational capacity of the CCP and, in particular, its ability to engineer mass conformity through the media and cognate "mobilization" practices. Both strands assigned considerable explanatory power to the cognitive foundations of social behavior, whether described as "values," "culture," "ideology," "psychology," or "belief." In *Ideology and Organization in Communist China*, sociologist and historian Franz Schurmann (1966: 58) described practical ideology—the "instrument of action" for political organizations—as a "system of communications" that created common categories of the thoughts and actions of individuals.[6] The mass communications strand further evolved in work by Alan Liu (1971), which integrated subnational perspectives and modernization theory into the image of the party-driven organization model proposed by Schurmann, underscoring ideological differences within the CCP as well as infrastructural limitations to media reach.

By the end of the 1970s, research on mass communications and culture as explanations of political change (and its disorders) had broken away from earlier post–World War II scholarship in two ways: first, by shifting the focus of comparative politics away from elites (e.g., Pool and Wright 1951; North and Pool 1952) and toward social dynamics and cultural practices; and second, by understanding totalitarian and developing societies from a cultural perspective, rather than through the more abstract lenses of communism and modernization theory. Continuities also existed, most centrally with regard to the role of communications as a shaper of values and the role of values as the critical variable in determining the outcomes of processes of change at the national level (Pooley 2008: 45). Organization-shaped ideology and static political culture were two manifestations of the same paradigm, which linked China's political development—the revolution led by the CCP—to the cognitive orientations of individuals.

China's History: Neoculturalism in State-Society Relations

Communications and political culture explained how politics in China did or did not change as a result of values distributed throughout society. Communications, which Schurmann had subtly incorporated into larger structures of organization theory, reshaped society through the imposition of values in the form of ideology or modernization. Political culture provided a complementary explanation for difference and divergence within the modernization process, particularly in societies that appeared as "traditional" and non-Western. This institutionalized social science also had a considerable influence on *historical* study by the 1960s (Chartier 1988: 2) and, as Paul Cohen (1984: 7, 57–58) has demonstrated, the view of "tradition" as an impediment in China's modernization process was the dominant approach taken by scholars of modern Chinese history within the anglophone academy until approximately 1970.

Historical research of the 1970s was more open-ended in approach, focused on recovering internal patterns of intellectual life (Schwartz 1972; Cohen 1974) and the dynastic cycle (Wakeman 1979). Modernization theory was upended by critiques alleging that Western imperialism, rather than China's response, accounted for the decades of tumult that followed (Marks 1985: 466–68). Theda Skocpol's *States and Social Revolutions* (1979), a landmark work of historical sociology that situated modern China in a comparative frame, argued that the modernization process itself created the socio-psychological preconditions of revolutionary crisis. Functional analysis and determinism (including varieties of Marxist determinism such as world-systems theory) were challenged by micro–case studies, sociocultural history, and history of mentalities (Chartier 1988: 6). "Culture" became separated from monolithic grand tradition, replaced with concern about the attitudes and values of ordinary people—popular culture (Burke 1992: 118–19). Within Chinese studies, more nuanced perspectives on cultural pluralism cast the equation of political culture with static Confucianism into doubt (Schwartz 1973).

As applied to China's political and social change, historical approaches initially replaced sweeping generalizations with more circumscribed case studies focused on individual thinkers, specific social strata, and local places. The modernization theory–defined object of "China" was, to a certain extent, smashed into pieces, even as the goal of much of this scholarship was to quickly rebuild it using interior perspectives and sources (Cohen 1984: 153–86; Marks 1985: 488–92). Local narratives superseded "national and patriotic mythologies" (Wasserstrom 2003: 6–7). Revolution, as a political process, was viewed through the lens of distinct regional ecologies and economic cycles (Hartford and Goldstein 1989). Institutions such as the Joint Committee on Contemporary China held the multidisciplinary China studies field together through symposia, conferences, and research awards that normalized "field-work" as the new dominant methodology (Marks 1985: 493–96). Research on change in values and consciousness likewise utilized a range of localized case studies—popular culture, religion, and grassroots governance—to explain the limitations of elite dominance (Johnson, Nathan, and Rawski 1985).

Social and economic history thrived during this period; accordingly, studies of the CCP-led revolution became tied to regional socioeconomic analysis and conflict theory rather than the communications-based values paradigm of earlier decades. Elizabeth Perry, author of an influential study of local peasant rebellions and its relationship to the revolutionary process in North China (Perry 1980), delivered a definitive critique of the political culture approach as practiced by Pye and Solomon in a 1992 essay titled "Chinese Political Culture Revisited," which sought to analyze patterns of protest in 1980s China, culminating in the 1989 protest wave leading to the Tiananmen Square Massacre (*Tiananmen datusha*), as instances of "innovation" within China's political culture and traditional protest repertoires (Perry 1992: 11). Perry (8) called the new approach "neoculturalism," taking pains to differentiate it from Pye and Solomon's work by critiquing their use of obsolete modernization theory and nonrigorous psychocultural explanations based on personal observation. The major error in Pye's political science, Perry argued, was the assumption of China's "unique cultural continuity" and, implicitly, the assumption that Chinese society was incapable of adopting new values and protest repertoires from other sources (e.g., Western culture, Europe) or generating unique patterns of state-society relations from within. Lacking a flexible understanding of tradition, earlier sinology had thus fallen into rigid repetition that failed to anticipate the events of 1989 and to explain them.

The return to tradition, culture, and experience—cognitive elements within the political process—as independent analytic variables may have been surprising after nearly a decade of drift toward materialist causality. However, Perry's return to the paradigm represented by Pye and Solomon appears to have been directly inspired by the work of cultural historian Lynn Hunt, whose analysis of political language, symbols, and rituals during the French Revolution was borrowed by Perry (1992: 22) to explain the dynamics of "resistance and repression" observable in 1980s China. Neoculturalism referred to the application of Hunt's popular culture approach—which stressed that political identities, like popular culture, were "constructed" by ordinary people (Burke 1992: 188–99)—to protest repertoires. At the level of overarching abstraction, *culture* (and, secondarily, experience) replaced *values* as the key to understanding change. Moreover, Perry and others writing in the neoculturalist mode seemed less interested in modernization, which Perry explicitly disavowed, and democratization; the new focus of interest was relations between society and the CCP-led state. While Perry still claimed a role for structural factors, these were less precisely defined. Neoculturalism was, in essence, a field-specific instance of a broader rejection of structuralist accounts of social and political change then sweeping the social sciences (Godwin 1996), as well as a critique of earlier sinology. Yet in terms of the scope of its method, it remained deeply attached to value and attitudes as bellwethers of social change, if not powerful forces of change in their own right. Neoculturalism thus substituted the political culture of Lynn Hunt for the political culture of Lucien Pye, yet remained aligned with the values paradigm of mass communication and modernization theory-derived area studies.

Theorizing Political Authority:
The Values Paradigm in Studies of Post-1949 China

Returning to the primacy of values over structural factors in explaining social change was not unusual in the context of a widening debate between materialists and culturalists taking place throughout academia following the cultural turn of the late 1970s and early 1980s (Burke 1992: 120). Whether considered as a paradigm in its own right or as simply an extension of earlier political culture approaches, neoculturalism represented a major strand in the analysis of Chinese society, particularly for historians. One reason was that research on culture, experience, and ultimately the cognitive functions of human behavior coincided with a massive explosion of new information about the present and past conditions of China's society—information that demanded explanation. China's "opening" in 1979 had already resulted in increased access to sources and research opportunities. Disciplinary knowledge increased as a result, particularly in economics, sociology, and political science (Walder 2004). Beginning in the 1990s, the availability of published state archival materials likewise created new opportunities for treating the history of China after 1949—"Party history" or "PRC history"—from a historical perspective (Strauss 2007).[7]

The early Party history field focused on the resilience of the CCP and of socialism. Focus on the origins of the Party-state was not initially driven by neoculturalist approaches; rather, its mode of analysis was mainly in line with earlier organizational studies (Barnett 1967; Vogel 1969). The edited volume *New Perspectives on State Socialism in China* (Cheek and Saich 1997) highlighted both how the CCP had first established order through organizational systems-building (spatial hierarchies of *hukou and danwei*; the united front; propaganda; and the military), and how the Party then managed the fracture and transformation of that order during the late 1950s. Other new scholarship, primarily written by political scientists using historical sources and techniques, analyzed organizational relations between state and society.[8] This research nonetheless marked a break with previous historiography of the PRC that had privileged elite politics as the principal location of change—a narrative periodized according to the rule of successive leaders ("eras") and Party-directed mass movements (MacFarquhar 1993). Moreover, it began to peel back the veil concerning Party efficacy on the ground by examining sweeping campaigns such as implementation of the 1950 Marriage Law, finding an ad hoc "bumbling state" in place of the organizational machine described in earlier studies (Diamant 2000).

New, state archive–driven perspectives overlapped with a preexisting tradition of studies grounded in relations between state and rural society, which took a bottom-up, realistic perspective concerning the "reach of the state" and its limitations (Shue 1988). Through increased contact with post-

Mao China, scholars across a range of disciplinary fields had already begun to dig beneath the smooth veneer of state propaganda and scripted interviews to identify gaps between rhetoric and reality with regard to the status of women, ethnicity, industrial workplace relations, and collective agriculture. Frequent purges during the Mao years, culminating in the Cultural Revolution, had demonstrated the existence of political and intellectual dissent after 1949; what became increasingly evident after Mao's death was the breadth of experience, viewpoints, and outcomes that had coexisted with seemingly monolithic CCP dominance over society. This outpouring of research, however, did not significantly alter the tenor of state-centric analysis. Following the earlier dominant China studies paradigm of explaining historical change through the analysis of values, other scholars recast the early decades of the PRC as consistent with China's unique political culture of state-making (Wong 1997; P. A. Kuhn [1999] 2002).

As it evolved, the new state archive–based scholarship followed both patterns of interpretation, while attempting to resolve the tension between them in a manner that directly followed from Perry's neoculturalist critique of analytic rigidity in the interpretation of how values—and which values—shaped China's society. The result was "PRC history": a field defined by access to subnational perspectives (whether through state archives, nonofficial sources, or interviews) but focused primarily on explaining how the CCP had seized and maintained political power over much of the former territory of the Republic of China after 1949. This more empirically granular, but still analytically state-centered, perspective was evident in signal works that combined scholarship from multiple researchers to produce new accounts of critical episodes in the history of the Mao Zedong era: the Cultural Revolution (Esherick, Pickowicz, and Walder 2006) and the early 1950s period of CCP political consolidation (Brown and Pickowicz 2007). The post-cultural-turn, neoculturalist perspective was evident in the topics of single-author monographs, the majority of which focused on aspects of public culture (Hung 2011); ideology and the Mao cult (Leese 2011); thought reform (Smith 2012); local state cultural production (DeMare 2015); historiography and museums (Ho 2017); and propaganda related to the changing political-legal system (Cook 2016; Altehenger 2018).

Earlier scholars of CCP politics had only glimpsed the dynamics of state-society relations fleetingly, through refugee interviews, local newspapers, and formerly classified materials released during the Red Guard period of the Cultural Revolution. Post-Mao openness made more widespread interviewing and collaboration with scholars in the PRC possible, and this in turn created the conditions of greater archival transparency and freedom of inquiry, which "new" PRC history scholars built on in claiming to reconstruct social realities of the 1950s and 1960s from the bottom up. Yet in a manner almost entirely consistent with the values paradigm which defined social science scholarship during those same decades—and for decades after—the dominant theory that defined the PRC history subfield focused on values, beliefs, and mass communications as engines of historical change. James Z. Gao's archive- and interview-based *The Communist Takeover of Hangzhou: The Transformation of City and Cadre 1949–1954*, one of the first studies to pair neoculturalist assumptions with local declassified sources, argued that the CCP's postrevolutionary "success" was the result of early governing methods, in particular, the use of "cultural weapons" as tools of state power to "consolidate the regime" in urban settings (2004: 2–3). Unlike Perry, Gao approvingly cited earlier political culture scholars Pye and Solomon in explaining why communications had been the crucial factor in creating conditions for smooth regime change, arguing that "communications between CCP cadres and the ordinary people involved a cultural process operating through political institutions and embodied in various forms of ritual that shaped public reactions to the political outcomes of the revolution" (Gao 2004: 4). However, in viewing the construction of political identities as an integral part of the political process, and a key variable in explaining political outcomes, Gao was, like Perry, already less culturally deterministic in outlook with regard to the influence of monolithic "tradition" on popular attitudes, attributing Party success to cognitive and cultural malleability.

The state-centered and neoculturalist approach of PRC history was further elucidated by two studies cited in numerous subsequent monographs and dissertations.[9] Like Gao's earlier book, Chang-tai Hung's *Mao's New World: Political Culture in the Early People's Republic* described "new cultural forms and keywords" as the principal means by which the Communist Party was able to "consolidate [its] hold on China" (2011: 2). Culture no longer meant "tradition," as it had in the context of more immediately postwar area studies, but rather referred directly to Communist "propaganda tools"; political culture was made up of the "shared values, collective visions, common attitudes, and public expectations *created by high politics*" (Hung 2011: 5, emphasis added). New values, as the foundation of political rule, were instilled through indoctrination and control. Elizabeth Perry's *Anyuan: Mining China's Revolutionary Tradition* represented another extension of the values paradigm into explanations of postrevolutionary political change, explicating the "distinctive" nature of the Communist revolution through appeal to "Mao's remarkable ability to convince millions of his countrymen to sacrifice for his revolutionary crusade long before he possessed the coercive means to enforce compliance" (2012: 1). In Perry's answer to this historical problematic, culture was paramount, whether referring to the "cultural capital and creativity" of early leaders and intellectuals; the strategic deployment of "symbolic resources" for purposes of political persuasion; the "use of cultural assets for purposes of mass mobilization"; the creation of an appealing and resonant "proletarian revolutionary culture"; or the leveraging of bureaucratic resources, media, and narratives for "political legitimation" (Perry 2012: 4–13). In line with earlier criticism of Pye and Solomon, Perry was careful to distinguish "culture"—as "meaningful invention within tradition"—from "unchanging Chinese culture" (Perry 2012: 5). Unlike Gao and Chang, Perry did appeal to some sense of overarching Chinese culture as an explanation for CCP success in consolidating power through popular values change. However, this tradition was multitudinous, at least within limits, and not a constant, but itself a changing field, albeit one subject to political domination.

Perry (2013: 2) would elsewhere refer to this model of domination through values change, with symbolic resources and mobilization serving the function of catalysts as *cultural governance*—a theory that seemed to displace political culture as explaining not only Communist political authority but also its resilience. Despite some reference to structure, cultural governance was overwhelmingly explained through analysis of policies, propaganda, and mass campaigns (the last sometimes in response to protests or, in the case of the Cultural Revolution, elite infighting). The idea that the Party-state was able to control, or "mobilize," society through appeals to shared values would not have been alien to Pye, Solomon, or the social scientists and mass communications researchers whose work had preceded and influenced area studies. Certainly, the focus on elites, symbols, and mass society—mutually interlinked through technologies of communication—had defined knowledge under the values paradigm of social change as constructed by policy-minded researchers and international relations managers from the 1950s onward. Yet notably missing from neoculturalism, cultural governance, and related frameworks was the emphasis on democracy and modernization as end points. Instead, the change that PRC history scholarship attempted to explain was the CCP's "success" and "resilience" in monopolizing political power after 1949. No behavioral base, which area studies had crudely represented as "traditional" culture (and thus an obstacle to modernization and normative political development), existed outside of the values communicated by Mao and other leaders downward to the rest of society. For this reason, much of the new PRC history, despite its local texture and empirical nuance, had much in common with ideology-and-organization studies of the 1960s and 1970s, which catalogued and evaluated the mechanisms of Party "control," national integration, and political self-renewal.[10] The persistence of the values paradigm was evident in arguments that the CCP ruled, and ruled successfully, because its leaders used control over symbols, rituals, language, and other media to align social beliefs with Party beliefs, social behaviors with Party behaviors, and social psychology with the receding fever dream of "Mao's revolution."

Conclusion and Reflection

In a broad sense, this article has argued that paradigms and path dependency, rather than the empirical afterimage of past realities, have determined the theoretical foundations of PRC history. The values paradigm first emerged from experiments in nonviolent social control and integration. Successive world wars taught researchers that insights drawn from psychology, sociology, and other social sciences, as well as professional advertising, had value to policymakers. Mass communication could be force multiplier as a well as a tool in its own right. As part of psychological warfare, it was effectively combined with selective use of violence to achieve "ideological, political, or military goals" (Simpson 1994: 11). During the Cold War, mass communication research was applied to key problems in American international relations such as development, modernization, and democratization. Division of the world into "areas" in order to better manage these problems resulted in the blending of mass communication and anthropological approaches to knowledge, making the values paradigm the basis for interpreting and predicting social change in external societies such as China. Belonging to this paradigm as part of "normal science" whose practices were established decades earlier is what unites theories such as political culture, neoculturalism, and cultural governance. Though theoretical alternatives to cognitive explanations of social change have appeared—examinations of the industrial transformation of core-periphery relations, ecological disruption, or conflict over the distribution of resources, for example—they have not yet triggered a paradigm shift, at least not where PRC history is concerned. If anything, the values paradigm has become synonymous with an increasingly narrow definition of "culture," one that reduces Chinese culture to tradition (even while allowing for variations within that tradition), and political culture to the values of elites.

The function of culture within the values paradigm is therefore as a metaphor for power. It is a misleading metaphor because, as I have suggested previously (Johnson 2018: 13), it functions to deny the existence of what historical sociologist Michael Mann (1986: 26) called the "concentrated coercive" form of power organization—meaning, the mobilization of violence as an instrument of sociospatial control. (Mann's theory and typology further includes two types of state power, coerced labor and terror, which other scholars have shown to have been particularly pervasive during the Mao years.[11]) This obscuration of violence in PRC politics is not itself hidden, however, but serves to support arguments for the uniqueness of the CCP's ruling style. Thus, Mao's use of mobilization to harness "emotional energy" is contrasted with Joseph Stalin's reliance on violent purges and secret police (Perry 2002: 121). Two forms of political power: one Chinese, persuasive and cognitive; one Soviet, cruel and corporeal. Yet terror, policing, and the criminalization of "enemy" groups were recurrent and systematically important elements of Maoist and post-Mao politics (Dutton 2005). These systems affected the lives of people who served not only as targets but also as informants and spies (Schoenhals 2013). To argue that "ideological as well as organizational imitation and innovation were key ingredients in the CCP's rise to power and after" (Perry 2012: 3–4) is not wrong, but incomplete. Though the logic underpinning this assertion is never stated, what makes ideological ingredients "key" can only be some prior assumption of significance, not any test against competing theories, as competing theories are never explored.[12] Here it seems germane to note that efficiency in reaching interpretable findings is one of the chief characteristics of paradigmatic research, in part because the rules determining validity are allowed to recede into the background (T. S. Kuhn 1962: 23–34).

And yet the rules are still there, and to test them is potentially to invite crisis, even if only crisis of a scholarly sort. Perhaps this is the reason that one of the most notable studies to place violence at the center of PRC historiography, Jung Chang and Jon Halliday's *Mao: The Unknown Story* (2005), was met with widespread academic condemnation on its release, including publication of an entire collection of critical essays in response (Benton and Chun 2009). In terms of method and sources, *Mao: The Unknown Story* was not unlike works of PRC history that rely on archives, interviews, and unofficial accounts to access the truth of past events that have otherwise been distorted or gone unremarked-on in official accounts. However, the book's Mao-centered, conspirational narrative turned off academic readers, even if no serious refutation of its claims concerning the extent of CCP violence was ever raised.[13] This quarantining and compartmentalization of the relationship between violence and state-making is not unusual (see Hooks and Rice 2005), nor is the policing of borders between "normal" and "anomalous" scholarship. But neither is it good history.

To conclude, I note that several articles in this special issue criticize a book I coedited and contributed to, *Maoism at the Grassroots: Everyday Life in China's Era of High Socialism*, for its empiricism and truth claims. I suspect that what provokes these criticisms is not really the method but the conclusions. In the volume's introduction, Jeremy Brown and I (Brown and Johnson 2015: 1–2) argued that prior scholarship on the PRC was primarily focused on top-down and state-centric issues such as policy implementation and group behavior;[14] that more diversity of social experience existed than had been accounted for by this scholarship; that policy-driven campaigns were limited and variable in their outcomes; and that "earlier generations of social scientists underestimated the extent of routine violence, resistance, and repression during the Mao period." We (2015: 5) also tried to demonstrate that "the 'grassroots' can be understood as both a methodological category and an objective structure of society"—or, in other words, that our focus and that of the other contributors to the volume was on interactions between individuals and Party-state institutions, written from a nonelite perspective. Like Yang Kuisong and other historians writing PRC history *in* the PRC, we wanted to prioritize the micro, the individual, and the social because these viewpoints did not seem widely represented in other studies of the same period that we were reading, whether written by American social scientists or CCP historiographers. The point bears repeating: existing studies assumed the importance of policy, state-sanctioned collective identity, and national events to individual lives; we were interested in testing those assumptions. While I have learned something from my fellow contributors' criticism of use of the "individual" as a category—mainly that I should be even clearer in stating why I think the category is important—I also think that they should ask themselves what it is about the volume's conclusions that troubles them. Is it politically bad form to put accounts of violence, religious belief, women's labor, ethnic persecution, or sexual behavior at the center of narratives about China's high socialist era? Are these subjects, unlike economic planning or the "nature of the state," of lesser importance to scholarship?[15] If so, why? Surely, we can all do better.

Notes

Early versions of this article were presented at the Lau China Institute, King's College London, and the "Empire and Modern China" seminar at the University of Bristol in 2013–14. I am grateful to the organizers, audience members, and graduate students who listened and provided feedback for their generous and critical attention. The editors of this special issue, along with three anonymous reviewers and my fellow contributors, have all provided inspiration for subsequent revisions. Responsibility for any errors of fact or interpretation belongs solely to the author.

1   "Cognition" refers to the activities of the human mind and its interactions with the environment in time and space. See Dúner and Ahlberger 2019. "Violence" refers also to the threat of violence; by violence I mean corporeal pain and damage. See Nieburg 1969: 5–6.

2   Similarly, violence is absent from most theories of Maoism's charismatic appeal, despite political violence having been noticeably intertwined with the creation and spread of the Mao cult. See Johnson 2021.

3   For a representative bibliography, see Pool 1997.

4   Pye's intellectual debt to anthropologists Kluckhohn, Mead, and Benedict was acknowledged some twenty years later. See Pye 1985: xii.

5   On cybernetics, systems science, and anthropology, see Kline 2015.

6   "The values and norms of the total ideology are tools with which the individuals are motivated to commitment and are given rational ideas for action. The values of the ideology are designed to bring about a moral and psychological transformation of the individual. By acquiring a pure ideology and internalizing its values, the individual develops commitment to the organization. The norms of the ideology give him [*sic*] practical ideas (principles and methods) for concrete action. By acquiring a practical ideology and learning its norms, the individual becomes an effective actor in the organization. When an organization consists of individuals with the same commitments and the same action ideas, it has a basis for solidarity" (Schurmann 1966: 45–46).

7   For those seeking to explore links between the cultural turn, neoculturalism, and Party/PRC history in greater theoretical and institutional detail, another important starting point is the Indiana East Asian Working Paper Series on Language and Politics in Modern China (easc.indiana.edu/resources/language-politics.html), which began publication in 1993. Contributors to the series included Michael Schoenhals, Elizabeth Perry, Timothy Cheek, and Barbara Mittler.

8   See Shue 1994; Perry 1994.

9   I base this judgment on citation tracing using Google Scholar.

10 Though the parallel was rarely acknowledged, similarities also existed between neoculturalist studies and earlier accounts of the Soviet Union that had likewise focused on propaganda, mobilization, and popular values change (Unger 1974; Fitzpatrick 1978; Kenez 1985) as critical tools of effective social governance, contrasting these with even earlier accounts describing Soviet society in terms of totalitarianism, militarism, and repression. See Engerman 2009: 286–308. Engerman points out that the rising generation of Soviet historians took pains to distinguish the Russian revolution of words from the Chinese revolution of bullets. As this article notes in the conclusion, scholars of China would make exactly the opposite argument decades later.

11 On "reform through labor," see Wu 1992; Williams and Wu 2004. On terror, including political terror, see Strauss 2002; Walder 2015. On Mao, the PRC political-legal system, and the death penalty, see Ning 2008.

12 An assumption that is paralleled elsewhere by the unexamined conflation of authority with legitimacy and acceptance. See Johnson 2018: 12–13.

13 Two of the Benton and Chun–edited volume's contributors, Lloyd Dittmer and Arthur

Waldron, found *Mao: The Unknown Story*'s chapters on PRC history convincing; among the (many) critics, the main objections seem to have focused on the authors' misrepresentation of Mao's motives and poor choices in narrative style. Above all, however, the book was repudiated for its "one-sided" portrayal of China's revolution (Benton and Chun 2009: 10)—that is, for its focus on violence.

14 Not, as one reviewer seems to have believed, that social scientists did not write "bottom-up" studies. See Thornton 2017.

15 See, respectively, Perry 2016 and Diamant 2018. Diamant in particular seems put out that *Maoism at the Grassroots* made outsized claims for novelty (though he produces no evidence of comparable studies) and failed to engage with theories of the state, link the Mao era to the "contemporary scene," or acknowledge the importance of local officials. Notwithstanding that our definition of "grassroots" specifically describes "provincial, commune, county, and village officials" as important social actors; that we addressed and argued against understanding of the state as a monolithic entity; and that we connected diversity of experience to particularism in both state and social structures across from the late Qing dynasty to the present (Brown and Johnson 2015: 4–5), this is a judicious and perceptive assessment.

References

Almond, Gabriel A. 1987. *Harold Dwight Lasswell, 1902–1978: A Biographical Memoir*. Washington, DC: National Academy Press.

Almond, Gabriel A., and James S. Coleman, eds. 1960. *The Politics of the Developing Areas*. Princeton, NJ: Princeton University Press.

Altehenger, Jennifer. 2018. *Legal Lessons: Popularizing Laws in the People's Republic of China, 1949–1989*. Cambridge, MA: Harvard University Asia Center.

Ankersmit, F. R. 2001. *Historical Representation*. Stanford, CA: Stanford University Press.

Barnett, A. Doak. 1967. *Cadres, Bureaucracy, and Political Power in Communist China*. New York: Columbia University Press.

Bell, Daniel. 1997. "Social Science: An Imperfect Art." In *Sociological Visions*, edited by Kai Erikson, 101–21. Lanham, MD: Rowman and Littlefield.

Beniger, James R. 1986. *The Control Revolution: Technological and Economic Origins of the Information Society*. Cambridge, MA: Harvard University Press.

Bennett, Wendell C. 1951. *Area Studies in American Universities*. New York: Social Science Research Council.

Benton, Gregor, and Lin Chun, eds. 2009. *Was Mao Really a Monster? The Academic Response to Chang and Halliday's* Mao: The Unknown Story. London: Routledge.

Brown, Jeremy, and Matthew D. Johnson, eds. 2015. *Maoism at the Grassroots: Everyday Life in China's Era of High Socialism*. Cambridge, MA: Harvard University Press.

Brown, Jeremy, and Paul G. Pickowicz, eds. 2007. *Dilemmas of Victory: The Early Years of the People's Republic of China*. Cambridge, MA: Harvard University Press.

Burke, Peter. 1992. *History and Social Theory*. Ithaca, NY: Cornell University Press.

Chang, Jung, and Jon Halliday. 2005. *Mao: The Unknown Story*. New York: Anchor Books.

Chartier, Roger. 1988. *Cultural History: Between Practices and Representations*, translated by Lydia G. Cochrane. Ithaca, NY: Cornell University Press.

Cheek, Timothy, and Tony Saich, eds. 1997. *New Perspectives on State Socialism in China*. Armonk, NY: M. E. Sharpe.

Chu, Godwin C. 1977. *Radical Change through Communication in Mao's China*. Honolulu: University of Hawai'i Press.

Cohen, Paul. 1974. *Between Tradition and Modernity: Wang T'ao and Reform in Late Ch'ing China*. Cambridge, MA: Harvard University Press.

Cohen, Paul. 1984. *Discovering History in China: American Historical Writing on the Recent Chinese Past*. New York: Columbia University Press.

Cook, Alexander C. 2016. *The Cultural Revolution on Trial: Mao and the Gang of Four*. New York: Columbia University Press.

Cumings, Bruce. 1999. *Parallax Visions: Making Sense of American-East Asian Relations at the End of the Century*. Durham, NC: Duke University Press.

DeMare, Brian James. 2015. *Mao's Cultural Army: Drama Troupes in China's Rural Revolution*. Cambridge: Cambridge University Press.

Diamant, Neil. 2000. *Revolutionizing the Family: Politics, Love, and Divorce in Urban and Rural China, 1949–1968*. Berkeley: University of California Press.

Diamant, Neil. 2018. "What the (Expletive) Is a 'Constitution'?! Ordinary Cadres Confront the 1954 PRC Draft Constitution." *Journal of Chinese History* 2, no. 1: 169–90.

Dúner, David, and Christer Ahlberger, eds. 2019. *Cognitive History: Mind, Space, and Time*. Berlin: De Gruyter Oldenbourg.

Dutton, Michael. 2005. *Policing Chinese Politics: A History*. Durham, NC: Duke University Press.

Engerman, David C. 2009. *Know Your Enemy: The Rise and Fall of America's Soviet Experts*. Oxford: Oxford University Press.

Engerman, David C., Nils Gilman, Mark H. Haefele, and Michael E. Latham, eds. 2003. *Staging Growth: Modernization, Development, and the Global Cold War*. Amherst: University of Massachusetts Press.

Eriksson, Kai. 2011. *Communication in Modern Social Ordering*. London: Bloomsbury.

Escobar, Arturo. 1995. *Encountering Development: The Making and Unmaking of the Third World*. Princeton, NJ: Princeton University Press.

Esherick, Joseph W., Paul G. Pickowicz, and Andrew G. Walder, eds. 2006. *The Cultural Revolution as History*. Stanford, CA: Stanford University Press.

Fitzpatrick, Sheila, ed. 1978. *Cultural Revolution in Russia, 1928–1931*. Bloomington: Indiana University Press.

Gao, James Z. 2004. *The Communist Takeover of Hangzhou: The Transformation of City and Cadre, 1949–1954*. Honolulu: University of Hawai'i Press.

Gilman, Nils. 2007. *Mandarins of the Future: Modernization Theory in Cold War America*. Baltimore: Johns Hopkins University Press.

Godwin, Jeff. 1996. "Symbols, Positions, and Objects: Toward a New Theory of Revolutions and Collective Action." *History and Theory* 35, no. 3: 358–74.

Hartford, Kathleen, and Steven M. Goldstein, eds. 1989. *Single Sparks: China's Rural Revolutions*. Armonk, NY: M. E. Sharpe.

Heilbron, J. L. 1998. "Thomas Samuel Kuhn, 18 July 1922–June 1996." *Isis* 89: 505–15.

Ho, Denise. 2017. *Curating Revolution: Politics on Display in Mao's China*. Cambridge: Cambridge University Press.

Hooks, Gregory, and James Rice. 2005. "War, Militarism, and States: The Insights and Blind Spots of Political Sociology." In *The Handbook of Political Sociology: States, Civil Societies, and Globalization*, edited by Thomas Janoski, Robert R. Alford, Alexander M. Hicks, and Mildred A. Schwartz, 566–86. Cambridge: Cambridge University Press.

Houn, Franklin S. 1961. *To Change a Nation: Propaganda and Indoctrination in Communist China*. New York: Free Press.

Hung, Chang-tai. 2011. *Mao's New World: Political Culture in the Early People's Republic*. Ithaca, NY: Cornell University Press.

Jiang, Yihua 姜义华. 2012. "Zouchu sixiang shang wenhua shang de 'bei zhimin'" 走出思想上文化上的 '被殖民' ("Moving On from 'Being Colonized' in Thought and Culture"). *Shehui kexue* 社会科学 (*Journal of Social Sciences*) 5: 155–56.

Jin, Dalu 金大陆. 2012. "Tuijin 'Wen ge' yanjiu ru lishi xueshu guidao" 推进 '文革' 研究入历史学术轨道 ("Pushing Forward the 'Cultural Revolution' onto the Track of Historical Study"). *Shehui kexue* 社会科学 (*Journal of Social Sciences*) 5: 160–64.

Johnson, David, Andrew J. Nathan, and Evelyn S. Rawski, eds. 1985. *Popular Culture in Late Imperial China*. Berkeley: University of California Press.

Johnson, Matthew D. 2018. "Political Culture in the Archive: Grassroots Perspectives on Party-State Power and Legitimacy in 1950s Beijing." *PRC History Review* 3, no. 1: 2–19.

Johnson, Matthew D. 2021. "Maoism and Charismatic Domination." In *Routledge International Handbook of Charisma*, edited by José Pedro Zúquete, 89–100. New York: Routledge.

Kenez, Peter. 1985. *The Birth of the Propaganda State: Soviet Methods of Mass Mobilization, 1917–1929*. Berkeley: University of California Press.

Kline, Ronald R. 2015. *The Cybernetics Movement: Or Why We Call Our Age the Information Age*. Baltimore: Johns Hopkins University Press.

Kuhn, Philip A. (1999) 2002. *Origins of the Modern Chinese State*. Stanford, CA: Stanford University Press.

Kuhn, Thomas S. 1962. *The Structure of Scientific Revolutions*. Chicago: University of Chicago Press.

Lasswell, Harold D. 1927. *Propaganda Technique in the World War*. New York: A. A. Knopf.

Lasswell, Harold D. 1935. *World Politics and Personal Insecurity*. New York: McGraw-Hill.

Lasswell, Harold D., and Nathan Leites. 1949. *Language of Politics: Studies in Quantitative Semantics*. New York: G. W. Stewart.

Leese, Daniel. 2011. *Mao Cult: Rhetoric and Ritual in China's Cultural Revolution*. Cambridge: Cambridge University Press.

Lerner, Daniel. 1958. *The Passing of Traditional Society: Modernizing the Middle East*. New York: Free Press.

Liu, Alan P. L. 1971. *Communications and National Integration in Communist China*. Berkeley: University of California Press.

MacFarquhar, Roderick, ed. 1993. *The Politics of China*. Cambridge: Cambridge University Press.

Mann, Michael. 1986. *A History of Power from the Beginning to A.D. 1760*. Vol. 1 of *The Sources of Social Power*. Cambridge: Cambridge University Press.

Marks, Robert. 1985. "The State of the China Field: Or, the China Field and the State." *Modern China* 11, no.4: 461–509.

Mattelart, Armand. (1991) 1994. *Mapping World Communication: War, Progress, Culture*, translated by Susan Emanuel and James A. Cohen. Minneapolis: University of Minnesota Press.

McGuire, William J. 2004. "The Poly-Psy Relationship: Three Phases of a Long Affair." In *Political Psychology*, edited by John T. Jost and Jim Sidanius, 22–33. New York: Psychology Press.

Nieburg, H. L. 1969. *Political Violence: The Behavioral Process*. New York: Palgrave Macmillan.

Ning, Zhang. 2008. "The Political Origins of Death Penalty Exceptionalism: Mao Zedong and the Practice of Capital Punishment in Contemporary China." *Punishment and Society* 10, no. 2: 117–36.

North, Robert C., and Ithiel de Sola Pool. 1952. *Kuomintang and Chinese Communist Elites*. Stanford, CA: Stanford University Press.

Perry, Elizabeth J. 1980. *Rebels and Revolutionaries in North China, 1845–1945*. Stanford, CA: Stanford University Press.

Perry, Elizabeth J. 1992. "Introduction: Chinese Political Culture Revisited." In *Popular Protest and Political Culture in Modern China: Learning from 1989*, edited by Jeffrey N. Wasserstrom and Elizabeth J. Perry, 1–14. Boulder, CO: Westview.

Perry, Elizabeth J. 1994. "Labor Divided: Sources of State Formation in Modern China." In *State Power and Social Forces: Domination and Transformation in the Third World*, edited by Joel S. Migdal, Atul Kohli, and Vivienne Shue, 143–73. Cambridge: Cambridge University Press.

Perry, Elizabeth J. 2002. "Moving the Masses: Emotion Work in the Chinese Revolution." *Mobilization: An International Journal* 7, no. 2: 111–28.

Perry, Elizabeth J. 2012. *Anyuan: Mining China's Revolutionary Tradition*. Berkeley: University of California Press.

Perry, Elizabeth J. 2013. "Cultural Governance in Contemporary China: 'Re-Orienting' Party Propaganda." Harvard-Yenching Institute Working Paper Series. dash.harvard.edu /bitstream/handle/1/11386987/Elizabeth%20Perry_Cultural%20Governance%20in%20 Contemporary%20China.pdf?sequence=1&isAllowed=y (accessed June 1, 2021).

Perry, Elizabeth J. 2016. "The Promise of PRC History." *Journal of Modern Chinese History* 10, no. 1: 113–17.

Pool, Ithiel de Sola. 1997. *Politics in Wired Nations: Selected Writings of Ithiel de Sola Pool*, edited by Lloyd S. Etheridge. New Brunswick, NJ: Transaction Publishers.

Pool, Ithiel de Sola, and Quincy Wright. 1951. *Symbols of Internationalism*. Stanford, CA: Stanford University Press.

Pooley, Jefferson. 2008. "The New History of Mass Communication Research." In *The History of Media and Communication Research: Contested Memories*, edited by David Park and Jefferson Pooley, 43–69. New York: Peter Lang.

Pye, Lucien W. 1963. Preface and introduction to *Communications and Political Development* (SPD-1), edited by Lucien W. Pye, ix, 3–23. Princeton, NJ: Princeton University Press.

Pye, Lucien W. 1965. "Introduction: Political Culture and Political Development." In *Political Culture and Political Development* (SPD-5), edited by Lucien W. Pye and Sidney Verba, 3–26. Princeton, NJ: Princeton University Press.

Pye, Lucien W. 1966. "Party Systems and National Development in Asia." In *Political Parties and Political Development* (SPD-6), edited by Joseph LaPalombara and Myron Weiner, 369–98. Princeton, NJ: Princeton University Press.

Pye, Lucien W. 1968. *The Spirit of Chinese Politics: A Psychocultural Study of the Authority Crisis in Political Development*. Cambridge, MA: Harvard University Press.

Pye, Lucien W. 1971. "Mass Participation in China: Its Limitations and the Continuity of Culture." In *China: Management of a Revolutionary Society*, edited by John M. H. Lindbeck, 3–33. Seattle: University of Washington Press.

Pye, Lucien W. 1985. *Asian Power and Politics: The Cultural Dimensions of Authority*. Cambridge, MA: Harvard University Press.

Schoenhals, Michael. 2013. *Spying for the People: Mao's Secret Agents, 1949–1967*. Cambridge: Cambridge University Press.

Schurmann, Franz. 1966. *Ideology and Organization in Communist China*. Berkeley: University of California Press.

Schwartz, Benjamin I. 1972. "The Limits of 'Tradition versus Modernity' as Categories of Explanation: The Case of the Chinese Intellectuals." *Daedelus* 101, no. 2: 71–88.

Schwartz, Benjamin I. 1973. "A Personal View of Some Thoughts of Mao Tse-tung." In *Ideology and Politics in Contemporary China*, edited by Chalmers Johnson, 352–72. Seattle: University of Washington Press.

Schwartz, Benjamin I. (1980) 1996. "Area Studies as a Critical Discipline." In *China and Other Matters*, 98–113. Cambridge, MA: Harvard University Press.

Shah, Hemant. 2011. *The Production of Modernization: Daniel Lerner, Mass Media, and the Passing of Traditional Society*. Philadelphia: Temple University Press.

Shue, Vivienne. 1988. *The Reach of the State: Sketches of the Chinese Body Politic*. Stanford, CA: Stanford University Press.

Shue, Vivienne. 1994. "State Power and Social Organization in China." In *State Power and Social Forces: Domination and Transformation in the Third World*, edited by Joel S. Migdal, Atul Kohli, and Vivienne Shue, 65–88. Cambridge: Cambridge University Press.

Simpson, Christopher. 1994. *The Science of Coercion: Communication Research and Psychological Warfare, 1945–1960*. Oxford: Oxford University Press.

Skocpol, Theda. 1979. *States and Social Revolutions: A Comparative Analysis of France, Russia, and China*. Cambridge: Cambridge University Press.

Smith, Aminda M. 2012. *Thought Reform and China's Dangerous Classes: Reeducation, Resistance, and the People*. Lanham, MD: Rowman and Littlefield.

Solomon, Richard H. 1971. *Mao's Revolution and the Chinese Political Culture*. Berkeley: University of California Press.

Strauss, Julia. 2002. "Paternalist Terror: The Campaign to Suppress Counterrevolutionaries and Regime Consolidation in the People's Republic of China, 1950–1953." *Comparative Studies in Society and History* 44, no. 1: 80–105.

Strauss, Julia. 2007. "Introduction: In Search of PRC History." *The History of the PRC (1949–1976)*, edited by Julia Strauss, 1–15. Cambridge: Cambridge University Press.

Thornton, Patricia M. 2017. Review of *Maoism at the Grassroots: Everyday Life in China's Era of High Socialism*, edited by Jeremy Brown and Matthew D. Johnson. *China Quarterly* 229: 250–51.

Unger, Aryeh L. 1974. *The Totalitarian Party: Party and People in Nazi Germany and Soviet Russia*. Cambridge: Cambridge University Press.

Vogel, Ezra. 1969. *Canton under Communism: Programs and Politics in a Provincial Capital, 1949–1968*. Cambridge, MA: Harvard University Press.

Wakeman, Frederic E., Jr. 1979. "The Shun Interregnum of 1644." In *From Ming to Ch'ing: Conquest, Region, and Continuity in Seventeenth-Century China*, edited by Jonathan Spence and John E. Wills Jr., 39–87. New Haven, CT: Yale University Press.

Walder, Andrew G. 2004. "The Transformation of Contemporary Chinese Studies, 1977–2002." In *The Politics of Knowledge: Area Studies and the Disciplines*, edited by David Szanton, 314–40. Berkeley: University of California Press.

Walder, Andrew G. 2015. *China under Mao: A Revolution Derailed*. Cambridge, MA: Harvard University Press.

Wasserstrom, Jeffrey N., ed. 2003. *Twentieth-Century China: New Approaches*. London: Routledge.

Whyte, Martin King. 1974. *Small Groups and Political Rituals in China*. Berkeley: University of California Press.

Williams, Philip F., and Yenna Wu. 2004. *The Great Wall of Confinement: The Chinese Prison Camp through Contemporary Fiction and Reportage*. Berkeley: University of California Press.

Wong, R. Bin. 1997. *China Transformed: Historical Change and the Limits of European Experience*. Ithaca, NY: Cornell University Press.

Wu, Hongda Harry. 1992. *Laogai: The Chinese Gulag*. Boulder, CO: Westview Press.

Yang, Kuisong 杨奎松. 2012. "Zhongguo dangdai shi yanjiu de qibu yu yiyi" 中国当代史研究的起步与意义 ("The Start and Significance of Research on China's Contemporary History). *Shehui kexue* 社会科学 (*Journal of Social Sciences*) 5: 147–49.

Yang, Yaping 杨亚平, and Cao Shuji 草树基. 2012. "Lilun, fangfa yu shizheng—dangdai Faguo xueshu dui Zhongguo dangdai shi yanjiu de qishi" 理论, 方法与实证 — 当代法国学术对中国当代史研究的启示 ("Theory, Methods, and Evidence—The Enlightenment of Contemporary French Academia on the Study of China's Contemporary History"). *Shehui kexue* 社会科学 (*Journal of Social Sciences*) 5: 166–69.

Yu, Frederick T. C. 1964. *Mass Persuasion in Communist China*. New York: Praeger.

Breaking with the Family Form: Historical Categories, Social Reproduction, and Everyday Life in Late 1950s Rural China

Alexander F. Day

Historians have crossed over the 1949 divide into the Mao period, once mainly the province of social scientists. This raises many questions as to how historians are to approach this period. One of the clearest answers comes from Jeremy Brown and Matthew D. Johnson (2015), who argue for a bottom-up history of everyday life. They highlight that historians focus on "individual people in villages, factories, neighborhoods, counties, and ethnic minority regions from the bottom up, and in everyday contexts that make the familiar analytical categories of 'state' and 'society' impossible to clearly distinguish from each other" (Brown and Johnson 2015: 1). Historians of the PRC have provided us with a more complex and messier picture, and therefore it is worth considering further what the implications of a history of everyday life are and how we are to understand what we are doing as historians of the PRC. In particular, here I want to consider how we move

positions 29:4　DOI 10.1215/10679847-9286740
Copyright 2021 by Duke University Press

between the messy level of everyday life and a higher level of abstraction, to make broader conclusions.

The great strength of the historians of everyday life has been their ability to find new sources through which the messy stories of individuals can be told, stories that often disrupt the typical "campaign time" narration of the period. As Brown and Johnson (2015: 4) say, "Focusing on everyday life means taking what people actually did as a starting point rather than starting with what top officials wanted people to do or to think" (see also Brown in this issue). Everyday life, of course, is historical, produced in different ways under different material conditions, structured and shaped by social forms in motion. In this sense, it is not an analytical frame through which we can view the real content of the Mao period underneath the thin veneer of Maoist high politics and its categories. Treating it as such would reinscribe the state-society dichotomy, with everyday life standing in for society, where real people, individuals, say and do things that do not clearly follow the dictates of the Party-state. And the Party-state in turn would stand outside of the real content of everyday life—a sphere of propaganda, unrealistic policies, faked figures (see Werner in this issue). In this article I will explore the way we use analytical categories by looking at the emergence of a divide between production and the social reproduction of labor (all the work that goes into producing and raising laborers) that transformed and structured rural everyday life during the Mao period. There is no simple starting point from which to view society; rather, historians dialectically tack back and forth to understand emergent social categories, practices, and forms.

Theory and History: Form and Content

The problem of the analytical categories we use in our work is at issue. As Georg Iggers (2005: 4) points out, social science–oriented historians admit that that relationship between their narratives and real historical events is "mediated by the concepts and mental constructs of the historians." So, do we apply social science categories from outside of the PRC to give comparative meaning and structure to the messy events of social and political life there? Can social scientists in China studies produce their own categories that would then change the general categories—general abstractions— of the social sciences more broadly (Perry 1999: 19)? The social sciences,

Immanuel Wallerstein (2006: 6) points out, are "nomothetic disciplines"—they aim at making generalizations—and their categories need to be shared across societies to allow them to do so. The discipline of history, however, sits at the edge of the social sciences as it is "idiographic" and "predicated on the uniqueness of social phenomena" (Wallerstein 2006: 6). Generalizations are problematic, therefore, and postcolonial and other critiques of the Eurocentrism of social science's general categories are rife.

Further complicating the situation for those studying the PRC, the three key nomothetic social sciences—economics, political science, and sociology—emerged out of the nineteenth-century liberal image of modern European society, with its social spheres of the market, politics, and civil society (Wallerstein 2006: 6). Yet this tripartite academic division was an uneasy fit for the PRC social formation, which lacked a similar state-society dichotomy, a problem with which social scientists in China studies have continued to wrestle (Brown and Johnson 2015; Perry 2016). In a critique of the treatment of China within the discipline of political science, Lin Chun (2017: 5) argues that "in the fixed disciplinary eye, 'China' is too specific to produce anything generalizable beyond descriptive and self-containing narratives." The contradiction is at the heart of area studies, which was an attempt to break from the idiographic Orientalism of earlier non-Western studies by bringing in social science generalizations. Maoist politics and ideology were the prevailing explanations for the PRC's differences.

Yet the clear problems of nomothetic rationalist approaches are not easily overcome through an empirical turn to the everyday life. We cannot ignore the analytical categories produced at various levels of social and political theory as impositions from the outside by focusing instead on the real of everyday life, as an empirical content of history. Histories of everyday life could tend in this direction when viewing politics "through the eyes of villagers and urbanites" in everyday life (Brown and Johnson 2015: 3). As historians of the PRC show in their work, however, the complex interaction of material conditions, politics, everyday life, and memory undermines any suggestion of transparency, as if our view through their eyes gave us direct access to the real (see Hershatter 2011). Thinking carefully about this relationship between form (analytical categories) and content (messy history) in our work is therefore vital to the project of PRC history.

This article argues that everyday life, far from a sphere resisting the impositions and dictates of the state, is fully implicated in the political-economic structuring of society. This is a call, therefore, to not simply replace an earlier focus on the political economy of the PRC with a bottom-up or empirical view of everyday life. Instead, we must begin with the fact that everyday life is already a structured terrain. Rather than bringing in social science analytical categories from the outside or searching for an empirical real view from below, we need to investigate the emergence of categories and social forms from the real material limits and tendencies of a rapidly changing PRC society. Here, we see a dialectical relationship between form and content, just as there is one between theory and history. The material content of production, accumulation, and reproduction shapes both the emergence of new social forms and dynamics and the emerging policy categories and forms within inner party debate, which in turn shape the further development of material content. The social and discursive forms of everyday life emerge there.

To explicate this further, I will now turn to rural China in the late 1950s to look at the developing relationship between material limits, emerging social forms, and policy categories that construct the gendered everyday life of rural social reproduction. Social reproduction (*shehui zaishengchan* 社会再生产) is a somewhat ambiguous category within CCP and wider Marxist theory: it can mean at once the structured reproduction of society as a whole and, more narrowly, though relatedly, the social reproduction of labor power—how society produces new laborers. Below I discuss why this category briefly emerged from the real material limits of social development as important in the late-1950s PRC, how it shaped policy discussions, and how it structured everyday life. Social reproduction emerged as a salient category as production broke from the grasp of the patriarchal family form and the attempt to socialize life was pushed to the limits. Everyday life, in other words, cannot be understood without first marking out the dynamics of the overall political economy. The first section of this article therefore focuses on the material content of agricultural production and how it fit within the overall PRC political economy. In the next two sections, I then argue that the material limits and developments of agricultural production and rural labor led to the emergence of new social forms in rural society and new discursive forms in party policy and politics. These developments in social and political forms in turn reacted to shape the material content of agricultural production. In other words, they dialectically interacted to restructure everyday life.

Agricultural Production and the Political Economy of Socialist Developmentalism

The fundamental economic goal of the "socialist developmental regime" (Chuang 2016) was to expand China's means of production and national material product, and the basic strategy was to raise the rate of accumulation—the percentage of the national material product that was reinvested to expand fixed capital assets, working capital, and reserves (Brodsgaard 1983a: 49; X. Xu 2009). Raising the accumulation rate, especially the funds reinvested into the production of producer goods, was to lead to rapid industrialization. Translated into rural policy, this strategy implied expanding direct control over as large an absolute rural surplus as possible while maintaining political legitimacy in the countryside. This does not mean that the PRC state had a purely extractive relationship to agriculture, for officials clearly saw the development of agricultural production as crucial to economic growth. The leadership recognized that agriculture imposed a fundamental limit on economic growth and development. State budgets included investment in the development and modernization of agricultural production; although, overall investment rates were biased toward industry and particularly heavy industry (Food and Agriculture Organization 1999: 129). Therefore, a fundamental tension existed within the political economy of Mao-era China between the accumulation of rural surplus for rapid industrialization and the limits of agricultural production. This was the most basic material tension shaping the rural social world and rural everyday life.

For economic planners, the goal was not to keep the overall growth rate of agricultural production equal to that of industry. Rather, what was crucial was that the growth of state-controlled agricultural surplus—production above rural consumption—grew fast enough for urban and industrial needs (Yan 1978). The two basic ways to do so were controlling markets, through supply and marketing co-ops, or directly controlling production, through breaking with the household as the unit of production, collectivization, and agricultural modernization (Hou 2010). The Nationalists had experimented with both forms before 1949, and the CCP used a combination in the 1950s. The PRC state used supply and marketing co-ops, for example, to incentivize households to collectivize (Barnett 1953: 195). In other words, there was no necessary contradiction between the two forms. Supply and marketing co-ops were folded into the unified purchasing and marketing system that was introduced in 1953 to control the agricultural market, initially the grain market, and this state-controlled marketing system was integrated with rural collectives as they expanded and deepened during the 1950s. Overall, the combination allowed the state to limit rural consumption as well as intensify labor inputs, yielding a larger absolute agricultural surplus, a surplus increasingly defined by the state, not "by peasant or even collective needs" (Oi 1989: 44).

Not all surplus was appropriated by the central state, as local accumulation also played important developmental and welfare functions (Yang 1958; Zhongguo Renmin Daxue 1958). After funds to address welfare needs were subtracted, local accumulation was primarily used for agricultural capital construction, particularly as the central state restrained agricultural investment and pushed for self-reliance, increasing the central accumulation rate. This divide between central and collective accumulation expressed the particular relations of production of the rural economy and the rural-urban divide of the period. Rural agricultural producers' cooperatives and even the communes that formed in the Great Leap Forward (GLF) operated as a form of "collective ownership" (*jiti suoyouzhi* 集体所有制) not the "ownership by the whole people" (*quanmin suoyouzhi* 全民所有制). Thus, unlike state-owned farms, collectives and communes were responsible for their profits and losses and for the overall welfare of their members, which depended on both local accumulation and central accumulation through taxation and state control over marketing rural surplus.

During the heyday of the GLF, however, the shift to a system of "ownership by the whole people" was believed to be possible in the near future.[1] The mobilization of collective surplus labor power (from the perspective of the state) and local accumulation was crucial to agricultural capital construction, as the percentage of central state investment in agricultural capital construction was always far below agriculture's contribution to the overall economic production (Food and Agriculture Organization 1999: 129; Colby, Crook, and Webb 1992: 33 and 36). From the mid-1950s onward, rural collectives and communes were supposed to use the majority of their accumulated funds for capital construction, which together with technological change constituted the material basis of agricultural modernization (Li 1963). With limited capital, however, national industrialization took priority, even at moments in which Mao called for the "simultaneous development of agriculture and industry" (Brodsgaard 1983a). Following the disastrous and unsustainable rural focus on agricultural capital construction during the GLF, the central government pushed rural areas to focus on agricultural production, and beginning in the mid-1960s the Dazhai became the key model of self-reliance. The accumulation rate again rose.

Furthermore, the fundamental material tension between accumulation for reinvestment and agricultural production generated a series of derivative or secondary tensions. One of the most salient and enduring of these was the conflict between accumulation and rural consumption (Yang 1958; Zhongguo Renmin Daxue 1958: 126–30), leading to the waning of peasant initiative and the decline in agricultural production. This temporal problematic would return as a pivotal issue at the end of the 1970s, leading to the return of the household as the basic unit of agricultural production (Teiwes and Sun 2016). Yet beginning in the 1950s, the party was well aware that propaganda, ideological work, and future promises could only do so much to alleviate this tension.

A confusing and unstable series of remuneration policies and forms emerged in the countryside to govern consumption from the 1960s onward, from various systems of tying remuneration to the quantity and quality of work and production, to the Dazhai system with its focus on attitudes and collective evaluation, to diverse responsibility systems, and to task rate systems. Seen in this light, the initial experimentation with responsibility systems in the wake of Mao's death was more continuous with earlier policies than is often admitted. All of these constituted forms of socialist accounting, linking work and consumption—"remuneration according to labor" (*gongzizhi* 工资制)—necessary once production decisions were divorced from the family form they had taken for so long. It was only during the GLF that rural production began to partially break from these regimes of accounting with the "free supply system" (*gongjizhi* 供给制) system, only to shift back to various accounting systems in the early 1960s.[2] Under the heavily promoted draft guidelines for the Weixing commune in the late 1950s, distribution for consumption (through both wages and supply systems) was oriented toward the rapid expansion of production. While consumption was supposed to increase each year, it was to do so more slowly than the rate of increase of production, allowing local accumulation, capital spending, and agricultural modernization to increase at a faster rate. The rate of growth of remuneration was to slow even further as average income of commune members reached the level of "well-off middle peasants" (*Weixing renmin gongshe* 1958). Nonetheless, a partial break from accounting of the GLF led to the emergence of new forms of social reproduction, reshaping everyday life. If at the level of material *content* the fundamental tension shaping rural everyday life was between the needs of accumulation and the limits of agricultural production, at the level of *form* this tension took on a twofold expression: of social forms and of policy and political discourse.

The Family and Social Reproduction: The Social Form of Rural Life and Production

The modernization of agriculture under the CCP was premised on breaking with the family form of production, a process that allowed the state to intervene in production decisions, mobilize labor, speed up capital construction, and accumulate surplus for the industrialization process. The patriarchal rural family was the center of production decisions and the organization of labor before 1949, and within it the production of goods and social reproduction of labor were not clearly differentiated, but rather fused under the general category of subsistence. Family-controlled and organized labor worked to produce for their own subsistence as well as producing commodities for the market, all of which aimed at adding to the overall subsistence and wealth of the family (Gates 1996; Huang 1990; Walker 1990). This social system could often tend toward an involutionary dynamic of declining labor productivity with increasing absolute production (Huang 1990). As party propagandists argued in the 1950s, agricultural and handicraft production were trapped within the cage of the feudal family, which had to be broken in the socialization process (Hu 1958: 29).

Accounting appeared with the end of the "small peasant economy" (*xia-onong jingji* 小农经济), within which the family had no need to account directly for labor power. Crucial to accounting was deciding what counted as formal productive activity in need of remuneration, and a new divide and relationship between production and social reproduction emerged, constituting one of the key structures of rural everyday life. The formalization of labor occurred at the level of social forms (how social relations and everyday life transformed once production was no longer organized primarily by the family) and policy discourse and its categories (how productive labor was to be named and what systems of accounting were to be used). The meaning and social role of work, production, sideline production, surplus, class, the family, and gender relations were all redefined in the process.

A main point here is that the divide between production and social reproduction—a key structure of everyday life—is historical. As Lise Vogel (1983: 27) points out, "Problems in defining the concept of reproduction derive from its wide range of potential meanings." Social reproduction theory emerged in the West during the 1970s, an important contribution of Western Marxist feminism. Overall, at stake in the project was a unitary theory that could give "an account of the systemic connection of gender and class relations" (Ferguson et al. 2016: 29). To construct such a theory, Vogel (1983) and others focused on the processes of "social reproduction,"[3] work that "highlighted and examined the logic of the contradictory but necessary internal/external relationship between gendered and economic productive relations" (Ferguson et al. 2016: 28). In the words of Ferguson et al. (2016: 29):

> Vogel argues that capitalist forms of gender oppression exist and persist because of the systematic—necessary and contradictory—relation between the production of labour-power (social reproduction) and the production of value or capital. Capital needs labour-power but does not produce it directly. Social relations outside of the direct labour/capital relation—Vogel and most [social reproduction feminist] theorists have explored those of gender in particular—shape the processes and institutions through which labour-power is (re)produced. But these relations are simultaneously shaped by, and exist in, articulation with the capitalist dynamic of accumulation.

The costs of social reproduction are externalized from the production process and usually located in the family. As Peggy Morton argued, the family was "a unit whose function is the *maintenance of and reproduction of labor power*" (quoted in Vogel 1983: 18). Under capitalism, the gendered labor of social reproduction within the family is cheapened and degraded (Ferguson et al. 2016: 30).

In Chinese debates in the 1950s, the concept of social reproduction comprised the reproduction of society as a whole, with the more specific connotation concerning the work that went into the social reproduction of labor power (*laodong li zaishengchan* 劳动力再生产) rising in importance as the GLF commenced (see Xu D. 1959: 279). The theorization in China, however, had a less critical and more instrumental purpose, the further development of the productive forces as they encountered material limits. Even in the most theoretically rich contributions, such as by Hu Sheng (1958), the focus remained on its role in producing a use value in the form of labor power. The "socialization of production" (*shengchan shehuihua* 生产社会化) in the 1950s required a distinction between production and social reproduction, as "productive" labor was no longer organized within the family. With the socialist formalization of labor—its separation from the family unit—the state defined certain tasks as productive labor (*shengchan laodong* 生产劳动) or social labor (*shehui laodong* 社会劳动), which deserved recompense, and other tasks as nonproductive labor/household labor/household tasks (sometimes *jiawu laodong* 家务劳动 but also *jiawu suoshi* 家务琐事), with a clear judgment of relative importance inherent in the dichotomy. As was noted by Western social reproduction theorists concerning capitalism, the socialist developmental regime likewise contained a necessary and contradictory internal/external relationship between the two spheres.

As with the term *social reproduction*, the definition of *productive labor* is historical and specific to social formations. It is important to note, therefore, that *productive labor* meant something different under the developmental regime than it does under capitalism. Under capitalism, *productive labor* is labor that produces surplus value; it entails a valorization process resulting in capital accumulation (Marx 1976: 644). Within the PRC, however, the line between productive and unproductive labor was shifting and never as clearly established. There, labor was productive if it produced an absolute quantity and particular quality of capturable surplus product. The state needed particular goods (particular amounts and qualities of grain, steel, cotton, etc.) that it could accumulate and reinvest for the national economy to develop and industrialize, as its goal was the expansion of the means of production, not of capital. This is clearly visible in the planning process, known as Material Balance Planning (Eckstein 1977).

These different logics have important implications for social reproduction and what counts as internal or external to the production process, although both are highly gendered. Under capitalism, the costs of social reproduction are usually pushed onto unpaid labor in the family, primarily women, constituting the externalization of reproduction costs. As more women enter the workforce, increasing aspects of social reproduction are commodified (from childcare and food preparation to the production of clothing). The trajectory in the PRC was quite different. Before the collectivization of agriculture in the 1950s, social reproduction was internalized in the household, within which reproductive and productive activity all contributed to the household's overall subsistence, and thus the distinction was not formalized. With collectivization and the socialization of *production*, some aspects of *social reproduction* were socialized. This process and the different forms through which reproduction costs are integrated within society have important consequences for social relations and the structure of everyday life. From the 1950s through the 1970s, from the perspective of the PRC state, social-reproductive labor in the household was not "productive," since its products were not directly accumulated and reinvested in the process of expanding the means of production. Thus, as rural production was socialized in the mid-1950s—raised to the level of the collective—social reproduction initially remained somewhat hidden within the family. Nonetheless, this does not mean the state ignored social reproductive labor, rather it paid attention particularly at times of labor shortage—at times in which the *efficiency* of social reproduction would lead to the inexpensive expansion of the labor supply for productive activities. Furthermore, this formalization process, in which a systematic link was drawn between one's productive labor and one's formal compensation, required a system of measurement or accounting of labor. Some work was privileged, deserving compensation, and other work disappeared from view within this formal system (Hershatter 2011: 138–39; Eyferth 2015: 134). This was a gendered process (Hershatter 2011). The moments in which socially reproductive labor became formalized, although usually weakly so, were at moments of rapid accumulation and labor shortage.

With the Great Leap Forward in the late 1950s, the accumulation strategy intensified and shifted, and the line between production and social reproduction shifted along with it. The accumulation rate rose dramatically during the GLF. The rate averaged 24.2 percent during the First Five-Year Plan (1953–57), a figure at which it was anticipated to stay during the Second Five-Year Plan. However, it rapidly rose from 24.9 percent in 1957 to 33.9 percent in 1958 and 43.8 percent in 1959 (Brodsgaard 1983a: 49). This entailed a massive increase in capital construction (including in agriculture, which received slightly more investment during the GLF years). And this in turn led to a shift of labor out of agricultural and often rural production, with more than twenty million people moving into cities during the GLF (Brown 2012: 79). The massive rural population was no longer seen as a potential detriment to socialist construction; rather, it became the foundation for a surge in capital construction. In a founding document of the GLF, Liu Shaoqi (1962: 431) stated in 1958:

> The great forward leap in agricultural production and construction this year has not only completely knocked the bottom out of [critics'] contention that agriculture cannot make quick progress but also blown sky high their argument that a big population impedes accumulation. All they see is that men are consumers and that the greater the population, the bigger the consumption. They fail to see that men are first of all producers and that when there is a large population there is also the possibility of greater production and more accumulation.

Under these conditions, the material limits of the labor supply forced an open inquiry into the relationship between production and social reproduction. Material limits, in other words, led to an investigation into and emergence of new social forms and categories, entailing the socialization of reproductive labor for the efficient reproduction of labor power. Collective cooking and dining, collective clothes making, birthing stations, collective childcare, and the machine milling of collective flour came to be known as the "five changes" (Hershatter 2011: 246). The rural labor shortage led to new social forms and the beginning of a break from labor accounting, a shift from a system of "remuneration according to labor" to a "free supply system" system.

The discussions of gender, household tasks, and labor at the time revealed the problems of governing the distinction between production and reproduction and of the accounting of the work-consumption relation. The suggestion at the time was to go one step further, in part expanding formalization (bringing some household tasks into the formal system of productive labor) and in part breaking with the formalization process and its accounting systems by delinking the measurement of work from consumption (forms of free distribution). Expanded formalization, always gendered, came before the end of accounting, or at least that was to be the trajectory. This was the communist horizon.

Yet the limit could not be transcended because of the developmental logic of accumulation and industrialization. The GLF, therefore, revealed the tension at the center of attempts to expand rural production and extraction at the same time. On the one hand, this necessitated the socialization of household tasks and the entry of women's labor into production. On the other hand, this had to be accomplished through self-reliance with little investment. The conditions of reproduction were exhausted.

The Emergence and Disappearance of the Debate on Social Reproduction

The appearance of new social forms was matched with an emerging theorization of social reproduction within political and policy discourse as the material limits of rural labor changed. Following the Eighth Party Congress in 1956, the state understood that both urban and rural labor was in surplus, and it expected this condition to continue for some time to come. This situation necessitated controls over rural-to-urban migration and led to an expansion of birth planning in 1956 (Zhongguo Renmin Daxue 1960: 436; Chao 1963: 119). During the First Five-Year Plan (FYP), eight million people moved from the countryside to the city, and another seven million were to have moved according to the Second FYP (Wang 1963: 144–45). At the same time, party officials called for urban unemployed people to move to the countryside when possible and for strong efforts to be made in finding productive placements for the unemployed (Zhou 1957). Rural "economic diversification" was seen as an answer (Zhongguo Renmin Daxue 1960: 436–37). An official of the National Planning Commission, writing in 1957, argued that agricultural producers' cooperatives should develop subsidiary productive activities to soak up surplus labor. Nonetheless, time for household work and private activities were to be recognized and set aside (Wang 1963: 147–48). In fact, household labor was not only recognized as a form that soaked up surplus labor, but also seen as an important support to national construction (Zhou 1957; W. Liu 2007). Already by 1956, rural collectivization showed that surplus labor could be productively used and that that would open the need to tap into the "great human resource" (*weida de renli ziyuan* 伟大的人力资源) of female labor power (Zhongguo Renmin Daxue 1960: 437).

The Third National Congress of Chinese Women in September 1957 linked "national construction through thrift" (*qinjian jianguo* 勤俭建国) to "thriftiness in running the household" (*qinjian chijia* 勤俭持家)" (W. Liu 2007). Household labor and particularly women's work was to make up for the lack of investment in light industry, which produced everyday household commodities, with the bias toward investment in heavy industry. Through 1957, however, this labor remained in the household, though no longer as hidden, with Zhou Enlai stating that "household labor was a part of social labor" and that it made important contributions to the nation and society (Zhou 1957).

The rapid transformation of the economy and everyday life called basic social categories into question. Early in 1958, Mao, in a call for continued debate on the nature of socialism, pointed to the persistence of the family under socialism as a key question, along with the investigation into the law of value and the criteria for setting wages (Mao 1967). The family, according to Mao, was historical, with a beginning and an end. It came into existence as a singular unit of production and consumption, but with the socialization of production, it only remained as a unit of consumption and reproduction of labor. The family only persists under socialism not because of the needs of production but because of the remuneration system of "to each according to labor" (*anlao fenpei* 按劳分配). Once society reaches the stage of communism, within which distribution would be "according to need" (*gequ suoxu* 各取所需), the social form of the family would die out and conceptual forms would be transformed as well. Mao saw this happening over several hundred or even as much as a few thousand years. But the ground was shifting fast in 1958 (Mao 1967).

Speaking to the Women's Association later in June 1958, Liu Shaoqi referenced Mao's discussion of the family, maintaining that the elimination of the family was still a task for the future. Yet under the new GLF conditions of a growing labor shortage, especially, but not only, in rural areas during harvest, Liu examined the social role of the family and women's labor, calling for the "liberation of women's labor power" (*jiefang funü laodongli* 解放妇女劳动力) (Liu Shaoqi 1958). Liu and others noted that the formation of urban industrial production cooperatives during the spring of 1958 was both partially responsible for urban labor shortages and was providing answers to the problem (Liu Shaoqi 1958; *Renmin ribao* 1958b; Hu 1958: 26). The same was true for the contemporary formation of the agricultural communes. The socialization of production was leading to the socialization of reproductive labor (*jiawu laodong shehuihua* 家务劳动社会化) and the organization of production to the organization of life (*zuzhi shenghuo* 组织生活). The period of women primarily working frugally in the household, as called for by the "Third National Congress of Chinese Women" just a year before, was over; women were now to leave the household and enter production.[4] Drawing examples from both rural communes and urban collectives, Liu called for the expansion of communal dining halls, nurseries, and other forms of socialized reproduction that had already been emerging. Nonetheless, this was a project for the masses to complete on their own, unaided by government investment. The self-reliance of the "thrifty and hardworking household" was to be replaced by the frugal collective organized by the masses (Liu Shaoqi 1958).

Xu Dixin, an economic planner and theorist of a socialist "law of value,"[5] likewise framed the problem of the social reproduction of labor in terms of its relationship to surplus population. Following Marx, Xu believed that capitalism produced a surplus population as it focused on raising labor productivity for the benefit of accumulating capital. Xu argued that this problem was being resolved as China moved into a socialist economy starting in the mid-1950s. The GLF, in fact, produced a labor shortage as production surged, and this led to the formation of the people's communes that "liberated the labor of women in the household" (Xu D. 1959: 279–82).[6] The Beidaihe resolution on the establishment of communes of late August 1958 also argued that because of the sharp increase in capital construction and rural industrialization, demands on labor transformed rural social life, including the institution of collective forms of social reproduction (Central Committee of the Chinese Communist Party [1958] 1962a: 454). Yet with the Beidaihe resolution, the discussion increasingly shifted from one primarily concerning the practical issues of labor shortages and the search for efficiency within social reproduction to one politically framed in terms of a move toward communism.

One of the most theoretically complex discussions on social reproduction came from Hu Sheng, a party propagandist and writer for the new party theoretical journal *Hongqi*. According to Hu (1958: 26), rural collectivization, and the surge of production that accompanied it, made it obvious that labor expended on household tasks held back continued advances. Even without technological improvements, the socialization of such activities would economize on labor power, while collectivization set the foundation for later mechanization. While reproductive labor was still necessary, with collectivization the character and status of reproductive labor were transformed from household labor to social labor. For Hu, this was a "second liberation of women," without which liberation would be incomplete.

But Hu goes further than the arguments of the early spring. On the basis of collectivizing production, other aspects of everyday life had to be socialized as well, and only by transforming everyday life was socialism and communism possible. "The content of everyday life" (*shenghuo de jingchang neirong* 生活的经常内容) could only be expanded by breaking with the family unit at an enlarged social scale (Hu 1958: 27). This led Hu to argue that the socialization of household tasks was not only a response to temporary labor shortages; rather its real content was the extension of collective life.

Nonetheless, this expansive vision was limited by overall political economy and the rural extraction on which it was based. According to Hu (1958: 27), there were two methods of socializing the activities of social reproduction: the state could provide them in a top-down manner through investments, or they could be "established mainly relying on the strength of the masses." Echoing Liu Shaoqi and others, Hu argued that the latter method would be quicker and more economical. Here, the inside/outside contradiction raised by social reproduction theorists is clearly expressed: while the social reproduction of labor was suddenly seen as crucial during the labor shortages of the GLF, its solution lay largely outside of state investment. "Crude and simple methods" of the masses had to be used; social reproduction would be transformed through self-reliance and "thrift" (Hu 1958: 28), echoing the language of the Third National Congress of Chinese Women. "Thrift" was transformed from a positive characteristic of household austerity, which allowed for more rapid accumulation, into a cheap way of producing more labor power (Hu 1958: 28; Xin B. 1958: 101). Communization only went so far.

Despite Mao's suggestion that the family would someday disappear, however, it is clear the Party worried about a reaction to its decline. Hu likewise pointed out that the family was a historical phenomenon tied to the economic system of production, to its class structures. The historical family bound up with class structures would be destroyed in the process of the socialization of everyday life. In its stead, the working-class family would be renewed, the way of life of the separate household would be brought to an end, and a new everyday life would be established. "The nuclear family (*fufu ernu zucheng de xiao jiating* 夫妇儿女组成的小家庭) would certainly persist for a very long time, even as the people's livelihood would far exceed the scope of the family" (Hu 1958: 30). Popularizing Hu's argument, Liu Song (1958: 93–4) stated that the new nuclear family would "naturally" continue to exist for a very long time, but "the enclosed, small family form of life" would be destroyed. An article in *Zhongguo Qingnian* argued that with the end of private property the family would be dramatically transformed but not eliminated. "If women continue to live in the pattern of a separate family life the broad masses of them will be still tied down to household chores . . . unable to participate in social production, lead an organized political life, learn techniques, and seek cultural advancement" (Zhai 1958: 7). Family life, redefined, would no longer be a burden on women, holding them and society back, but families would still participate in the raising of children and care for the elderly (Zhai 1958). The texts, in other words, attempt to manage expectations: while suggesting rapid advances in material production, families did not have to fear the complete disappearance of the family anytime soon, as the social organization of everyday life would take a slower progressive climb through historical stages.

By the late fall of 1958, the party leadership, including Mao, attempted to moderate the enthusiasm for a rapid shift to communism (Teiwes and Sun 1999: chap. 4). Criticizing both those unenthusiastic and those overly enthusiastic about the shift to communism in the countryside, Xu Liqun ([1958] 1962) argued in *Red Flag* that the full transition to a communist system of supply, in which need alone was the criterion of distribution, was impossible at a time in which the majority of one's income was taken up by expenditures for food. While discussions of social reproduction had begun as a practical reaction to labor shortages at a time of rapid capital accumulation and construction, in the spring and summer of 1958 discussions were inflected as a political issue concerning the shift to communism. By the fall they had swung back. For Xu and others, the key standard was whether a change in systems of distribution would advance production or not, and the answer was not yet. The December Central Committee ([1958] 1962b: 491–92) resolution on communes called for a consolidation of the commune movement, stressing the gradualness of the shift to "ownership by the whole people"—taking twenty or more years—and the communist principle of redistribution according to needs, which would take even "much more time." The communal "free supply system" expressed the "first shoots of . . . communist principles," but wages would "occupy an important place over a long period:" "premature" transition was "utopian" (Central Committee [1958] 1962b: 493–94). In his April 1959 work report to the National People's Congress, Zhou ([1959] 1962: 514–15) noted that, despite the commune's liberation of women from household chores, there was still a shortage of rural labor power, and this affected agricultural production. Agricultural work should consume at least 80 percent of the rural labor force, and urban districts should send surplus laborers back to the countryside. Over time, increasing agricultural labor productivity from mechanization and agricultural modernization would relieve the problem.

The Socialist Developmental Regime, Capitalism, and the Critique of Categories

In some ways, it would be easier to construct a political economy of the PRC and its everyday life if it had been capitalist from the mid-1950s on, for capitalism's categories and social forms are brought into concert through the mediation of its value form in a way that does not occur within the socialist developmental regime. Marx's critique of political economy focused on the field's rationalist construction of fixed and ahistorical analytical categories. The political economists produced seemingly timeless, presupposed, and self-evident categories that they would apply to capitalism from the outside. But Marx showed that the categories themselves were historical and emerged with and within the development of capitalism. As Geoff Pilling (1980: 28) states, "Capital was, for Marx, a definite social relation in which the labour process took on a determinate historical form, the form of a value-creating and *a fortiori* a *surplus-value*-creating process." Abstract labor, or human labor in general irrespective of its concrete attributes, became the crucial "relation of social mediation" under capitalism, a relation that "requires a specific objective manifestation which it first obtains in money" (Heinrich 2015). Money, in Marx's words, is abstract labor's "immediate form of existence" (quoted in Heinrich 2015). Such a relation only emerges, however, once the commodification of labor power is generalized, the concrete labor of individuals across society becomes commensurate, and thus a commodity's value expresses the socially necessary labor time of its production. But for the political economists Marx critiqued, the process of commodification becomes naturalized and hidden: theory (discursive form) becomes separated from history (material content). Following Marx, Ferguson et al. (2016: 31) state that "the task of theory is incomplete if it remains in the realm of the abstract. Theory's task is to comprehend and articulate the concrete unity of the diverse." The theorization of capitalist categories, therefore, had to be immanent to the historical emergence of capitalism.

From around the mid-1950s onwards in China, however, labor power was not commodified, and abstract labor was not a dominant form of social mediation. Labor power produced only specific goods in the production process, not value, as it did in capitalism. The resulting social formation did not have the same degree of coherence as capitalism. This does not mean there was no structure, but rather that the structure that existed was only unified at the level of the central state through domination of purchasing, marketing, and taxation, the control of labor allocation and remuneration, and the regulation of production decisions. Most dramatically, rural and urban flows were institutionally divided and regulated by the state, and, unlike in capitalism, there was no easy way to compare the value of rural and urban labor. Whereas in capitalism there is a sharper divide between state and market, within the PRC the state increasingly took on the mediating role of the market. Only at the level of the state was there any unity of society.[7]

None of the systems of labor remuneration that developed allowed for a measure of socially necessary labor time to emerge as a value form, through money, even when people were paid wages or received goods in return for labor. Unlike in capitalism, within which prices reflected the socially necessary labor time of a commodity, within the PRC social formation prices were used to guide the planned economy. Within capitalism, in other words, prices were expressions of the value produced by labor; within the socialist developmental regime, prices were top-down impositions of the planners (Eckstein 1977; Perkins 1966). While the Chinese debate on social reproduction in the 1950s stressed the increased efficiency brought about by the dining halls, nurseries, sewing teams, and the like, the goal was how much absolute labor could be then put into agricultural and industrial production, which was considered "social productive labor." Productive labor was defined, from the standpoint of the developmental regime, as a productive force that produced a specific set and quantity of absolute product. And as such there was no mechanism through which different specific qualities of labor came to be commensurate with an abstract quantity or value, as abstract labor.

In the PRC, therefore, the dialectical emergence of categories (form) out of material conditions (content) was a much more fractured and halting process, yet it was nonetheless still structured by the overall political economy of the social formation, namely, the state's direct domination of the specific products of absolute social surplus. Within different sectors of PRC society, the state's demand for specific surplus product had different measures, colliding with specific material limits and producing particular social effects. Out of this process new social forms and discursive categories emerged. It was here that everyday life was produced.

The implication for drawing broader conclusions about the period are important. Following Elizabeth Perry, Brown and Johnson (2015: 1) suggest that they can be formed by "putting together our local case studies . . . like a jigsaw puzzle." But this metaphor is somewhat misleading and does not really represent the way most PRC historians work. As Pilling (1980: 26) suggests, "The 'general' for the empiricist is mechanically constructed out of a series of 'concrete' experiences and in this way all dialectical relations are set aside, since the universal is merely analysed from the empirically concrete." This article suggests that a more general understanding of the production of everyday life in 1950s rural China can only be arrived at through an analysis of the development of social and discursive forms, forms that emerge in dialectical relationship to the material developments and limits of society. The forms of everyday life, not only their particular content, are at issue.

Notes

I wish to thank Angelina Chin, Chris Connery, Gail Hershatter, Fabio Lanza, Huaiyin Li, Aminda Smith, Malcolm Thompson, and the anonymous reviewers for comments and for opportunities to present and discuss material in this piece.

1   On these different forms of relations of production, see Hebei Provincial Committee (1962: 474); Central Committee of the Chinese Communist Party ([1958] 1962a: 456); *Renmin ribao* (1958a).

2   On these shifts in the remunerative systems, see X. Xu (1959: 142); Y. Xin (2011: 132).

3   For a recent discussion on social reproduction theory, see *Viewpoint Magazine* (2015).

4   Liu is explicit in noting this break from 1957 Congress's slogan of "national construction through thrift, thriftiness in running the household" (*qinjian jianguo, qinjian chijia* (勤俭建国, 勤俭持家) (Liu Shaoqi 1958).

5   For the best discussion of the debates on the "socialist law of value," see Thompson (forthcoming 2022).

6   For a contemporary Marxist theorization of the capitalist tendency to produce a surplus population, see *Endnotes* 2010.

7   See *Chuang* 2016 for a similar argument.

References

Barnett, A. Doak. 1953. "China's Road to Collectivization." *Journal of Farm Economics* 35, no. 2: 188–202.

Bowie, Robert R., and John K. Fairbanks, eds. 1962. *Communist China, 1955–1959: Policy Documents with Analysis.* Cambridge, MA: Harvard University Press.

Brodsgaard, Kjeld Erik. 1983a. "Paradigmatic Change: Readjustment and Reform in the Chinese Economy, 1953–1981, Part I." *Modern China* 9, no. 1: 37–83.

Brodsgaard, Kjeld Erik. 1983b. "Paradigmatic Change: Readjustment and Reform in the Chinese Economy, 1953–1981, Part II." *Modern China* 9, no. 2: 253–72.

Brown, Jeremy. 2012. *City versus Countryside in Mao's China: Negotiating the Divide.* Cambridge: Cambridge University Press.

Brown, Jeremy, and Matthew D. Johnson, eds. 2015. *Maoism at the Grassroots: Everyday Life in China's Era of High Socialism.* Cambridge, MA: Harvard University Press.

Central Committee of the Chinese Communist Party. (1958) 1962a. "Resolution of the Central Committee of the Chinese Communist Party on the Establishment of People's Communes in the Rural Areas (Peitaiho Resolution)." In *Communist China, 1955–1959: Policy Documents with Analysis*, edited by Robert R. Bowie and John K. Fairbanks, 454–56. Cambridge, MA: Harvard University Press.

Central Committee of the Chinese Communist Party. (1958) 1962b. "Resolution on Some Questions Concerning the People's Communes (Wuhan Resolution)." In *Communist China, 1955–1959: Policy Documents with Analysis*, edited by Robert R. Bowie and John K. Fairbanks, 488–503. Cambridge, MA: Harvard University Press.

Chao, Kuo-chun. 1963. *Economic Planning and Organization in Mainland China: A Documentary Study (1949–1957).* Vol. 1. Cambridge, MA: Harvard University Press.

Chuang. 2016. "Sorghum and Steel." Issue no. 1. chuangcn.org/journal/one/sorghum-and-steel/ (accessed June 1, 2021).

Colby, Hunter W., Frederick Crook, and Shwa-Eng Webb. 1992. "Agricultural Statistics of the People's Republic of China, 1949–1990." ideas.repec.org/p/ags/uerssb/154783.html (accessed June 1, 2021).

Eckstein, Alexander. 1977. *China's Economic Revolution.* Cambridge: Cambridge University Press.

Endnotes. 2010. "Misery and Debt: On the Logic and History of Surplus Populations and Surplus Capital." endnotes.org.uk/issues/2/en/endnotes-misery-and-debt (accessed June 1, 2021).

Eyferth, Jacob. 2015. "Liberation from the Loom? Rural Women, Textile Work, and Revolution in North China." In *Maoism at the Grassroots: Everyday Life in China's Era of High Socialism*, edited by Jeremy Brown and Matthew D. Johnson, 131–54. Cambridge, MA: Harvard University Press.

Ferguson, Susan, Genevieve LeBaron, Angela Dimitrakaki, and Sara R. Farris. 2016. "Introduction." *Historical Materialism* 24, no. 2: 25–37.

Food and Agriculture Organization. 1999. "Poverty Alleviation and Food Security in Asia: Lessons and Challenges." www.fao.org/docrep/004/ab981e/ab981e00.htm#Contents (accessed June 1, 2021).

Gates, Hill. 1996. *China's Motor: A Thousand Years of Petty Capitalism*. Ithaca, NY: Cornell University Press.

Hebei Provincial Committee. 1962. "Directive of the Hopei Provincial Committee of the Party on the Building of People's Communes." In *Communist China, 1955–1959: Policy Documents with Analysis*, edited by Robert R. Bowie and John K. Fairbanks, 470–77. Cambridge, MA: Harvard University Press.

Heinrich, Michael. 2015. "Too Much Production: Postone's New Interpretation of Marx's Theory Provides a Categorical Critique with Deficits." libcom.org, March 18. libcom.org /library/too-much-production-postone%E2%80%99s-new-interpretation-marx%E2%80 %99s-theory-provides-categorical-crit#:~:text=deficits%20%2D%20Michael%20Heinrich -,Too%20much%20production%3A%20Postone's%20new%20interpretation%20of%20Marx's %20theory%20provides,critique%20with%20deficits%20%2D%20Michael%20 Heinrich&text=Postone%20opposes%20to%20this%20a,at%20the%20center%20of%20 analysis.

Hershatter, Gail. 2011. *The Gender of Memory: Rural Women and China's Collective Past*. Berkeley: University of California Press.

Hou, Xiaojia. 2010. "'Get Organized': The Impact of Two Soviet Models on the CCP's Rural Strategy, 1949–1953." In *China Learns from the Soviet Union, 1949–Present*, edited by Thomas P. Bernstein and Hua-yu Li, 168–97. Lanham, MD: Lexington Books.

Hu, Sheng. 1958. "Jiawu laodong de jitihua, shehuihua" 家务劳动的集体化,社会化 ("The Collectivization and Socialization of Household Labor"). *Hongqi* 红旗 (*Red Flag*), no. 7: 24–30.

Huang, Phillip C. C. 1990. *The Peasant Family and Rural Development in the Yangzi Delta, 1350–1988*. Stanford, CA: Stanford University Press.

Iggers, Georg G. 2005. *Historiography in the Twentieth Century: From Scientific Objectivity to the Postmodern Challenge*. Middletown, CT: Wesleyan University Press.

Li, Fuchun. 1963. "Report on the Achievements of the First Five-Year Plan of Our Country and the Tasks and Directions in Socialist Construction in the Future." In *Economic Planning and Organization in Mainland China: A Documentary Study (1949–1957)*, vol. 1, edited by Kuo-chun Chao, 35–45. Cambridge, MA: Harvard University Press.

Lin, Chun. 2017. "Discipline and Power: Knowledge of China in Political Science." *Critical Asian Studies* 49, no. 4: 501–22.

Liu, Shaoqi. 1958. "Tong quanguo fulian dangzu de tanhua" 同全国妇联党组的谈话 ("A Talk with the National Women's League Party Group"). June 14. www.marxists.org/chinese/liushaoqi/1967/111.htm.

Liu, Shaoqi. 1962. "Report on the Work of the Central Committee of the Communist Party of China to the Second Session of the Eighth National Congress." In *Communist China, 1955–1959: Policy Documents with Analysis*, edited by Robert R. Bowie and John K. Fairbanks, 416–38. Cambridge, MA: Harvard University Press.

Liu, Song 刘松. 1958. "Guanyu jiawu laodong de jitihua, shehuihua" 关于家务劳动的集体化,社会化 ("Concerning the Collectivization and Socialization of Household Labor"). *Qingnian gongchanzhuyizhe congkan* 青年共产主义者丛刊 (*Youth Communist*) November: 89–96.

Liu, Weifang 刘维芳. 2007. "Zhongguo funü gongzuo 'liang qin' fangzhen queli de qianqian houhou" 中国妇女工作 "两勤" 方针确立的前前后后 ("The Whole Story of the Establishment of Chinese Women's Work 'Two Diligences' Principle"). *Dangdai Zhongguo shi yanjiu* 当代中国研究 (*Contemporary China Historical Studies*) 14, no. 6: 100–107.

Mao Zedong 毛泽东. 1967. "Zai Chengdu huiyi shang de jianghua" 在成都会议上的讲话 ("Fourth Talk to the Chengdu Conference" [March 22, 1958]). In *Mao Zedong sixiang wansui* 毛泽东思想万岁 (*Long Live Mao Zedong Thought*). N.p.

Marx, Karl. 1976. *Capital: A Critique of Political Economy*. Vol. 1. London: Penguin Books.

Oi, Jean C. 1989. *State and Peasant in Contemporary China: The Political Economy of Village Governance*. Berkeley: University of California Press.

Perkins, Dwight H. 1966. *Market Control and Planning in Communist China*. Cambridge, MA: Harvard University Press.

Perry, Elizabeth. 1999. "Partners at Fifty: American China Studies and the PRC." Paper presented at the "Trends in China Watching" conference, George Washington University, Washington, DC, October 8–9. www2.gwu.edu/~sigur/assets/docs/scap/SCAP7-Trends.pdf.

Perry, Elizabeth. 2016. "The Promise of PRC History." *Journal of Modern Chinese History* 10, no. 1: 113–17.

Pilling, Geoff. 1980. *Marx's Capital, Philosophy, and Political Economy*. London: Routledge.

Renmin ribao 人民日报 (*People's Daily*). 1958a. "Cong 'Weixing' gongshe de jianzhang tan ruhe ban gongshe" 从"卫星"公社的简章谈如何办公社 ("A Discussion on How to Form a Commune Based on 'Weixing' Communes General Regulations"). September 4.

Renmin ribao 人民日报 (*People's Daily*). 1958b. "Chengdu daban jiedao fuwuzuzhi shi xuduo funü cong jiawu laodong zhong jiefang chulai" 成都大办街道服务组织使许多妇女从家务劳动中解放出来 ("Chengdu's Great Organization of Residential District Services Has Led to the Liberation of Many Women from Household Labor"). September 4.

State Planning Commission. 1963. "Chubu yanjiu di guanyu dierget wunianjihua di ruogan wenti" ("Certain Problems in the Preliminary Studies of the Second Five-Year Plan"). In *Economic Planning and Organization in Mainland China: A Documentary Study (1949–1957)*, vol. 1, edited by Kuo-chun Chao, 29–35. Cambridge, MA: Harvard University Press.

Teiwes, Frederick C., and Warren Sun. 1999. *China's Road to Disaster: Mao, Central Politicians, and Provincial Leaders in the Unfolding of the Great Leap Forward, 1955–1959.* Armonk, NY: M. E. Sharpe.

Teiwes, Frederick C., and Warren Sun. 2016. *Paradoxes of Post-Mao Rural Reform: Initial Steps toward a New Chinese Countryside, 1976–1981.* London: Routledge.

Thompson, Malcolm. Forthcoming 2022. "From the Law of Value Debate to the One Child Policy in China: On Accounting and Biopolitics." *positions.*

Viewpoint Magazine. 2015. "Issue 5: Social Reproduction." July 5. www.viewpointmag.com /2015/11/02/issue-5-social-reproduction.

Vogel, Lise. 1983. *Marxism and the Oppression of Women: Toward a Unitary Theory.* New Brunswick, NJ: Rutgers University Press.

Walker, Kathy LeMons. 1990. *Chinese Modernity and the Peasant Path: Semicolonialism in the Northern Yangzi Delta.* Stanford, CA: Stanford University Press.

Wallerstein, Immanuel. 2006. *World-Systems Analysis: An Introduction.* Durham, NC: Duke University Press.

Wang, Guangwei. 1963. "Duiyu anpai nongye laodongli di yijian" ("How to Organize Agricultural Labor Power"). In *Economic Planning and Organization in Mainland China: A Documentary Study (1949–1957)*, vol. 1, edited by Kuo-chun Chao, 143–51. Cambridge, MA: Harvard University Press.

Weixing renmin gongshe 卫星人民公社. 1958. "Weixing Renmin Gongshe shixing jianzhang (caoan)" 卫星人民公社实行简章(草案) ("Putting into Practice Weixing People's Commune General Regulations [Draft]"). *Renmin ribao* 人民日报 (*People's Daily*), September 4.

Xin, Bing 新兵. 1958. "Chayashan Weixing Renmin Gongshe de tuoer zuzhi" 嵖岈山卫星人民公社的托尔组织 ("The Organization of Childcare at Chayashan Weixing People's Commune"). *Qingnian gongchanzhuyizhe congkan*, 101–3.

Xin, Yi. 2011. "On the Distribution System of Large-Scale People's Communes." In *Eating Bitterness: New Perspectives on China's Great Leap Forward and Famine*, edited by Kimberley Ens Manning and Felix Wemheuer, 130–47. Vancouver: UBC Press.

Xu, Dixin 许涤新. 1959. *Zhongguo guodu shiqi guomin jingji de fenxi (1959 xiudingben)* 中国过渡时期国民经济的分析 (1959 修订本) (*An Analysis of China's National Economy during the Transition Period* [1959 rev. ed.]). Beijing: Kexue chubanshe.

Xu, Liqun. [1958] 1962. "Have We Already Reached the Stage of Communism?" In *Communist China, 1955–1959: Policy Documents with Analysis*, edited by Robert R. Bowie and John K. Fairbanks, 479–83. Cambridge, MA: Harvard University Press.

Xu, Xianchun. 2009. "The Establishment, Reform, and Development of China's System of National Accounts." *Review of Income and Wealth* 55, suppl. 1: 442–65.

Yan, Shaochun. 1978. "Agricultural Production Planning." In *Chinese Economic Planning: Translations from Chi-hua Ching-chi*, edited by Nicholas Lardy, 24–36. Armonk, NY: M. E. Sharpe.

Yang, Bo 杨波. 1958. "Tantan renmin gongshe shouru fenpei zhong jilei he xiaofei guanxi" 谈谈人民公社收入分配中积累和消费关系 ("Discussing the Relationship between Accumulation and Consumption within People's Commune Income Distribution"). *Qingnian gongchanzhuyizhe congkan*, 131–35.

Zhai, Xiangdong. 1959. "How We Should Regard Communist Family Life." *Extracts from China Mainland Magazines*, 6–11.

Zhongguo Renmin Daxue xinwenxi Chayashan gongzuozu 中国人民大学新闻系嵖岈山工作. 1958. "Nongcun renmin gongshe de fenpei wenti" 农村人民公社的分配问题 ("Distribution Issues for Rural People's Communes"). *Qingnian gongchanzhuyizhe congkan*, 115–30.

Zhongguo Renmin Daxue zhengzhi jingjixue jiaoyanshi 中国人民大学政治经济学教研室. 1960. *Zhongguo shehuizhuyi jingji wenti: Wenjian zhailu* 中国社会主义经济问题:文件摘录 ("Economic Problems of Chinese Socialism: Document Extracts"). Beijing: People's University.

Zhou, Enlai 周恩来. 1957. "Guanyu laodong gongzi he laodong fuli zhengce de yijian" 关于劳动工资和劳动福利政策的意见 ("Opinions on Labor Wage and Labor Welfare Policy"). September 26. cpc.people.com.cn/GB/64184/64186/66664/4493153.html.

Zhou, Enlai. (1958) 1962. "Report on Government Work." In *Communist China, 1955–1959: Policy Documents with Analysis*, edited by Robert R. Bowie and John K. Fairbanks, 503–29. Cambridge, MA: Harvard University Press.

Afterword: Conversing with the Good Left about PRC History

Jan Kiely

Something Unusual

This has been an unusual experience. As an outsider to the PRC History Group and an anonymous reviewer, I had not expected to be invited to add this commentary at the last minute. How could I say no? Aminda Smith, Fabio Lanza, and their group's engagement with the criticisms and questions posed to them, their passion for the subject, and their commitment to substantive dialogues with those who think and work differently from themselves are admirable. I am happy to continue the conversation.[1]

There is much to recommend in these pages that I will assign to my graduate students. This includes useful sections on sources and methodology, especially the innovative sources analyzed by Sigrid Schmalzer and Smith's call to "map the grain" of Maoist sources. The inquiries into the relationship between methods and theoretical frameworks for this period

positions 29:4   DOI 10.1215/10679847-9286753
Copyright 2021 by Duke University Press

opens a path well worth pursuing with sustained effort. The self-reflection called for throughout—to ensure the "same level of empirical and epistemological scrutiny," as Smith puts it—is always important for historians. Even if not exhaustive, the range of theoretical genealogies traced offers much to explore and question about the common terms, categories, and assumptions with which we often think and write. I will also assign those sections I do not endorse, for the benefit of alternative perspectives and for the productive reflections stimulated by our differences.

Of course, not all that divides us inspires constructive debates. Let me simply note and set aside several of my less stimulating quibbles. Like Matthew Johnson (this issue), I do not perceive a crisis-level deficiency of understanding of Maoism in the scholarship. Nor do I consider the "demonizing" of Maoism to be dominant in the field tout court. The terms *irrational* and *illogical* (Smith foreword, this issue) may be common characterizations of Great Leap Forward economic policy, implementation, and persistence in the face of overwhelming evidence of disaster and of the political chaos of the Cultural Revolution, but hardly seem widespread, definitive judgments on the entirety of Maoism. The notion that the so-called "garbology" approach associated with Johnson and Jeremy Brown's targeted edited volume, *Maoism at the Grassroots* (2015), is hegemonic appears peculiar to a North American vantage point or "siloed" presumptions within the subfield. The assertions of these perceived problems contribute, at points, to erecting caricatures of existing scholarship that will be justifiably contested.

What I find more interesting is the fabric of the logics that distinguish this project. Of course, there is a lot going on in these articles, so, against my predilection, I will be reductive. As I read several versions of this project in the making, I thought of the contributors, in Maoist vocabulary, as consisting of a "backbone" core of the PRC History Group—the Good Left—and a few of their "friends." It is to the Good Left, and its proposed diagnosis of the problem in the field and prescription for a cure, that I address my comments, starting with the cure.

The Passion of the Good Left

To "Good PRC history is Left history" (Smith foreword, this issue), I reply: Left history can be good history *if* its theorizing and analyses enrich and sharpen our historical understandings and explanations. The Good Left's passion for inhabiting Maoism, seeing it from the inside out, in all its complexity, formation and evolution, fullness and limitation, as vision, theory, propagation, implementation, variant manifestations, lived experiences, reproductions, and imaginations promises much to our collective historical endeavor. Recapturing emancipatory visions and social inspirations surely is central to this. Yet I remain perplexed by the minimizing of scholarship that has made such contributions[2] and of commonalities across subfield periodization. There is no acknowledgment, for instance, that the much targeted Elizabeth Perry, in her most recent historical monograph (2012), sought to recover veins of inspiration in an initially nonviolent, moral vision for the oppressed in the CCP revolutionary tradition; see in this issue the views expressed by Smith, Lanza, Jake Werner, and Alexander Day. Their notion of inhabiting also seems particular to Maoism, and not meant to be extended, for instance, to the study of the Qing, the KMT, or the Wang Jingwei state. Why grant this twenty-seven-year period such an aura of exceptionalism?

A significant move in this project involves salvaging the reputation of Maoists in their time of governance; see in this issue, Smith (foreword and article); Lanza; Werner; Covell Meyskens. Defending Maoism's importance and against charges that it was "irrational," "dogmatic," "bumbling," and ineffective recalls previous salvage projects, such as the studies that challenged once standard narratives of the KMT's incompetence and inevitable failure (Kirby 1984; Wakeman 1995; Strauss 1998; Van de Ven 2003). Yet, in this comparison, I am struck by the Good Left's anxiety about the judgment. Something they see in the dismissals of Maoism and its import to their own hopes for recovering value seems responsible for this disquiet.

Recovering positive aspects of Maoism for the sake of a fuller, richer historical picture than we currently display does not seem to be enough for this project. The aim appears to be the resuscitation of an elementally Good Maoism. This is evident in arguments defending Maoist leadership and activists' authenticity, sincerity, and good intentions and in claims for a "popular legitimacy," not in Mencian, but in republican-popular sovereignty terms (in this issue, Smith foreword; Werner; Day). This deep desire to see, omnisciently, the essential honesty and moral good in the motives of historical actors concerns definitive judgments whose potential for substantiation and relevance to historical illumination can only be limited. This is not solely because of the difficulty of demonstrating such points with evidence, but also for the reason that historical records abound with cases of destructive, abusive human actions initiated by the sincere and well intentioned "on their own terms." More problematic, such an immutable, a priori determination asserts itself at the expense of the historian's struggle to comprehend the complexities of human thought and action in motion and context. Why insist to this extent?

The drive for this, as articulated most thoroughly by Smith in her foreword, is a product of dissatisfaction. The Good Left appears to be as disillusioned with the state of the field, with their teachers, and with China now as the "disillusioned scholars" they take to task were decades ago. Surely this would be a moment to draw on our historian's "empathetic imagination" (Wakeman 2009: 416, Bonnin 2013: xxv) and extend it to some of our colleagues and predecessors. I read in the ample discussions of the place of politics and presentism in this corner of historical studies tones and principles that evoke much about our recent present, especially looking out from within North American academia. There is an understandably strong desire for emancipatory visions and a feeling of profound repugnance with the notion that our histories might unconsciously, as William Sewell (2005) argued, abet, and that we would be "disarmed" before, powers and forces remaking the world for the dominant and destructive few. Disillusion can be creatively productive, as is evident in both generations, and the mutual recognition of our predicaments in different moments may be as helpful to our practice as mutual criticisms. We all seek to communicate intelligibly to our present in terms that are never free of our aspirations for the future, and, in doing so, cannot abrogate our principal mission to make sense of the past. The tensions involved are inherent to these aims and aspirations. To add a variation to Johnson's criticism in this issue, I would argue that all forms of politics, consciously and unconsciously reflected in history writing, can lose their potential for illumination and careen into obfuscation if they become unassailably dominant or demonstrably yoked in service to the powerful. Self-reflection is necessary for all of us, as this project has emphasized.

To this end, let me raise more questions. First, why does this project appear more interested in identifying good Maoism and asserting the Mao era CCP's socialist bona fides than developing its own coherent Marxist-inspired critique? The long tradition of Marxist criticism of Maoism, inside and outside China, are, with the exception of some maneuvering around the shadow of Moishe Postone, unmentioned (see in this issue Meyskens; Werner). Is this a move away from Marxist theorizing for the sake of the salvaging project? Second, why, after repeated assaults on "state-society" frameworks, does this discussion leave the impression that the centrality of the Party-state to PRC history, which closely reflects that state's claims to ubiquitous dominance, remains unchallenged? Third, why does this project, which states its aims so forthrightly, still often engage in mercurial qualifying statements about the "dark sides" and exercises in selective good Maoism? Is good Maoism just in the "early years" or mainly "the radical potential that never belonged to Mao or the PRC state"? (See in this issue, Smith foreword; Meyskens; Day.) Does the latter statement include figures like Yu Luoke, who were labeled "counterrevolutionaries" and executed under Maoism for their Maoist criticisms of Mao (Wu 2014: 75–79)? I ask these questions not as rebuttal, but to suggest that a better Good Left history would not blind itself to those avenues just as they shed light on others discovered missing. I urge direct confrontation of the subjects that fit least well with the broader critique and, above all, a willingness to balance the productivity of critical skepticism with an open curiosity that keeps our imperfect art breathing with the question "After all, was there not more than this?"

More Than This

Good Left history should not be satisfied with just acknowledging that violence, coercion, and exploitation were "fundamental" to Maoism. The interest in showing that tragedy and brutality are "not the whole story" best proceeds if it does not, as Johnson notes, "sidestep" the violence or leave the impression that those who suffered were the "collateral damage" price of radicalism (see in this issue, in addition to Johnson, Smith; Lanza). In fact, theorizing and narrating of that "whole story" requires confronting Maoist violence, as Jake Werner's approach in this issue suggests. This does not mean enumerating statistics and sketching images of horrors detached from context and thin on explication. The inhabiting of Maoism requires, as for all such phenomena, seeing up close its theoretical commitment to and legitimation of violence, the policies, institutions, and means of its practice, and the intimacy of the pain, destruction, and trauma it wrought on specific human beings, families, and communities; the imprints it left and transformations it coerced, induced, and informed. In recording the inhumanity of humanity to humanity, to paraphrase Primo Levi (1988: 44), we have to find the capacity to make sense of not just the coexistence of compassion and brutality in a single society, community or episode of violence, but also bear witness to its coexistence "in the same individual, and in the same moment."

Land Reform violence in the villages from the mid-1940s into the early 1950s, for instance, demands such interrogation of specific cases and of the uniform Maoist statement that the violence was justified because "the masses demand[ed] we suppress counterrevolutionaries" (Smith, this issue). In my research on rural Northern Jiangsu communities, places with long histories of violence, Land Reform violence was common and something different. It rarely involved interclan hostility or vendetta, even when it employed the language of vengeance. It was mob murder in which some villagers, guided and sanctioned by CCP officials, used specially prepared long, wooden "turning over big clubs" (翻身大棍) to beat to death fellow villagers in full view of the community, before relatives and children. The bloodied long-clubs were retained, in cases displayed, as symbols of the new authority. Even if we set aside the troubling matters of who the killers and killed were in their social settings and the validity of any kind of mob-justice killing, we cannot avoid what its practice and its justification meant in these communities. Whatever emancipatory changes and visions would be advanced in those places were inextricably founded not in an abstraction of war or revolutionary violence, but in intimate, bloody murder. Acceptance of this willing of the murder was the initiation into membership in the new political community, "the masses." And, in village terms at that time, it extended moral responsibility for the death, before gods, ancestors, and relatives, to all who accepted its justification. Since this was almost an entirely rural phenomenon, the Maoist knowledge act aspect alone expanded on the modern epistemological creation of "the peasant" (Cohen 1993; Eyferth 2009), requiring that the apparent barbarousness of this class would be manifested in its original act of liberation. As in all Maoist epistemology of the Mass Line, elements of practical power and ideology openly went hand in hand, and the ideal visions of the ends were inscribed in the structures of the means.

The Good Left's emphasis on the significance of Maoism as epistemology is a view I share (Lanza, this issue). Yet, it is essential that we recognize (1) that by design it was expressly backed by armed force and (2) that all ways in which this transformative, revolutionary epistemology was productive of possibility were bonded to the ways in which it was reductive through what it excluded and redefined with powerfully simplifying labels. Maoist political and historical theory and practice were both formulated this way (Gao 2018). Can the Good Left really align its historical practice with this epistemology? Can it just replace a liberal values reductive model (Smith foreword, this issue) with a Maoist one? Is this the better theory we need to correct a presumably unhinged empiricism? We do not necessarily have to agree on Timothy Cheek's (2016: 307) view of Maoist "epistemological elitism" or cite generations of scholarship on this point (U 2019; Eyferth 2009). I agree with this group that Maoists stated their theories quite plainly. And I concur that Maoist epistemology set out its vision and recorded much about how it was being limited and contested *in their own Maoist terms.* Smith acknowledges that there was much the PRC state "never came to know" (Smith foreword, this issue). Still, I would be more concerned by a historical practice based on what Maoists claimed to know in their own way.

This is where Brown and Johnson (2015) entered with their quest for something "more than this." Under Maoist epistemology, what will be missing about the past, about lives lived partly before 1949, about all forms of difference of opinion and expression, politics, morality, aesthetics, creativity, language, religion, cultural and social practice, ethnicity, locality, bodies, gender, sex, approaches to making a living, of being born, living and dying? Will the Maoist version capture fully, on its own, the historical significances of subalterns, or as Lanza (this issue) has it, "those who work with their hands"? As Smith and Lanza know, I have argued that local family and religious "language and practices," in the most basic matters of life and survival, "were the idiom through which rural people were expressing their experience in troubled times" in the 1950s (Kiely 2019; see also Wang 2020). Some evidence for this was drawn from archives and government documents depicting abundant phenomena defined as "feudalism" and "superstition" targeted for elimination. I would hope we can see more than this—a space for emancipatory visions and expressions of "moral autonomy and human dignity," both "central to the socialist project" (Wu 2014: 56) *and* to Buddhist, Daoist, Confucian, Christian, local religious, family, and other articulations identifiable under Maoism.

Debates will continue about the privileging of the details of our empirical work set against the meaning making and abstractions of our theories. For historians, there is no way out of this—much as is the case with our posture toward social reality. These are tensions inherent to our craft. Neither can be discarded or overlooked. So, let us embrace the tensions as creative and recognize how much this demands of us. We can afford neither free-floating evidence nor theories of an abstract social totality, flattened and lifeless. Nor can we get bogged down in complaining about our sources. All historical sources are remnants or remembered fragments, shards, and glimpses, even when they claim comprehensiveness; limited, distorted, obscured by both the conditions of order and those of disorder we find them in. All require strenuous cross-examining and decoding in relation to what we can comprehend of their symbolic and social contexts. In keeping with this Good Left project, let us continue to interrogate method in relation to frameworks and, in the manner that Smith and Werner attempt, pursue theories that can explain more fully, not less. Let us continue to open up the aperture of our inquiries, surely to those whose contributions are least understood and yet not at the expense of all others. In doing so, let us not reject what might be learned from different generations and types of scholarship, including those of social scientists.[3] We need all the help we can get.

Smith (foreword, this issue) and I agree on the significance of the "squat in a spot" (*dundian* 蹲点) approach, in my case as a practice of historical anthropology. I take inspiration in not being alone in this, from the collective engaged in this work before, now, and coming after; those who have put the time into localities and viewed them over extended periods (Siu 1989; Dubois 2005; Grove 2006; Li 2009; Eyferth 2009; Hershatter 2011; Harrison 2013; Guo 2013); those who have pioneered collaborations across borders, like Gail Hershatter (2011) and Gao Xiaoxian and Andrew Walder (a social scientist) and Dong Guoqiang (a historian) (Dong and Walder 2020); and especially the new generations of Chinese scholars setting the standard for "squatting" (Liu et al. 2015) and producing rich histories likely to shape understandings of China's history for an approaching time when English language scholarship will be globally less prominent than it is today. The complexity with which we are coming to think of the early history of the PRC is not a minor matter, even if it is not itself a revolution.

The Good Left and I can hopefully share an appreciation of the resonances from Mao Zedong's 1941 criticism of Marxist historians' knowing "only ancient Greece but not China and . . . in a fog about the China of yesterday and the day before yesterday. With this attitude, a person studies Marxist-Leninist theory in the abstract and without any aim" (Mao [1941] 1960: 799). And yet I hope we can agree that, whatever our politics, we cannot act like Promethean revolutionaries when we are doing the onerous mental labor of historical research. If often seemingly modest and limited in its rewards, the historian's contributions to "progressive intelligibility" or "good enough" history (Bloch 1954: 10; Hershatter 2011: 3) has values to our attempts to inquire into and make sense of ourselves and our predicaments that, history shows, are most recognized when they are abruptly denied to us.

Notes

1   I first took part in conversations with Smith and Lanza at the International Symposium on Conjuring the Socialist Rural: Locality, Economy, and Imagination of Village Life in 1950s China, Chinese University of Hong Kong, May 16–18, 2019, which I co-organized with Rebecca Karl and Pang Laikwan.

2   The relevant works in English are too many to note here. For recent examples, see Wu 2014 and Mittler 2012.

3   Among many examples, most relevant and recent are Dillon 2015 and Andreas 2019.

References

Andreas, Joel. 2019. *Disenfranchised: The Rise and Fall of Industrial Citizenship in China.* Oxford: Oxford University Press.

Bloch, Marc. 1954. *The Historian's Craft,* translated by Peter Putnam. Manchester, UK: Manchester University Press.

Bonnin, Michel. 2013. *The Lost Generation: The Rustication of China's Educated Youth, 1968–1980,* translated by Krystyna Horko. Hong Kong: Chinese University Press.

Brown, Jeremy, and Matthew D. Johnson, eds. 2015. *Maoism at the Grassroots: Everyday Life in China's Era of High Socialism.* Cambridge, MA: Harvard University Press.

Cheek, Timothy. 2016. "Making Maoism: Ideology and Organization in the Yan'an Rectification Movement, 1942–44." In *Knowledge Acts in Modern China: Ideas, Institutions, and Identities,* edited by Robert Culp, Eddy U, and Wen-hsin Yeh, 304–27. Berkeley, CA: Institute of East Asian Studies.

Cohen, Myron L. 1993. "Cultural and Political Inventions in Modern China: The Case of the Chinese 'Peasant.'" *Daedalus* 122, no. 2: 151–70.

Dillon, Nara. 2015. *Radical Inequalities: China's Revolutionary Welfare State in Comparative Perspective.* Cambridge, MA: Harvard University Asia Center.

Dong, Guoqiang, and Andrew G. Walder. 2020. *A Decade of Upheaval: The Cultural Revolution in Rural China.* Princeton, NJ: Princeton University Press.

Dubois, Thomas D. 2005. *The Sacred Village: Social Change and Religious Life in Rural North China.* Honolulu: University of Hawai'i Press.

Eyferth, Jacob. 2009. *Eating Rice from Bamboo Roots: The Social History of a Community of Handicraft Papermakers in Rural Sichuan, 1920–2000.* Cambridge, MA: Harvard University Asia Center.

Gao, Hua. 2018. *How the Red Sun Rose: The Origins and Development of the Yan'an Rectification Movement, 1930–1945,* translated by Stacy Mosher and Guo Jian. Hong Kong: Chinese University Press.

Grove, Linda. 2006. *A Chinese Economic Revolution: Rural Entrepreneurship in the Twentieth Century.* Lanham, MD: Rowman and Littlefield.

Guo, Yuhua 郭于華. 2013. *Shoukuren de jiangshu: Jicun lishi yu yizhong wenming de luoji* 受苦人的講述:驥村歷史與一種文明的邏輯. (*Narratives of the Suffering: The History and Cultural Logic of Ji Village*). Hong Kong: Chinese University Press.

Harrison, Henrietta. 2013. *The Missionary's Curse and Other Tales from a Chinese Catholic Village.* Berkeley: University of California Press.

Hershatter, Gail. 2011. *The Gender of Memory: Rural Women and China's Collective Past.* Berkeley: University of California Press.

Kiely, Jan. 2019. "The Way of Not Being Transformed in the Socialist Rural Revolution of the 1950s: Evidence from a Northern Jiangsu County." Paper presented at the "International Symposium on Conjuring the Socialist Rural: Locality, Economy, and Imagination of Village Life in 1950s China," Chinese University of Hong Kong, May 18.

Kirby, William C. 1984. *Germany and Republican China.* Stanford, CA: Stanford University Press.

Levi, Primo. 1988. *The Drowned and the Saved*, translated by Raymond Rosenthal. New York: Simon and Schuster.

Li, Huaiyin. 2009. *Village China under Socialism and Reform: A Micro History, 1948–2008.* Stanford, CA: Stanford University Press.

Liu, Yonghua 刘永华, Kan Zhang张侃, Weixin Rao 饶伟新, Xiangchun Huang 黄向春, Xing Ying 应星, Meibao Cheng 程美宝, and Chang Liu 刘昶. 2015. "Shehui jingjishi shiyexia de zhongguo geming" 社会经济史视野下的中国革命 ("China's Revolution in the Perspective of Social-Economic History"). *Kaifang shidai*开放时代 2: 11–80.

Mao Zedong 毛澤東. (1941) 1960. "Gaizao women de xuexi" 改造我們的學習 ("Reform Our Study"). In *Mao Zedong xuanji* 毛澤東選集, vol. 3, 795–806. Beijing: Renmin chubanshe.

Mittler, Barbara. 2012. *A Continuous Revolution: Making Sense of Cultural Revolution Culture.* Cambridge, MA: Harvard University Asia Center.

Perry, Elizabeth J. 2012. *Anyuan: Mining China's Revolutionary Tradition.* Berkeley: University of California Press.

Sewell, William, Jr. 2005. "The Political Unconscious of Social and Cultural History, or Confessions of a Former Quantitative Historian." In *Logics of History: Social Theory and Social Transformation*, 22–80. Chicago: University of Chicago Press.

Siu, Helen F. 1989. *Agents and Victims in South China: Accomplices in Rural Revolution.* New Haven, CT: Yale University Press.

Strauss, Julia C. 1998. *Strong Institutions in Weak Polities: State Building in Republican China, 1927–1940.* Oxford, UK: Clarendon Press.

U, Eddy. 2019. *Creating the Intellectual: Chinese Communism and the Rise of a Classification.* Berkeley: University of California Press.

van de Ven, Hans. 2003. *War and Nationalism in China, 1925–1945.* London: Routledge.

Wakeman, Frederic E., Jr. 1995. *Policing Shanghai, 1927–1937.* Berkeley: University of California Press.

Wakeman, Frederic E., Jr. 2009. "Reflection: Telling Chinese History." In *Telling Chinese History: A Selection of Essays*, selected and edited by Lea H. Wakeman, 410–30. Berkeley: University of California Press.

Wang, Xiaoxuan. 2020. *Maoism and Grassroots Religion: The Communist Revolution and the Reinvention of Religious Life in China*. New York: Oxford University Press.

Wu, Yiching. 2014. *The Cultural Revolution at the Margins*. Cambridge, MA: Harvard University Press.

Contributors

Jeremy Brown is professor of history at Simon Fraser University in British Columbia. He is the author of *June Fourth: The Tiananmen Protests and Beijing Massacre of 1989* (2021).

Alexander F. Day is associate professor of history and chair of East Asian studies at Occidental College. He is the author of *The Peasant in Postsocialist China: History, Politics, and Capitalism* (2013).

Matthew D. Johnson is an associate professor of the University of Pittsburgh Asian Studies Center. He recently edited *Redefining Propaganda in Modern China: The Mao Era and Its Legacies* (2021).

Jan Kiely is professor and director of the Centre for China Studies at the Chinese University of Hong Kong and associate editor of *Twentieth-Century China*. He is the author of *The Compelling Ideal: Thought Reform and the Prison in China, 1901–1956* (2014) and coeditor of *Modern Chinese Religion II, 1850–2015* (2015), *Recovering Buddhism in Modern China* (2016), and *Fieldwork in Modern Chinese History: A Research Guide* (2019).

positions 29:4   DOI 10.1215/10679847-9286767

Fabio Lanza is professor of modern Chinese history at the University of Arizona. His recent publications include *The End of Concern: Maoism, Activism, and Asian Studies* (2017).

Covell F. Meyskens is assistant professor of history at the Naval Postgraduate School. He is the author of *Mao's Third Front: The Militarization of Cold War China* (2020).

Sigrid Schmalzer is professor of history at the University of Massachusetts Amherst. She is the author of *Red Revolution, Green Revolution: Scientific Farming in Socialist China* (2016).

Aminda Smith is associate professor of history at Michigan State University. She is the author of *Thought Reform and China's Dangerous Classes: Reeducation, Resistance, and the People* (2013).

Jake Werner is a postdoctoral research fellow at the Global Development Policy Center, Boston University. His research interests include labor, nationalism, everyday life, and the trajectory of global capitalism. He is currently completing a book manuscript, "Everyday Crisis and the Rise of the Masses: Life in Shanghai, 1925–1972."

Keep up to date on new scholarship

Issue alerts are a great way to stay current on all the cutting-edge scholarship from your favorite Duke University Press journals. This free service delivers tables of contents directly to your inbox, informing you of the latest groundbreaking work as soon as it is published.

To sign up for issue alerts:

1. Visit **dukeu.press/register** and register for an account. You do not need to provide a customer number.

2. After registering, visit **dukeu.press/alerts**.

3. Go to "Latest Issue Alerts" and click on "Add Alerts."

4. Select as many publications as you would like from the pop-up window and click "Add Alerts."

read.dukeupress.edu/journals

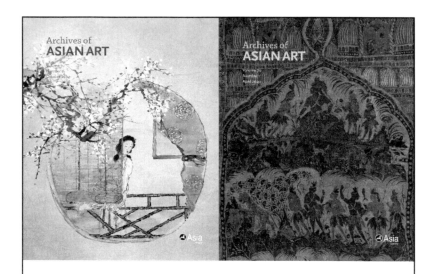